A LAMENT

Was Partition Inescapable?

The author has penned down his memories of a lost culture, the pain and agony caused by partition, his movement from the other side of the shadow line i.e., Pakistan to India, his post-partititon struggles and his tussle with life.

ॐ

असतो मा सद गमय
तमसो मा ज्योतिर्गमय
मृत्युर्मा अमृतागंमय

LEAD ME, O' LORD
FROM UNTRUTH TO TRUTH
FROM DARKNESS TO LIGHT
FROM DEATH TO IMMORTALITY

A LAMENT

Was Partition Inescapable?

V.N. Sekhri

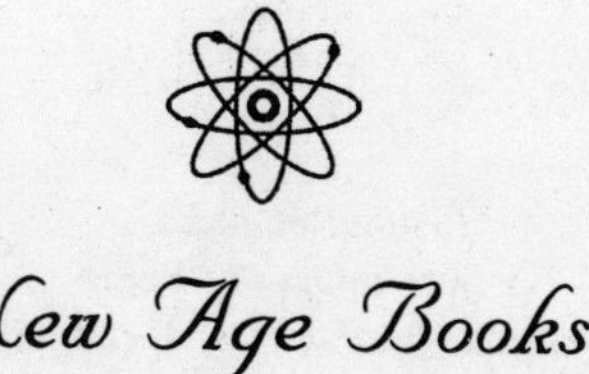

New Age Books

ISBN: 81-7822-206-x
First Edition: Delhi, 2007

Published by
NEW AGE BOOKS
A-44, Naraina Industrial Area, Phase I
New Delhi 110 028 (INDIA)
Email: nab@vsnl.in
Website: www.newagebooksindia.com

Printed in India
at Shri Jainendra Press
A-45 Naraina Phase-I New Delhi-110 028

DEDICATION

To
the known and unknown sons and daughters of my great Motherland
who
fought and sacrificed their lives for her freedom
and
those who were mercilessly murdered in the areas now forming Pakistan.

THANKS

To Shri S.K. Vasudeva, who first suggested to me to write; to my wife—Santosh Sekhri, who further prompted me to go ahead; to Dr A.K. Monga (Reader in philosophy, Hans Raj College, Delhi—retired), who edited my amateur writing and encouraged me to get it published for commercial sale; to my children who gave me all the facilities to complete this book.

My affectionate indebtedness is due to my grandmother and father whose telling of the stories of my ancestors and that of the originator of our clan, has enabled me to retell these stories in the book.

FOREWORD

Vishwanath's anguish is understandable because a country where people belonging to different religions and different regions had lived for centuries was divided on the basis of religion. But his lament for Hindus alone is not justified. Muslims were as mercilessly cut off from their routs as non-Muslims. On the Indian side, victims were Muslims and on the Pakistan side, Hindus and Sikhs.

I too travelled from Sialkot to the Indian border and saw murder and the worst. But it was the killing all the way, this side of the border or that. There was no difference in brutality.

It was late in the afternoon on Sep.13, 1947, when we reached the outskirts of Lahore. We halted; nobody knew why. Word was that a convoy of Muslims had been attacked in Amritsar and that the Muslims of Lahore were waiting to take revenge. We were ordered to get down from the trucks which were then parked in a circle to form a sort of first line of defence. The men took up positions behind the trucks and the women and childeren were asked to sit in the middle. We waited in silence. There was some stray shooting in the distance and from the nearby fields came the strench of decomposed flesh. Slogans of Allah ho Akbar, Ya Ali, Pakistan Zindabad came to our ears. But there was no attack. After a long wait our fears were proved wrong. We were off again.

I saw piles of bodies on both sides of the road, empty trucks here and there bore testimony to the looting which had taken place either before or after the killing.

There was nervousness as we neared our destination. And then we heard Bharat Mata Ki Jai (Slaute to Mother India).

It was an avalanche of migration; humanity was on the move on both sides. None expected it; none wanted it, but none could help it. The two countries blamed each other as they tried to grapple with this and other chaotic problems of Partition after the first few heady days of independence.

The refugees carried with them to the country they went not only bitterness and vengeful thoughts but also stories of atrocities in the villages where they had lived peacefully with other communities for centuries. If partition was on the basis of religion, these instances only furrowed it deep.

On paper, both India and Pakistan declared that "there shall be no discrimination against those who before 15 August may have been political opponents." In practice, there was no accommodation, no forgiveness. The two countries behaved as the Congress Party and the Muslim League had done before partition; it was the same old effort to see the other side go down.

Whoever was to blame—or, rather, more to blame—the few weeks of madness on both sides of the border embittered the relations between the two countries, for two generation and more. The two countries differed on every subject, at every step. Fear and mistrust of each other made even trivial matters major issues.

I am glad that Vishwa had his grievance off his chest. But there are in Pakistan many Vishwas who too want to tell their tale of woes. They too left their homes and hearths, friends and neighbours, businesses and factories. They too were broken on the wrack of history. They too became refugees.

Kuldip Nayar

PREFACE

I attempted to write this book very late in my life and now when I have finished it, I am 83 years old. I had been pushed into it by a highly accomplished gentleman, who once heard my experiences of the partition of India. He suggested that I might put my experiences in writing as those were extraordinary such that he had never heard or read. When I laughed at his suggestion and told him that I could not put my stories in writing, he promptly offered his cooperation for editing it if I wrote in English as he is an MA in English. But I remained unconvinced.

My wife, when told of this, gave an affirmative reaction. She felt that the book would reveal to our children, the type of situations their father had to face in his young life. That clinched the subject and early next morning I sat with a copy and pencil.

It was September 1999 and I had to spend two/three days in searching my way to begin and for that I had to look into all the autobiographies on my bookshelve. I started from my birth and very soon realized that I had a bagful of unusual stories to write about. I wrote and re-wrote my manuscript at least six times so as to do justice and be true to my experiences.

Though the book is mainly my autobiographical account, it actually epitomizes all those who suffered, struggled and survived the tyranny, chaos and pain of partition.

It was in November 2005, that I handed over my final manuscript to my publishers. But for the strength given to me by the Almighty God, it would not have been possible to complete this project.

CONTENTS

PART - I

— 1 —

MASSACRES AND EVICTIONS

It was in Bengal first. In August 1946, in response to the "Direct Action" call by Jinnah, it started with "the great killings of Calcutta" followed by "rivers of blood flowed in Noakhali". The Punjab made the beginning in March 1947. A passenger train coming from Peshawar was stopped near Hasnabdal, a border town on the north-west Punjab province. The Muslim mob, waiting nearby, surrounded the train and ordered all Hindu men, women and children to come out of the train. They were then butchered with swords, daggers and other weapons. It was the start of the massacre of Hindus and Sikhs in the Punjab. The whole province was rudely shaken. The Hindus and Sikhs residing in the neighbouring places of the train massacre were alarmed and scared at that dastardly act. They had been watching for sometime the Muslim leaders of their town holding meetings and threatening them. They decided to save their families and so left their homes and hearths in groups and took shelter in the large Gurdwara of Punja Sahib. Soon the Gurdwara was filled to its capacity. But there was an unending flow of people. Finding no space in the Gurdwara, the people started sitting in the open spaces around it.

In the last election in Britain the Labour Party came into power and Lord Attlee became the Prime Minister. He had declared that the British would leave India by June 1948. Lord Wavell was replaced by Lord Mountbatten as the Viceroy of India in March 1947. The same month, the massacre was planned by Jinnah's Muslim League, to put pressure on the new viceroy for early decision in favour of creation of Pakistan.

The Hindus all over the province were shocked and soon the *Punjab Hindu Raksha Samiti* was formed. They appealed to the government to make suitable arrangements for the protection of the Hindus of the province and especially for the help of those who had been driven out of their homes and had taken shelter in and around the Punja Sahib Gurdwara. The government then opened a refugee camp at Wah, which was the area that belonged to the erstwhile Chief Minister, Khizar Hayat Khan, of Punjab. The people gathered in Punja Sahib were told to occupy the barracks at the Wah camp. The camp was put under a military commandant and was guarded by the military. However, the government did not promise any relief to the refugees who took shelter in the camp. The *Raksha Samiti* made appeals to all the Hindus of the Punjab for sending aid to the people taking shelter in the camp. Hindus all over the Punjab rose like one unit and generously contributed for this purpose. The major role was played by RSS, whose members were foremost to collect aid in the form of money, provisions and clothing by going from house-to-house in each city of the province.

Lahore was the first city which sent its collections in a few trucks to the Wah camp along with an adequate number of *swayamsewak* volunteers. The camp commandant handed over two barracks to those volunteers and allowed them to unload their trucks and stay there to manage the distribution of those provisions among the refugees in that camp. Every city and town from Rohtak, Ambala to Peshawar collected aid and transported it to Wah by trucks. From Sialkot, we collected provision to fill three large trucks. Each truck manned by one *swayamsewak* reached Wah without any problem. The three escorts with the trucks were Kapur Chand Jain, Dwarka Nath

Rakra and myself. We handed over the collected contents to the volunteers and decided that after a night's stay in the camp we would return to Sialkot.

The Wah camp was the same place where the Indian government had kept Italian prisoners in the Second World War. There were barracks for a few thousand prisoners, but they were not sufficient for a multitude of 60,000 refugees who were housed there. The relief work for providing food and clothing was wholly managed by the RSS volunteers. There were about 25–30 school and college going boys working as volunteers under one head, who was a mature person. Young boys had no experience of such type of relief work earlier. When I stayed there for a night and watched the way the relief work was conducted, I opted to stay back.

Staying back I continued watching the work for another two days and on the third day, I sought to discuss the matter with the incharge. I explained how I felt the service should be handled. He agreed with me and arranged a meeting with all the other volunteers. He introduced me to them and also told them about my suggestions which would improve the services rendered to the refugees. I suggested that instead of the refugees coming to our barracks, to collect their needs we should go to their barracks and deliver the articles to them. All boys gladly accepted my suggestion.

Some other suggestions included were that the volunteers would be visiting the barracks and shall be responsible for distribution of provisions; batches of volunteers would go to the barracks, allotted to them in the morning and would enquire from each family their requirements; they would prepare a list of each barrack, come back with the list and collect all the articles and in the evening they would carry all the articles on their heads and deliver them in the barracks.

This way it would be a real service, which would be appreciated by the refugees. This would also give them a feeling of inner satisfaction.

The second point that I explained to the boys was that whatever the stocks of clothing and food we had there in our centre, had been donated by the public primarily for the use of the refugees. Therefore, the volunteers had a right to use only the minimum possible for their sustenance.

My words had the right effect on them and they readily agreed to my suggestions. After all, those young boys, only school or college going, had left their homes and had volunteered to do service.

At the end of the meeting, the incharge, having confirmed that I would stay there handed his charge to me and told the volunteers to consult me for any of their problems. The changed distribution system attracted the attention of all, particularly the medical department for the refugees, set up by the government. There was only one government doctor with whom our volunteers had not made any contact. I told our boys that since we had no medical facilities to offer, we must cooperate with the government doctor. So our volunteers were told to prepare a separate statement of each barrack with regards to their medical needs. The medical requirement statements were passed on to the government doctor. The doctor felt very happy to find the change and therefore made it a point to come to our centre. He met me and we discussed how we could coordinate our services in the field of medical aid in a more effective way. Some of the standard medicines for common cold, headache, constipation, dysentery, etc. were stored under the care of the doctor in the camp. Those were handed over to our volunteers with instructions for their disbursement. In just one week, the entire system of service was streamlined.

There after I started attending to the stock of provisions considered necessary for the centre. We had to buy vegetables from a place which was a few miles away from our centre. The centre had its own jeep and a driver and someone was sent daily to buy the vegetables. Milk was a very important item for children and was out of stock quite often. We advised the refugees to use milk only for children or sick people; and the adults should use it only for making tea. All the refugees were very cooperative. Supplies from the Refugee Relief Committees of different cities kept on arriving to replenish our stocks. More trucks came from Sialkot and I used to get news about the city and other places from the people accompanying those trucks.

Once it so happened that milk supplies went very short and the incoming trucks from all over Punjab, did not include any type of tinned milk. We were alarmed as the lives of the small children depended on that supply. We tried to get fresh milk from places all around, but it was not enough. I went to Punja Sahib where the Gurdwara people were running daily *langar*. I sought the help of the *Mahanta* but he could not assist us. As a last resort, I personally went to Nawashehar in the NWFP, which was the nearest big city, but could not get any supplies from there too. After failing there, I proceeded to Peshawar. It was a Sunday and the markets were closed. As our need was urgent, I tried for help through Dev Prakash Shastri, the local RSS *pracharak* for the NWFP, stationed in Peshawar. He knew Mr Salwan, the owner of the largest provision store in Peshawar and got his store specially opened for our requirement of powdered milk. They had only 20 cases of powdered milk, in their stock which they delivered to me. I booked those cases on my lorry ticket for Hasnabdal and boarded the bus.

At the Attuck river bridge, there was a police check post, to check the luggage, for any contraband or harmful items. When our bus was checked, the checkers reported to the inspector of police incharge that there were powder-milk cases in the bus. An announcement was made to find out who was carrying the milk. I stood up and claimed the possession of those cases. I was asked to show the permit for taking out of the province a banned item. I was surprised to hear that and told the officer that I never knew that milk was a banned item. I further explained that I was not a trader but a volunteer serving at the Wah camp and that milk was very badly required for the babies and children in the camp. The officer showed me a rule-book which stated that milk was a prohibited item for export from the province. As the bus was being delayed and other passengers were objecting to the delay, the police officer got all the cases removed from the bus and told me that I and my milk cases could only be released after my bail and the production of the required export permit. I was required to be present in the magistrate's court the next day in connection with my case.

I was a complete stranger in that city. How could I arrange for my bail. I requested the police inspector to allow me to make a phone call to the camp commander who was a military colonel. Over the phone, I explained the whole situation to the colonel. He said that I should wait there and he would arrange to send someone. Late in the afternoon, an elderly person arrived in his jeep with a certificate from the camp commander. He stood my bail and on my release carried me in the jeep to the camp.

Next day, the colonel issued another certificate and a letter requesting the Deputy Commissioner of Nawashehar for issuing a permit to export milk for use in the government refugee camp of Wah. We took those documents and appeared next day in the magistrate's court for his permission so that we could get the permit from the Deputy Commissioner. He waived the penal clause applied in my case and after setting me free, he agreed with our request and forwarded our application to the Deputy Commissioner along with the camp commandant's recommendation. Simultaneously, we could get an introduction letter for a local Red Shirt Leader who was very influential in Nawashehar. With his help, we could get the permit from the Deputy Commissioner's office the same day. It meant tremendous relief for us. The confiscated milk was released and necessary transport arrangements were made for taking it to the camp.

In the meantime, the political conditions in the country were deteriorating. The agitations of the Muslim League were becoming more aggressive and provocative all over the country. The Radcliff Commission appointed by the Viceroy to demarcate the borderline between East and West Punjab had started working with a directive to submit their final report to the Viceroy on or before August 15, 1947. The position of some areas situated in the middle like Lahore, Gurdaspur and Shekhupura was not clear and both the Hindu and Muslim leaders were pleading their respective cases. But the Muslim League did not rely on such verbal wrangling. They had started literally cutting the throats of the Hindus wherever they could to put pressure on the British government and on the Radcliff Commission.

Tension in all the cities of Punjab was increasing. Staying in Wah camp, I was getting the reports from the *swayamsewaks* who came to the camp, accompanying the trucks of relief material. The RSS of the different cities of Punjab had decided to be prepared to defend Hindus in their areas, in case of mass attacks on their *mohallas*. The RSS *pracharaks* in the cities like Peshawar and Haripur Hazara, offered to procure any quantity of small arms like pistols, grenades and rifles, from their areas for those who may need them. Haripur Hazara was situated in the remote interior of the West Punjab and Peshawar was the capital city of the north-west Frontier Provinces. Since I stationed myself in the Wah camp for refugee service, I received a message from Sialkot about growing tension there and their need to prepare for protection. I was told to transfer my relief work responsibilities to some other person and devote my attention for the protection of my own city. Our people had assessed the situation of all the localities where Hindus were living. As in most of the cities, the Hindu and Muslim populations in Sialkot were concentrated almost in separate *mohallas* but in the old city, all those *mohallas* were interconnected and were located alongside each other. Our city might be one of the very few where Hindus and Muslims in general were on very good terms. It was an industrial town having large as well as small scale industries. An overwhelming majority of the large scale industries were owned by the Hindus and the small scale industries were mostly run by the Muslims. About 90 per cent of workers and labourers were Muslims. Again the small Muslim manufacturers sold their products to the Hindu shopkeepers. In this way they had been bound together in a close relationship for centuries.

The leaders of the Muslim League were spreading their venom every where among the innocent people of their community and were fully exploiting them in the name of their religion. The most effective slogan in their armour was that "Islam was in danger" and in those times the danger was from the rich and exploiting Hindu community. In that surcharged atmosphere in the entire country, our city was also affected and reports in the possession of our *swayamsewaks* were that in Sialkot, the Muslims were preparing to attack the Jain *mohalla*, which was the richest and was surrounded on three sides by Muslim *mohallas*. The Jains were also considered to be the weakest and the most timid members of the Hindu community. Although this *mohalla* had the maximum membership of *swayamsewaks* and a few of them were most courageous and stout-hearted, the geographical situation made it prone to a big risk. Their demand for protection was large and urgent. The other two *mohallas*, which stood in danger of an attack were Dharowal and Greenwood Street.

In the Wah camp, ample funds were placed with me for whatever useful could be bought in the markets of Haripur Hazara and Peshawar through our own men. Haripur Hazara was closer to Wah and approachable by road. I went there in our jeep. It was around 80–90 miles from Wah and reaching there in the evening, I saw Harish Bhanote who was the in-charge of RSS of that district. I had met him for the first time and stayed with him in the RSS office for the night. He knew the purpose of my visit and was already engaged in procurement of whatever small and big items of armament were available from the local Muslim population for the needs of various cities in the Punjab. It seemed to be the local Muslim longtime business. There were available countrymade arms as well as the imported ones of various brands. I was surprised to know from Harish that the whole thing was so open and so easy there. I handed him the list of arms which I needed to buy. He told me that I should leave my holdall there and he would procure whatever was readily available, pack those properly and keep it ready for me to collect during my next visit. At night we slept on the roof, spreading our beddings on the floor. As we lay down in our beds, Harish told me about himself and his work there in that district as a *pracharak*. Hindus in the district might not be more than 10 per cent but they were rich landlords. So far the atmosphere had been calm but the Muslim Leaguers had started penetrating and were trying to provoke the local Muslim population. He was maintaining good relations with some of the important Muslims, and was being invited to their homes for dinner. He had been able to organise the *sangh* work very well and almost every Hindu landlord or *sahukar* was either a *swayamsewak* or a firm supporter. He talked in such a manner and language that I felt mesmerised by his courageous words and tone. He was a totally fearless person who foresaw no trouble for himself, in case things turned bad and some mischief-makers attacked his office-cum-home. He was fully prepared to face them, and was sure that he could defend himself and his office from all sides from the top of his house. No one dared come near him as long as he held a gun in his hand. He was totally fearless and had a plan ready for escape if the things went out of control. I had never seen such a bold and courageous person. Harish was of a medium height and a lean body. It's amazing how he could pack so much of courage in his lean frame.

After two days, I collected my material wrapped in a holdall. Early in the morning, Harish got it placed in my jeep and I drove straight towards the camp. In our service barrack, I got one corner cleared to keep such material. I visited Haripur Hazara almost twice a week. I was advised to visit Peshawar also where some different types of material were available.

Later, when I read the history of the Sikhs in Punjab under *Maharaja* Ranjit Singh, I learnt that Hari Singh Nalwa who was one of the greatest generals in the formidable Sikh army, was assigned the command of the most troublesome *Pathan* territory. He chose Hazara for his headquarters. He took his force there and lived there for fifteen long years. As a result of his prolonged stay, a new city was created with his name Hari attached to it and it was called Haripur Hazara. Considering this I wonder about the coincidence. Hari Singh Nalwa was a lion-hearted general and so was Harish. There is a commonality in the names of the two—one is Hari Singh and the other Hari-ish. It becomes Harish when Hari and Ish are joined. Harish too lived there for many years. He continued to live in Pakistan even after independence and left the country on his motorcycle following Muzzaffar Nagar–Srinagar road in October end to inform his comrades in Srinagar of the attack of Pakistan army in the guise of the tribal *Pathans*.

Peshawar was about three hours run from the Hasnabdal railway station by mail train. I reached there and went straight to our RSS office. Dev Prakash Shastri, whom I had met earlier for the milk procurement, could easily guess the purpose of my visit. I gave him a copy of a list of items we needed. He discussed with me the situation in our city and gave me his opinion for defence. He was a different type of a commander—very deep, creative and courageous. Peshawar was the deepest post the RSS had established in the farthest part of Western India. Shastriji had travelled further deep wherever even a single Hindu lived. He visited Charsadha, at the end of NWFP, and had crossed into the Khyber Pass and visited Landi Kotal, the last railway station at the end of the pass. He used to mention with pride that he had visited Jamrud Fort, built by Hari Singh Nalwa, a great general in the army of *Maharaja* Ranjit Singh. Shastriji had easy access to all of illicit arms manufacturing centres in that area. He helped me to my satisfaction and also trained me on how to manage the gun running effectively. As a result, I developed courage and used his instructions intelligently with maximum effect. As in Haripur Hazara, here also the arms I needed were packed in a large and strong holdall. I carried it upto Hasnabdal station from where our Wah camp jeep carried my baggage and me to the camp. Hitherto I confined my activities to three places— Wah camp, Haripur Hazara and Peshawar. I collected and stored the material in our barrack in Wah camp from where the Sialkot boys collected it.

By the month of July 1947, the position in the towns of West Punjab had worsened, which made many Hindus shift their bank accounts and families to places beyond Amritsar. This development further incensed the Muslim leaders who then incited their followers to restrain the Hindus from doing so. They told them that if the Hindus took away their riches from there, what would remain for them would be an empty shell of Pakistan. And that was never the intention of the promoters of the Pakistan scheme. All the riches, lands and properties, which were in Pakistan must remain there and Muslims must not accept any position whereby they might have to inherit a ruined country. The so-called Muslim promoters or originators of the Pakistan idea were highly educated and intelligent persons. They wanted the division of the country where the Muslims would be in a majority and thus would be rulers of that area. Hindus would continue to live there as before. But the smaller leaders at the state and district level misunderstood and misinterpreted the original scheme and started acting in a way which forced the enterprising Hindu population to migrate to the other parts of the country.

Stabbing was thus resorted to with the intention of keeping the Hindus indoors. Side-by-side meetings of the city elders were held to reassure the Hindus of their safety. They were told not to get scared by the stray acts of a few mischief mongers, who would be controlled by the saner people. But some of our Muslim friends came to us privately to inform us that the mischievous sections were planning mass attacks, looting and killing. They advised us to remain alert.

As the conditions in Sialkot were getting out of control, I received a message to change my manner of operation. Rather than having my centre at Wah camp, I had to shift to Sialkot and conduct my operations from there. That way I would be getting a direct feel of the situation in the city and also I could participate in the meetings and know all plans for protection. I therefore, took leave from Wah camp with the promise that I should be visiting them almost every week.

During my stay in the Wah camp, the relief work had been well established to the satisfaction of all concerned. Dr Jai Gopal Jolly, the medical officer of the camp, appointed by the government, was now working in close association with our volunteers. He had also developed a very close and sweet relationship with me. Even after a lapse of 53 years, he continues to be one of my closest and dearest friends.

At the call of my city, I had to shift my responsibilities immediately and reach Sialkot. Once there, I got a detailed information on the planning made for defence of different *mohallas*. The part of the city where I lived was away from the old city and was considered as one of the safest colonies and also the nearest to the railway station. In the meetings of the inner circle where detailed discussions were held, I was told to continue the procurement with my headquarters at Sialkot.

From Sialkot I had to travel to Peshawar by rail; it was a long journey with a change of train on the way. I had to carry a lot of cash for fulfilling my purpose and therefore, for safety I chose to travel by first class. I selected a special outfit with a Jinnah cap for my head, a Kashmiri basket containing all the necessities required during a long journey and a book on the life of Prophet Mohammed written by K.L. Gaubha. The book was titled *The Prophet of the Desert* and its author was the estranged son of Lala Harikishan Lal Gaubha, a former congressman with legendary courage. He defied the infamous Martial Law of Amritsar in the year 1919 and was condemned to death for doing so. Later, he got a reprieve and after the reçall of the notorious Punjab Governor, O. Dwyer, the perpetrator of the Jallian Wala Baugh massacre, Lala Harikrishan Lal was appointed as the first Indian minister of the Punjab for finance, education and rural development. K.L. Gaubha developed differences with his father, converted to Islam to marry a *nautch* girl and changed his name from Kanhya Lal Gaubha to Khalid Lateef Gaubha, retaining thereby his initials.

Getting the list of the city's requirements for defence, I travelled by train first to visit the Wah camp. From there I reached Haripur Hazara in a jeep early in the morning. Arriving there, I discussed the Sialkot situation with Harish giving him the details of our plans. He told me that he would make arrangement for all my requirements by the night and that I could leave early in the morning. I spent that night with him as I had done on an earlier occasion. The night was very pleasant and before sleeping I talked to Harish about his latest assessment of his district. He told me that it continued to be calm so far and the people were very simple and good. As he was generous with them, the local people, irrespective of their religion were happy with him. But he felt that some of the mischievous elements were slowly trying to propagate the Muslim League's ideology. People by and large were peaceful and were influenced by Khan Abdul Gaffar Khan of NWFP. He then added that he was fully prepared for any trouble. He and a few of his very sincere local *swayamsewaks* stayed with him in the office building. In the event of an attack on his office, he had thought out and made adequate arrangements about how to face it or escape from there.

As per our plan, I left early with my cargo, reached Hasnabdal station and boarded the first mail train towards Lahore. Changing at Wazirabad I reached Sialkot and got my baggage carried to my house, which was very close to the station. I heaved a sigh of relief to have successfully executed for the first time the dangerous act of gun running for such a long distance. The material was sent to the designated places.

My next trip was to Peshawar. I was careful to avoid those things, which had created problems for me during my first trip. One was, not to carry a brand new holdall because it attracted unnecessary attention. The other was about the weight of the cargo. On the first occasion, the weight of my cargo was so heavy that it was difficult for one coolie to carry it. I had to pay the coolie a high wage and had to tell him in advance that my bag was heavy in order to check him from complaining. The whole month of July, I continued running different errands. During this period, there had been some anxious moments but I could come out safely. Once, after I left with my dangerous cargo from Haripur Hazara in our jeep, we were driving at our normal speed of 60–65 miles per hour. Midway between Haripur Hazara and the Wah camp, I saw before me on the road an English cavalry officer on a horseback with his hand raised in a gesture to stop our jeep. He was followed by his cavalry men on horses. My heart just sank and as I looked at my driver I found that he had also turned pale. We thought that somebody might have spied on us and informed the government. The road was too narrow for escape. The driver slowed down and as we reached near the cavalry, the officer started moving his raised arm up and down to signify that we should slow down in order not to disturb the horses. The driver was obliged to go slower and, being an old military man, gave a stiff salute to the officer while controlling his steering with his left hand. As we passed the troops, we laughed heartily at our imaginary fear.

There was another occasion when another *swayamsewak* from some other city travelled in the same train from Peshawar with his cargo. He travelled in the third class carrying a new holdall which he placed in the upper berth of the same compartment. I could recognise him from his dress and cap. I called him out of his compartment and told him to be careful as the new holdall in third class attracted instant attention. He, therefore, took his seat on the opposite side of the compartment away from his baggage. I was in the same train but in the first class with my own baggage. The train stopped at Hasnabdal, which was the first station after crossing from NWFP to the Punjab. Men from the Excise Department normally came to that station to check the compartments to see if anybody was travelling with any illegal or contraband items out of NWFP. It was one of those days when there were checkers at the station. One of them entered that third class compartment where our man was carrying his dangerous cargo. The checker noticed the new holdall and pricked it with his stick. He became suspicious and enquired to whom did that holdall belong? When there was no response he shouted and asked again. Finally, at the third announcement a villager travelling in that compartment thinking that the owner of the holdall may have forgotten to take his baggage, decided to claim it and answered the excise man in his rustic language, *"Mehnda Ayie"*— "it belongs to me". He was asked to bring it out on the platform. The compartment was crowded and on reaching the holdall he moved it with his two hands to bring it on his head. It was too heavy for the frail villager to hold it on his head. It fell on the legs of the passengers sitting there. Two of them on whose legs the holdall fell, hurting them slightly, swore but helped to place it back on his head. He was scared at its heavy weight but somehow carried it outside and threw it on the platform. He was asked to open it; and as he tried to open his hands trembled. One of the excise men helped him; and when it was spread open, it revealed the firearms. The man started crying, "No! It is not mine, it is not mine". The two excise men started hitting him; and as the train was getting late, the guard told the excise men that he was flagging-off the train and they allowed the train to leave. The train started and the *swayamsewak* continued sitting quietly on his seat. He was saved but the ammunition was lost.

Some days later, there was another experience at the Hasnabdal station when I had only four revolvers in my small attaché case in the first-class compartment, in which I was the only passenger. I boarded the train at Peshawar and as it stopped at Hasnabdal station, what I saw at the platform alerted me. About ten soldiers led by a colonel were marching from the main station gate towards my compartment. Seeing them I immediately got up from my seat, opened the door of my compartment and stood there looking towards them. As they marched straight towards me, my heart started beating very fast. The officer stopped before my compartment and asked my name. When I gave him my name, he looked into my compartment and enquired who else was travelling in that compartment? I told him that I was all by myself there. He then passed me and went to the first-class next to my compartment. I shut my compartment door, came out on the platform and walked few steps towards the adjacent compartment. The colonel called four of his men and entered that compartment after ordering the stationmaster to let the train go. The train moved on, and I reached Sialkot safely.

It was the end of July and although I had handed over the refugee camp charge some time back to another *swayamsewak*, I kept in touch with him on a regular basis. On one of my visits, three Sialkot ladies, all with congress sympathies, accompanied me to the Wah camp. They wanted to stay there for a few days and watch and console the suffering refugees. They might have carried with them some gifts for refugee women or children for which I had no idea. I remember them even now. They were Gauran *Behenji*, wife of Dr L.C. Dutt and her younger sister. Both these noble ladies were social workers. The third was a young girl named Kamla Ahuja, sister of a *swayamsewak*, Dharam Bir Ahuja. All of them stayed in a separate barrack for a few days and went back to Sialkot on their own.

On my last visit there, I promised the volunteers that I would visit sometime in the beginning of August. But in the first week of August it was not possible for me to leave the city because the situation there had become quite nasty. Stabbing had started in a small way in certain areas. The general relationship beetween Hindus and Muslims being quite good, the chances of widespread disturbances were rather remote . But the Muslim League had become more aggressive with their propaganda and the stabbing had caused all the business to come to a standstill. The Hindu shopkeepers in the city closed their business houses and did not move out freely because of the risk of attacks.

The RSS decided not to retaliate as it could result in a widespread trouble. I was told to remain in the city and participate in the defence arrangements of the vulnerable *mohallas*. I therefore, threw myself in that work and attended meetings daily till midnight. Distribution of whatever weapons we could collect was being done according to the needs of different *mohallas*. Main attention was given to the rich Jain *mohalla*. I also had a friend who had retired from the army and was then living in the contonment. At that time, he became our local source of small arms through the army canteen contractor. He could procure a few revolvers and a big wooden case full of 303 cartridges for us. The delivery of a case of 303 cartridges presented me with a dangerous situation. It was a very heavy wooden case bearing all the markings and arrow signs. I was not at home when my friend delivered the case outside our main gate. When I reached home, one of the workers of my father's workshop informed me that a wooden case was delivered by my *sardarji* friend and it was lying there on the road near our main gate. I saw the case and was alarmed. With the help of the same worker, I managed to carry it in and then to the top roof of my house. I was terribly scared that my father might see it. It was so heavy that both the worker and I were profusely sweating after carrying it to the top. My hands got scratched and bled at some places. As the worker was leaving, I warned him not to mention anything to anybody about it and gave him a generous tip for his service. I then caught hold of a chisel and a hammer and with great difficulty broke the wooden case. Inside there were printed cardboard boxes containing one gross of cartridge in each box. I put all the wood of the broken case in a tandoor fixed in one corner of the top roof and ignited it. The cardboard boxes were carried slowly to my room and placed under my cot. After putting everything at a safe place, I rode on my motorcycle and informed the receipt incharge. He immediately arranged to collect all the boxes from my house.

It was the end of the first week of August and we were busy day and night in preparing several plans of protection and their trials. A *Punjab Raksha Samiti*, or some other organisation having a similar name, had been functioning for some time with its headquarters at Amritsar. Our Sialkot RSS *sanghchalak*, who was also the city president of the *samiti* in Sialkot, had attended its meetings at Amritsar. When he came back to Sialkot after one of such meetings, he told our city incharge that very good quality daggers were available at Amritsar. Our *sanghchalak* had ordered hundred pieces for Sialkot, which were to be collected from Amritsar. Again, I was told to collect those. The address of Amritsar source with an introductory letter was handed over to me for immediate action. I took a direct train to Amritsar. The place where the daggers were available was a big bungalow with extensive lawns and a beautiful garden. The inside of the house looked like a palace with high ceilings, carpeted rooms and lavish furniture. I was entertained very affectionately and was shown my bedroom to spend the night. The gentleman responsible to look after me promised me that next morning, hundred daggers in a steel box would be delivered to me at Amritsar station in front of my first class compartment seat. The room was too cosy and luxurious for me to spend the night comfortably, but I was ready early in the morning. At around 8:00 AM, somebody knocked at my door. I was told that my goods had been packed and sent to the railway station. My seat was reserved and handing me my ticket, I was told to finish my breakfast and get into their car, which would drive me to the station. Reaching the station, I found my seat and the man with a steel trunk waiting for me. The trunk was placed under my seat. When I reached Sialkot, I got the trunk carried to my house and from there the contents were removed to its right place the same night.

That was my last trip outside Sialkot. My journeys for the relief work or for procurement of arms came to an end. The conditions all over the West Punjab, where I had been moving all those months were getting worse. The movement of Hindus to safer places had started. My father and my uncles had gone to Ludhiana and transferred some money in a bank there. Similarly, many others had gone to different places. Some people were sending their families outside Punjab to spend some time with their relatives. From our family, my grandmother, with two children each from her three sons, had gone to Shimla to stay with one of her daughters.

It was certain that Sialkot, like all the districts on the west of the river Ravi, was to go to Pakistan. Still the Muslim League propaganda continued and provoked their community members to take revenge on the Hindus who had been dominating the poor Muslims because of their superior financial position. It did create more tension and fear among the Hindus . On the eleventh of August, there was a fatal stabbing case outside Dharowal *mohalla*. Kartar Singh Ghura was stabbed to death and his licensed revolver was snatched away from his dead body. He was the father of my friend who was living separately from his father's family, in cantonment area. My friend had an Italian wife, whom he married when he was in Italy serving the British Army in the last Great War. I was riding my motorcycle to cover all the Hindu localities of the city when I was informed about the stabbing. At once, I went to the cantonment and informed my friend about the murder of his father. He had already received the news by telephone and was ready to leave for the Deputy Commissioner's bungalow, because his father was employed under him in the intelligence. He sat on the back seat of my motorcycle and I drove him up to the place he wanted to go. While coming back to the city, I made another round of different *mohallas* to see whether their defence preparations were adequate. The entire business community and all the big factories were closed for two days now. The city looked like a deserted place with not a single soul seen on the road in the Hindu populated areas. On that day, one bus load of Hindus was ready to go to Jammu. After visiting several areas all over the city to watch the situation, I came to have a look at that bus. I saw that my closest friend and near relative, Lakshmi Chand Khanna was sitting inside with all his family members. I greeted him and told him that I would watch the safe passage of their bus beyond the border. During those days, I always carried a loaded revolver in my pocket for any emergency. I did follow that bus and saw that it passed safely beyond the Sialkot limits, greeted my friend and rode back on my motorcycle to the city.

In the Old City, the Hindu and Muslim *mohallas* were built centuries back using the same layouts and same type of the construction materials . Though these were separate from each other, yet they were connected and one could go to a Hindu *mohalla* from a Muslim *mohalla* and *vice versa*, easily. The Hindus and the Muslims could be easily distinguished by their looks, dress and many a time by their language and the way they spoke. The Hindus were richer, more educated, better dressed, more cultured and had a much better sense of hygiene. There were more Hindu doctors, lawyers, teachers, businessmen and government servants. The Muslims had more artisans, blacksmiths, masons, carpenters, leather tanners, gut makers, farmers and wrestlers. In every Muslim *mohalla* they had one or two Masjids which normally had a small *Madrassa*. There were some localities, which were also established long back on the city's outskirts. Those were mostly inhabited by Muslims. Only on one side of the city, where the Britishers chose to build their cantonment and the railway station, did the new Hindu localities develop. Those were all built as per modern construction plans. All the government bungalows and the best buildings with beautiful gardens were built on that side.

With such clear differentiations and delimitations of the Hindu and Muslim populations, the RSS workers had taken full charge of the Hindu *mohallas*' protection. The maximum attention was given to the areas in the Old City, which were most vulnerable to the attacks by the Muslim League rowdies. They had openly declared that their main target was the Jain *mohalla*, and that they had planned to start their major attacks from the Kashmiri *mohalla*. Most of our protection and defence arrangements were therefore concentrated on that side. The other *mohallas* in the Old City had also their adequate defence arrangement. But in spite of all this we could not control the panic, which was spreading in the majority of the Hindu families. The news of attacks on the Hindus living in the towns and villages of western districts beyond the Chanab river, and the stories of the crualties and bestialities committed by the Muslim mobs on the innocent Hindus especially on the young girls and women, created more terror in their minds.

Day and night there were slogans from the Muslim *mohallas* of "*Allah Hu Akhbar*", "*Pakistan Zindabad*", "*Qaed-E-Azam Zindabad*". Some of the Hindu localities too replied with "Har Har Mahadev"or "*Jo Bole-So-Nihal, Sat Sri Akal*". All this further added to the panic and on the eleventh of August, the Hindus started moving out of the city, either to Jammu by rail and by bus or to safer areas like the cantonment. There were many good Muslims who visited their Hindu friends or Hindu owners of the factories in which they were working, and gave them assurance that they would guard their houses and properties in case the rowdies attacked. But the Hindus were not convinced as they knew that the good persons among the Muslim community would not be a match for the trouble makers. Their sincerity they thought, would be of no avail.

On the eleventh evening our elders also decided to leave for Jammu with the ladies and children for a week or so and come back after the fifteenth August when Pakistan was created and there was peace. But I refused to leave. All others left except me and my father who would not go without me. On the twelfth of August, more Hindu families started leaving their houses, but due to lack of sufficient transport facilities, they were crowding the areas around cantonment. To cope with that situation, the local government had to open camps by pitching tents to provide shelter for those people. With the outflow from the city increasing, the authorities had to stretch their arrangements and also provided armed protection in that area. The general condition in the city continued to deteriorate. It was only the Jain *mohalla*, from where nobody was allowed to move out and it was here where the Muslim mobs attacked on the evening of the twelfth August. The *mohalla* had prepared well to face the attack from all sides. Some of the most courageous of the *swayamsewaks* of the city had been entrusted with the defence and they withstood all attacks successfully throughout the night. The attackers used guns, rifles and grenades with all the ferocity they could muster. They had come well prepared to attack, enter the *mohalla* and start murder and mayhem, loot and plunder. But they had not the slightest idea of what they had to face there. Their guns and rifles shots were answered with guns and rifle shots from the positions held at some important posts. Grenades were retaliated with grenades. This most unexpected but adequate reply not only stopped their advance but was also instrumental in putting some fear in them. Some of our boys repeatedly shouted from their positions that they would not allow the attackers to return to their families on their legs. In support of that declaration, the boys, first started with 303 shots from the highest positions in the Jain *mohalla* into the far-off houses in the Muslim *mohalla* from where the attackers appeared to have emerged. There were loud cries from the inhabitants of those houses. At the break of dawn on the thirteenth there were no attackers to be seen anywhere near the Jain *mohalla*. But the hostile attitude of the civil authorities made the Hindus leave the city in a planned manner from the inner Hindu *mohallas*. Some Hindus became the victims due to their Congress inspired over confidence. They flatly refused to follow the organised evacuation under the *swayamsewaks* of different *mohallas*. One such family headed by Dr Badri Nath Chawla, a Congress leader of Sialkot, was entirely massacred when they left their home. Not even the ladies and their children were spared.

—2—

MAYHEM — CREATION OF PAKISTAN — OUR MIGRATION

By midday on the thirteenth August, the Deputy Commissioner ordered imposition of penal 144 in the city, allowing only the evacuating Hindus on the roads. Most of the Hindu population then left their homes. The government had also announced that those of the Hindus who wanted to leave their homes might find a place in the refugee camp opened in the protected cantonment area. I too left with my father and went to the railway station where a train full with passengers stood, on its first platform, destined for Jammu Tawi. The railway station too was full to its capacity. The Jain *mohalla* was totally evacuated. Some families were going into the government camps and some of them were pouring into the already crowded railway station.

The stationmaster and most of his Hindu staff were managing to accommodate the inflow on that train. All the additional coaches, available in the yard, were attached but even those could not cope with the inflow at the station. People were still steaming in, and there were many *swayamsewaks* to help them find some space in the already full compartments. Ladies, small children, young girls, and old people were allowed the preference for finding space inside the compartments. The young people rode on the top of the train, as there was no room available inside. Then some adventurous young men found accommodation for themselves in the space between two coaches. The reports had reached the stationmaster that the train would be attacked by the Muslim murder squads somewhere before it reached the next station. He therefore, sought military protection force from the cantonment to travel with the train. So far no soldiers had arrived. In the absence of the defence guards to go with the train, the stationmaster was not moving the train. The train stood at the station having been filled with people to every inch of it and the whole railway station compound was also overflowing with people.

All the available buses had already been hired by groups of evacuees and had left for Jammu Tawi. Then came the turn of the trucks till those were also fully availed of. The people who could not find any scope for their families to get onto the train, had started moving to the camp in the cantonment in groups. Late in the afternoon, news reached the stationmaster's office that a train full of massacred passengers was reaching there from Wazirabad. It was stopped at Nizamabad, a suburb of Wazirabad, and all the passengers were massacred totally. The train was to arrive in a few minutes at platform number five. The stationmaster appealed to people on the platform through a loudspeaker to help vacate the train full of the badly wounded passengers by providing him with ten volunteers. I and nine others offered our services to the stationmaster. We were told to reach platform number five as the train had already arrived.

On reaching there, as the door of one of the coaches was opened and we looked in, a terrible shudder passed through our bodies. The hand that had grasped the handle of the door to open dropped, and all of us stepped back looking at each other with faces turned pale. What we saw was ghastly beyond our wildest imagination.

Six boys, without uttering a single word, turned their faces and started vomiting on the platform. The other four of us, were then shaken to the realisation that we had been entrusted to do some duty. We told the six boys to go back to the stationmaster, tell him about the gruesomeness of the situation and request him to send more boys who were stout-hearted and strong-bodied. If possible, he should also arrange a few stretchers.

We then opened the door of the same coach again and allowed the scene inside to register in our mind fully so that we could decide the way to handle the work. There was blood all around with human bodies thrown topsy-turvy, totally mauled and blood-smeared. A slow groaning sound told us that there was still some life. We again shut the door and discussed the manner to start the job. We decided to first drag out those bodies which were near the door and could be reached without entering the coach.

O' God ! what kind of job was thrown our way? Our hands slipped when we tried to drag out the first body. All of us then jointly tried with determined effort to pull the nearest body to bring it near the edge. Meanwhile, six other boys arrived with two stretchers. Two of the boys suggested some guidelines using their experience of scouting in their school.

It was decided that we may pull out the bodies, one by one, to the gate. Check it whether it was dead or still breathing. The living shall be placed on the platform near to the coach and the dead at some distance from the train. Some boys showed better capability to handle the grim job. We formed two groups with a stretcher each and started doing the job in two coaches separately.

The arrival of boys with scouting training and the stretchers made our work easier. After clearing the door, our groups entered the coach, very carefully to avoid slipping on the blood plastered floor. Slowly and cautiously, we were able to clear the entire train. But what we saw and tackled cannot be adequately described in words.

In the group with which I worked, I may just try to write about two cases. In one case, we saw an old woman sitting with the head of her middle aged and very healthy son in her lap. The man must be breathing when she might have seen the body wounded badly of his son but as we reached her, he was dead. The woman was sitting like a statue, bemoaning in a slow voice of painful helplessness. The other case was that of a badly wounded and dead young girl lying flat on her back with a small baby crying at her stone like breasts. We lifted the crying baby and handed it over to one boy and asked him to give it a wash at the platform water tap and then entrust it over to some elderly and kind woman.

Both the dead and the still breathing were all brought out from the coach. Some from under the seats, others on them and yet others half inside the toilet. After washing our arms and legs at the platform water tap, we reached back and reported to the stationmaster about the completed work. It was the most abominable type of job which even the slaughter house butchers may find difficult to perform. Today I cannot imagine that I was one of those who cleared the train full of the massacred human bodies. A very large amount of mental and physical strength with a deep sense of duty must have enabled me to do that job and not desert the scene in despair and helplessness.

The stationmaster, in the meantime, had arranged some scavengers from the railway establishment. They washed the blood splattered coaches, lifted the living from the platform and placed them on the seats of the washed coach. That coach was brought to the first platform and was attached to our train.

The sun was about to set when six riflemen, all *gurkhas*, arrived at the railway station. They positioned themselves in the train—two each in the middle and last bogies and two in the engine. The stationmaster had already received confirmation about a big armed gathering somewhere before or after the Sialkot cantonment, which was the next station. The train started with a long whistle and the hooting of the engine. All the people on the train shouted, "*Har Har Mahadev*" and "*Jo*

Bole-So-Nihal, Sat Sri Akal". The train slid in inches and very slowly gained speed. The engine drivers and the guards were very considerate about the safety of all the people on top of the train, between the bogies and specially the wounded. It reached Conley Park, the playground for all school and college boys. Slowly it arrived at the Sialkot cantonment station and passed the deserted platform. Hardly had it gone a little distance away from the cantonment station when suddenly we heard the screeching sound from the engine wheels and the train stopped. A storm of dust enveloped our coach which had tilted to its right. I could not understand what was happening and tried hard to keep standing where I was, as my body reclined towards the windows. I looked in my coach and saw my father and others sitting or standing as they were in fully crammed condition, somewhat stunned at the sudden stoppage of the train.

As the dust cleared, I saw from the window a big mob appearing from nowhere, at some distance from our train, with raised weapons in their hands, flashing in the rays of the setting sun. They ran towards our train shouting, "*Allah-Hu-Akhbar*".

I jumped out of the window and stood outside to face the murderous crowd. The two *gurkha* soldiers took their positions in a minute and I moved near the engine by their side with my loaded revolver. The *gurkhas* shouted at me to get back as my revolver was of no use against a big gang of attackers. Next minute, six rifle shots flew towards the assailants who instantly stopped their advance. Another six shots were fired and the entire mob turned back and ran away.

Our train had been derailed by removal of the fish plates of the rails. The engine touched the unbolted rails, and slid off the track with its right side wheels digging into the earthy ground raising a storm of dust and barely stopped short of falling to its right. My compartment was second from the engine and next to the wounded people's bogie.

It was getting dark and the loud cries from the train did not stop even though the murderers had retreated and disappeared as quickly as they had appeared.

Some of the *swayamsewaks* in the train then took charge of the whole train clearing it as soon as possible and lead the people to the other side of the track. We saw several military trucks arrive at site; soldiers alighting from those trucks encircled the derailed train. Their presence helped build the confidence of the crying women. There was a big plot of vacant land on the cantonment side. All the occupants of our train were asked to stay there during the night, which had come around without notice.

People tried to find space for themselves in groups, helped by the moonlight. I sat at one place with my father and tried to assure him of our safety. He was quite nervous after seeing what had happened. I told him to rest peacefully and keep his head on my lap. He stretched there for a while but instead of resting his head on my lap, he put his turban under his head. I told him that I might be going around among the people and would come back after seeing the protection arranged by the military. The *gurkhas* then took position on top of the empty train. The total area, where the people from the train were resting, was guarded by an adequate number of soldiers. When I was fully satisfied, I returned to my father. He was lying with his eyes closed and chanting the *Gayatri Mantra* in a low voice.

I sat down reflecting about all I had witnessed and experienced that day. Soon, I was dozing when suddenly I was jolted by the loud and piercing cry of a girl. I stood up and saw a group of ladies encircling a girl who was crying with intense pain. I enquired from one of the ladies and was informed that a young girl was giving birth to a baby. It was a rather shocking news; I could only feel pity in that situation because I could be of no help to her. One of the women surrounding the girl shouted for some water. Some of the boys ran out to enquire from one of the guards about how and where to get a bucket of water? There was a tanker full of drinking water nearby, but no bucket was to be found. Some ladies offered their *patilas* which were filled with water and carried to the place of happening. The girl was still in intense pain and was crying helplessly. After about half-an-hour, she stopped crying and the ladies surrounding her, heaved sighs of relief. After all the panic and pain, their frantic efforts could save the baby and the mother. It was God's gift in that horrible situation when time seemed to have stopped.

The painful cries of the girl reminded me of the cries and groans heard by me from the massacred train. Then I thought about the fate of those persons who were loaded in the compartment attached with our train. I tried to go back and find about them but the guards around the train did not allow me. They told me that the military must have taken care of that compartment. But I felt that nobody in that compartment could survive after what happened to the train. Only the Omniscient God knows about such things.

At the first sign of dawn, I took leave from my father for a short while and located Kapur Chand Jain in that miniature humanity. He was considering their next move in consultation with his relatives. As I stood with them, I saw my friend Balwant Singh, who resided in the cantonment, approaching us. Reaching me he said that he had come to take me along to his bungalow. I told him that I was with my father and we would, together with Kapur Chand's family and relatives, go to the government camp. But he insisted and took me with him, along with the Kapur Chand's group which included his family and friends. That group also included Shiv Kumar Sharma and his family. At his bungalow, he arranged to serve all of us tea, biscuits and bread. But clearly it was not possible for him to look after all those persons any longer. Considering this fact, Kapur Chand and his party left for a camp after thanking Balwant. I and my father were not allowed to leave. We passed that day and night with Balwant talking most of the time about the unexpected developments.

After the murder of his father, Balwant while carrying his father's dead body from the city had also brought his mother and other family members to his bungalow. His mother reminded him that he had to collect his father's ashes from the cremation ground on that day—the August 14.

It started raining in the morning that day and Pakistan celebrated her independence, in their capital city of Karachi. In Balwant's house, the atmosphere was gloomy. We were preparing to go to the cremation ground to collect Balwant's father's ashes. It was raining heavily and knee-deep waters had collected around the cremation ground. The shed at the cremation ground was practically of no use in that kind of weather, and the spot at which the dead body was cremated had been washed away with rainwater. There was nothing there and we had to search for the bones scattered around. With the joint efforts of all, we could barely find a few bones here and there. We placed those and also some flowers and petals in a small bag. We brought the bag back to the bungalow and showed it to Balwant's mother telling her that the God of rain had already washed the remains of her *sardarji*. She was a woman of rare courage and extreme patience. She directed her son in a very poised voice to place the bag at some clean and secure place outside the bungalow.

On August 15, the commandant of the cantonment announced that rail track had been repaired. The steam engine and all the coaches were moved to the railway yard for complete check up and inspection. Further, we were informed that the train to Jammu Tawi would leave on the nineteenth from the cantonment railway station.

We had nothing to prepare to catch the train on the nineteenth. Leaving our house on the thirteenth, I carried only a small attache case, which had been left inside our bogie when the train was derailed and I jumped out. Next morning, when I went to the derailed bogie, there was nothing inside. I thought that people who were deputed to search all the bogies took it into possession.

I helped Balwant in the packing of his household goods as he had also decided to leave on the nineteenth by the rescheduled train to Jammu Tawi. Everything he possessed was packed in nine steel trunks and sacks. We were quite concerned as to how we could catch that train with my father and Balwant's family. But Balwant was very resourceful and had been an achiever all his life. He met the commandant who was responsible for transportation of the refugees from the cantonment station. The commandant issued him a special permit to board the train with eleven other people, after hearing from him about, his military service during war, his Italian wife, and about the recent murder of his father.

Somehow, we passed those four days and nights in extreme anxiety. There appeared to be no change in the people in the city even after achieving what they wanted. They continued shouting daily "*Pakistan Zindabad*" and other offensive slogans against India and Hindus. Pakistan had been created. The Hindus and Sikhs had been driven out of their homes. The Muslim League leaders had got the full control of the entire land they demanded. We could not understand, why were they continuing raising slogans and what was it they wanted more.

One night while sleeping on the roof of the bungalow, I was awakened by a hissing sound arising from the lawn. The first thought that came to my mind was that some Muslim fanatics had entered the lawn of our bungalow stealthily to attack us. I immediately took out my revolver from under my pillow, crept near the stairs and tried to locate the invaders. But nothing was visible though the hissing sound continued. It was a dark cloudy night and nothing could be seen from the roof. I then awoke my friend and told him about the hissing sound in the compound. He confirmed that there was some sound but could not figure out anything. Finally, we decided to go down the stairs and face the intruders. We started moving cautiously. After covering half the compound, we saw a buffalo grazing in our lawn, moving freely in the dark night. We looked at each other with amused faces at our mental pre-occupation with danger of attack by the Muslims and went back to our beds.

On the day of departure, we were all ready early in the morning to board the train. Priority was accorded to the camp refugees who were being transported in military trucks from the camp to the train. We reached the station and with the help of the permit, were allowed to board the train immediately.

The train was again crowded and there was not an inch of space left anywhere. The military personnel adequately guarded the entire station and the train was also provided full military protection. The rail track up to Suchetgarh, the first railway station in the Jammu and Kashmir state, was also guarded by the military police. The train moved out of the station slowly. It continued moving at a very slow speed without stopping anywhere and reached Jammu station safely. The entire platform and the open space outside were full of people who had come to receive their kith and kin. The Jammu and Kashmir government had also opened refugee camps and arranged transportation for those who wished to go there. My youngest uncle was also there to receive us as he hoped that we would be on that train. Similarly, everybody who had come to the station had done so with the simple hope and prayer that their relatives might be on the train. The political position had deteriorated so much that no Hindu remained in the old part of

Sialkot city. A group of *swayamsewaks* of Jammu were the most conspicuous among the other people at the Jammu station. Many of them were well known to me. We left in a *tonga* to our place, which uncle had arranged for our family. My mother had been almost half dead with anxiety due to our staying back in Sialkot after our entire joint family had moved out to a safe place. During those eight days that we remained in Sialkot, she had been assailed by all sorts of apprehensions about our safety. The union of the whole family after days of extreme anxiety was considered as a blessing of God. After 2–3 days, we sat discussing the current situation and the future plan. Everything depended on what my father and his two brothers would decide. Among the younger generation, only I was capable of thinking independently about the family and also about my future course of action.

My friend Balwant Singh stayed in a hotel with his wife and two kids. His mother and other members of her family had gone to the refugee camp. Shiv Kumar Sharma had also gone to the refugee camp with his family. Kapur Chand Jain stayed with one of his relations, a police inspector. With the police officer's influence, his family could manage to stay in a portion of the old palace of the *Maharaja* of Jammu and Kashmir. After their stay there for a few days, the police inspector arranged transportation of Kapur's family to Pathankot. They then stayed in Amritsar for a few days and finally reached Ludhiana where they had planned to settle. I maintained contact with Balwant and Shiv Kumar. Balwant was in a peculiar situation being married to a European and having kids. Even then we had been considering our future actions jointly.

Like many of the refugees from Sialkot or other places, who stayed in Jammu, we hoped against hope that the Muslims, having achieved their aim, had nothing left to agitate for. They had their Pakistan and their own leaders were running the government in their country. The conditions in Pakistan would become normal shortly and we would go back to our homes where our ancestors had lived for centuries under the Muslim kings. The only fear was that our moveable possession would have been looted. As long as our, houses, factories and shops were there, we would go back and again re-establish our households and businesses by working a little harder. After all our intelligence and experience could not be snatched away from us. With such fond hopes, many of the migrants considered it a temporary phase and were looking forward to the change in the situation. Our family were a little more sanguine because our Muslim foreman came to Jammu to show his sympathies. He also assured us that when we went back to Sialkot, everything would be safe and we would get full co-operation from all our workers. They had all been missing us and cursing the bad times and the few mischief-mongers. Those bad people would repent and their families would curse them when they would have nothing with them to run their households. On the basis of good relations, which went back to centuries, most of us hoped and waited for that moment.

Leaving all the responsibility to my father and mother, I spent all my days with my comrades in the RSS. The incharge of Jammu RSS, Jagdish Abrol was from Sialkot and we had a special relationship and deep affection for each other. Besides the regular *shakha* work, the dynamic incharge of the Jammu region, had managed to render full service to the refugees in the camps through volunteers from his *shakhas*. Side by side, he was arranging to find room in the state for the Hindus who had come and who had still not gone to the refugee camps. He had not given me any job or work of any sort.

One day at the RSS office, Jagdishji assigned me a job which I would have to execute with all precision and efficiency. He explained in detail what I had to do and called four other young boys to assist me. I thought about the job and told him that I would like to speak to him in private. He asked the four boys to leave and looked at me in anticipation. I told him that on the Sialkot railway station, after clearance of the massacred train, something very strange had happened to me. It seemed to me that all the spirit and initiative had been drained out of me. At that moment I felt that I was incapable to do the job he wanted me to handle. He was looking at my face, all that time and when I ended my explanation, he told me very tenderly that he understood my feelings.

I went home and felt ashamed for my reply. After that I never met him during my days in Jammu. But I kept on thinking about the conversation between us and how he had responded to my unexpected and unusual acknowledgement of my weakness.

It revealed to me something new about the character of the man and his affection for me. He was a lion-hearted man, leading people with courage and daring. He never hesitated, even for a moment, to jump into any type of dangerous situation. He must have fought scores of times, broken many heads and had fought many battles where he was wounded badly. But he did not reprimand me for my lack of courage to do the job. He had lots of hope from me, as he knew that in many situations, I too had fought courageously and came out a winner. But those fights were limited to the use of *laathis* or hockey sticks and I might have also broken a few heads. It had never come to such a situation where I had to intimidate or beat an innocent person.

It is also a strange aspect of my character. I had seen trains full of innocent men and women, old and young, butchered mercilessly by the Muslims. I had off loaded bloody trains full of dead and dying people, mothers killed with their babies crying on their naked bosoms and had witnessed many other gruesome scenes which I cannot forget througout my life. These incidents and experiences had a very deep effect on me but they did not turn me into a cruel person. I always carried weapons to face an emergency but Providence had always kept me out of any such situation where I had to kill a person. All my life I had never fired a single shot with a gun, even for practice.

During my stay in Jammu, I was told that all the Hindus have left Sialkot except a small community who lived in their colony alongside the Aik stream. Their main profession was frying and selling fish. After a few months they also left, and Sialkot was then without any Hindu.

Another few months and the entire area from Peshwar to Lahore was cleared of all Hindus.

—3—

PAKISTAN ATTACKS KASHMIR

While spending our time in Jammu, some of our family members proved more practical. On one of those days when the Sialkot-Jammu train still operated, my uncle Dwaraka Das and younger auntie Phoolanwanti went to Sialkot. They reached our home, collected whatever they could manage and reached back Jammu successfully by the same train. That incident justified the assurance given by our foreman from Sialkot. From my father's family, neither my father nor I cared to do so. Personally, my robust and daring mind had become almost paralysed after my experiences on the thirteenth August.

Our family continued their stay in Jammu in a totally confused state of mind. They discussed daily, but could not decide where to go from there. Our loyal workers continued visiting us in Jammu and assured us that both our homes and business were safe in Sialkot. On the other hand we heard daily the shouting of slogans from across the border. The slogan had become more nasty. They included among their slogans a new one as, "*Hus Kay Liya Hai Pakistan Lad Kay Lengay Hindustan*".

In beginning of October, the Jammu governor deciding to dismantle refugee camps requisitioned as many buses as he could and started evacuating the refugees from the camps to the East Punjab. There was a primitive and undeveloped outlet to India from the state via Samba, Kathua and Lakhanwal which was then used for evacuation, but the buses could go only upto Kathua. From there the evacuees were to arrange their own transport. After Kathua there was a wild stream to cross on boats, then a thick Ghati forest to pass through its mud track on horses or *tongas* to reach Lakhanwal. From there, after crossing the bridge on the river Raavi, there was Pathankot.

It was then that our elders decided that they should leave Jammu and reach Amritsar. There, the brothers shall decide what they had to do and where they might chose to go and settle.

I planned with Shiv Kumar and when their turn came to leave the camp I smuggled myself into the bus with his family. The bus dropped us at Kathua. From there upto Pathankot, the journey was very arduous. Somehow, we managed to cover it. From Pathankot we took a train to Amritsar. Reaching Amritsar, I accompanied Shiv to his elder sister who was waiting for them. I stayed there and waited for my family to arrive in Amritsar where Balwant was allotted a house in Shareefpura. His mother and her family had already shifted from Dhariwal to that house. It was a double-storey house and the upper floor was kept vacant for my family. Before leaving Jammu, I informed my father that I would receive our family at the Amritsar station.

Staying with Shiv Kumar at his sister's house, I went to the station daily to look for my parents on the trains that arrived from Pathankot. It was nearly one week but there was no sign of them. Naturally, I became worried. I told Shiv that I should go back to Jammu and find out why my parents had not arrived as yet.

I left by train to Pathankot. At Pathankot railway station I met someone from Sialkot who told me that he had seen my father in the Kathua bazar purchasing some provisions. He had been waiting for the rains to stop so that he could leave with his large family. I immediately proceeded towards Kathua. The Ghati forest at the end of Lakhanwal town stopped me. It was drizzling and getting dark. There were no tongas serving in that weather and after sunset, I had to cross that dense forest all alone, as there was no one else travelling in the dark and rain. I stood there with my shoulder bag not knowing how to cross that thick jungle when suddenly a local man appeared there.

He saw me and enquired the reason for my standing there. I told him I wanted to go to Kathua and could not find the way through the forest. He advised me not to go into that thick jungle at night and in that weather. But I insisted that I needed to reach Kathua that night itself and requested him to put me on the right track. He then gave me directions to the best of his ability and put me on a mud track. He advised me to follow the mud route very attentively. He further told me that in case the track was merged in the rainwater, I might have to divine its place by seeing the space between the trees. I entered the forest with the name of God on my lips and went ahead as directed. Going ahead some distance, I tugged up my pants to my thighs and moved faster in the darkness. The rain started falling heavily and I lost the track in the heavy downpour and thick darkness. Stopping for a few seconds, I looked for any space between the trees to indicate the route but could find nothing. In that desperate situation, I pushed myself to run wherever my luck took me in the ankle-deep water. I had no idea whether I was running towards my destination or to some other place. But by my intuition I felt that I might at long last reach safely out of the jungle.

The rainwater falling from the dense tree leaves combined with that which my running steps shuffled up, made me thoroughly drenched. My shoulder bag too had become heavier. The lightning and the thunder made me further stupefied and I tried to run faster to somehow reach out of that damned forest. With no hope to find any help in that place, I kept running without a break. At one place when there was a lightning, I saw something in front of me moving zig-zag, crossing my way on the water. Thinking it to be a snake, I instantly increased my speed and after travelling some distance I started feeling that under my drenched shirt and *baniyan*, I was actually sweating. But I was almost like a possessed person running on and on, oblivious of my fate. I had no idea how far and how long I had run directionless with all my faculties numbed with fear of the unknown. But then, that state had to end somewhere. It ended when I reached out of the jungle and stopped there before a human being. The rain had also stopped by that time.

It took me sometime to regain my full senses. The man before me was bewildered to see my water drenched body emerge out of the jungle in that ungodly situation. It was he who spoke first and asked me what I was doing in that weather in that thick jungle? I told him that I was coming from Amritsar and wanted to go to Kathua. He did not stop me and told me to go ahead and make sure to cross the Ujh stream from a safe point and I may find the way to Kathua on reaching the other shore of the Ujh. On reaching the stream some village folks sitting on the bank told me that they would take me along after a few minutes when they had finished smoking their tobacco. I waited there till they were ready and then followed them into the stream. They knew the right place to cross the stream where it was the shallowest. I safely went across to the other bank with those men and as they had also to go through Kathua to their villages, I continued to follow them upto the Kathua main bazaar.

In the bazaar I met a person who knew my family and told me that they had planned to leave Kathua in the morning. However, he had no clue regarding their residence. I remembered the name of my grandmother's cousin—Sohan Lal Sehgal–and enquired about his address from a shopkeeper. He directed me to the *mohalla* and the distinctive mark of their house and I reached there without any problem. It was a big *haveli* with a big door. There was no life at the ground floor and I ascended the dark stairs to reach the first floor where I saw the glimmer of an oil lamp. Going a few steps forward, I heard the sound of my family members talking. I reached there and offered my greetings to the elders. Everyone looked at me and there was a spontaneous chorus of welcome from them. For a moment they did not even notice my drained physical condition. But soon, they realised the late time of the night and my totally drenched figure. They became anxious and, asked me how I had reached there so unexpectedly and in such a bad weather? My younger sister ran towards me and took away my shoulder bag. My mother stood up to find a towel for me to rinse my head and face. Then she gave me a new set of clothes to change.

After I washed and changed, I sat among the ladies who were cooking the meals and had my dinner. After I finished eating, I started feeling the ache in my legs and back. As the rest of the family sat to eat, I fell into the bed and went to sleep immediately.

I got up from my bed when I heard the ladies trying to wake up the small children. The men folks had already arranged for a boat to take the whole family, across the Ujh. In the morning, the elders thanked the host profusely and took his leave. The host accompanied us to the boat and bid the family farewell. As the boat moved away from the shore, I and my father jumped into the water and swam with the boat to the enjoyment of the children. The boat reached the other end and I helped everybody to get out of it. I had to carry the youngest baby on my back from the boat. Luckily it was not raining and the footpath through the jungle was visible. Strangely, all the water of the previous night's rain had flowed out to clear the path. But it was all muddy and the *tongawallas* were charging much more than usual. There were also many other families who wanted to hire them. In the situation, we straight-away hired three tongas, loaded our luggage and then made the ladies and children get onto them first before the menfolk.

The way through the forest was uneven and at certain places the *tonga* drivers wanted the males to come down to help their horses pullout of the deep mud. The journey was very tiring, was full of jerks and at times, making it all the more difficult for the ladies to keep their balance on the seats especially those who held their kids on their laps. The *tongawallas* did warn the passengers every time there appeared some hazard on the way. Somehow, to the immense relief of all of us, we reached Lakhanwal. Everybody felt hungry after the long and tiring journey, through the muddy track which caused some of the mud fly to our clothes and some parts of our bodies. Finding on the roadside a hand water pump, we washed our hands and faces. There were many *dhabhas* but as we had our own food, we found a tea shop, where we found seats, ordered tea for all and had our food on the benches there. Lakhanwal is the last town of the Jammu and Kashmir State. It is on the bank of the river Raavi when it enters the plains. We crossed the long Raavi bridge to reach Pathankot, the first border town of the East Punjab from the Jammu and Kashmir State. Pathankot is a commercial town primarily for timber. It has a terminal railway station from where we reached Amritsar. There the families parted as pre-planned. I took my family to Shareefpura house and occupied the vacant upper floor. We spent a few days in Shareefpura, but our minds were not at rest. Political conditions were going from bad to worse. In Amritsar, we witnessed daily trainloads of the Hindus arriving from Pakistan and trainloads of Muslims going to Pakistan from our side. It was the middle of October.

There was no peace of mind as we were witnessing gruesome scenes all around. The news that we were getting, added to our unrest further. My mother was particularly agonized on account of total obscurity about the survival of her old mother, brother and their children in a small village, in Pakistan surrounded by Muslim villages and, with no scope for getting any transport to cross over to the Indian territory.

However, in Amritsar we saw batches of people coming on foot from Dera Baba Nanak border and some of them were from the villages around that of my maternal parents. One day, in the Shareefpura Bazaar, we met a man who told us that, a few days back he had seen my maternal uncle at Dehra Baba Nanak, crossing over to Amritsar. He had told him that they would be going to Jalandhar.

When my mother heard that her mother's family was safe, she was very anxious to meet them. But there was no address. She wanted to go to Jalandhar to find them. We, therefore packed up and taking leave from Balwant's mother, made to the railway station to leave for Jalandhar.

To get into the train when it arrived at the platform, was a job which required all the strength and grit. Somehow, I succeeded in pushing all my family members into a compartment in which, I managed to be the first to jump. At Jalandhar railway station, we were again lucky to hire two *tongas* which carried us to our people. We found about their whereabouts from a provision shop in the main bazaar from where my uncle purchased material for cooking.

When the two families met, the joy was limitless. It was a spontaneous burst of emotions on both sides with an uproar of joyous cries and sentimental outbursts. It all happened when one *tongawalla* went into a temporary looking quarter to check the name of my maternal uncle, and came back with him, followed by his wife and mother, all with dazed and expectant faces. Then it all happened with the speed of an electrical current. The three who accompanied the *tongawalla* would not allow my mother to come down from her seat in the *tonga*. She was physically lifted from her seat by her brother and there arose a medley of sound and confused activity between my mother and her three relatives. Finally, it was my father who brought some order and made his family members alight from the *tongas* safely. All of us went inside the premises with our luggage. After the elders exhausted their emotions, the turn came for the younger members, from me downwards.

After exchanging information in bits and pieces, we settled down on the *charpoys*, which had been spread for us. My aunt attended the kitchen for preparing tea and drinks. I inspected the accommodation where our family would have to stay. A poor evacuee's hut, outside the city—it was inadequate—only one large room and a temporary kitchen. The remaining portion was a compound with walls. All construction, including the flooring inside the room and outside, were simply made from mud and bricks. There was a hand pump but no *latrine*. Everyone, big or small, male or female had to go out in the fields for this purpose. Exit for water was also quite unsatisfactory, as there was no drainage worth the name.

Being very tired, we had early dinner and went to sleep. Next day I asked my uncle about their escape from a remote village surrounded by all the notorious Muslim villages. He told his story thus :-

My *Nani* was a strong-willed, self-reliant old lady who was widowed at a young age. She had suffered a lot during her life, first by losing most of her children and then by the most tragic death of her husband. She had to take the place of her husband as a landlady and lived her life doing all his jobs. For her qualities she was respected by all her Muslim tenants. Even after the creation of Pakistan, she refused to leave her home. Her family consisted of her only son and daughter-in-law with three grandsons and a granddaughter.

When she saw that the Muslim Leaguers had come in the village and were inciting the Muslim farm workers against the Hindus and providing them with guns, she made up her mind. She had six other members of her family. She planned like a very sagacious person to leave home in three separate groups. First she let her eldest grandson aged 14 leave with her youngest grandson, accompanied by a very sincere servant, a Hindu water supplier from the village wells. They accompanied a village group of Hindus going to Narowal, a *tehsil* town and a railway station about four miles away from her home. After two hours she allowed her son and daughter-in-law to leave with another group. Last, she prepared herself to leave. Took out all her gold and wrapping it in two parts tied those on her thighs. She then put on her white clothes and covered her head and body with a white *chadder*. She locked her house and left with a group along with her granddaughter and a grandson. She was escorted by one of her most loyal tenants who carried his son's gun with him. Thus, the whole family reached Narowal and joined there a big convoy headed by *Sant* Fateh Singh Akali.

The three groups had faced some anxious moments on their way to Narowal. The water server with the first two boys was killed in an attack. He wore a turban and was mistaken as a Sikh by the attackers. The third group too was attacked as they wanted to rob the rich old woman. But her Muslim tenant shot dead one of the attackers and the others ran away.

From Narowal, the big convoy reached Amristsar, walking along the rail track and covering 50 miles distance in five days. On the way they faced several attacks on their convoy but *sant's* swords carrying followers did not allow them to do any damage. After arriving safely at Amritsar every family went their own way.

My grandmother was totally averse to occupying any house where the Muslim had lived. After many days of search, a small place under construction was found outside Jalandhar city which she agreed to live in and the family stayed there for many years. My grandmother could survive the last tragedy only for a year or so.

I had known my maternal grandmother very well. But after hearing the story of her escape with her family, my respect for that serious looking old lady had increased many times.

Living in Jalandhar for few days, we heard one day the radio broadcasted a news which shook everyone out of their slumber. Pakistan had stealthily attacked Kashmir from the Rawalpindi side, in the garb of the Pathan Tribals. The meager forces of *Maharaja* Hari Singh withered under the surprise onslaught of the superior forces of the attackers. The *Maharajas's* administration and the Indian government were taken unaware when they got the information that the raiders had reached Bara Mula on October 25. The *Maharaja* immediately signed the letter of accession to India and sent it through his Prime Minister with a request for its acceptance and to save the state from the attack of the Pakistani raiders. The Indian government acted as swiftly and adequately as it could do. In its emergent cabinet meeting, the Indian government accepted both the *Maharaja's* accession of his state with India and his request for sending urgent help. The crack Indian troops were flown in the only available Dakota planes immediately to save the Srinagar airport from the raider's occupation. We in the Punjab heard the buzz of the planes in the sky and our eyes were fixed towards those messengers of mercy.

After one or two days, I told my father that the place was not fit for our living. My father agreed with me and told me to find something better somewhere in or near Delhi. In the meantime, he proposed to pass time there. He said, that he might also contact his brothers who had decided to settle together at one place, which was suitable for living and starting of their business. My mother was comfortable to live with her old mother and only brother. Discussing all this, I decided to leave Jalandhar. Before leaving Amritsar I had planned to meet Balwant on a particular date at the Jalandhar station from where we were to go to Delhi to meet Shiv Kumar at his sister's house. I therefore left on the day and time fixed with Balwant.

— 4 —

ARRIVING DELHI OCTOBER 30, 1947— GANDHI MURDERED JANUARY 30, 1948

I reached the Jalandhar station in time but Balwant arrived in the afternoon. We waited for the train going to Delhi and around sunset, a goods train stopped there. There were covered wagons and open-top bogies. Deciding to travel by that train, we looked in the covered wagons one-by-one. Most were full with army horses, cows and buffaloes. The others were locked. The only choice left for us was to get onto an open-top bogie; most of them were also occupied by the refugees. At last we found one bogie where there was some space. We both jumped into it and found ourselves some room in one corner. There was some hay inside which we gathered to sit on.

It was night when the train moved out. Being the month of October and having had lots of rain in September, the nights were cold. In the open wagon of the running train it was chilling but we lowered our heads into our folded legs, brought our arms round our legs and huddled into each other as close as possible to get a little warmth. Being tired, we both fell asleep. A violent jerk woke us up and we found that the train had stopped. We stood up and looked out to find a very low platform with flicker of light at one spot. Both of us told our *hookah* smoking neighbours in the wagon to guard our shoulder bags as we had planned to jump out of the wagon. We were feeling very hungry but found nothing on that platform. We entered the room with a dim light. A man sat there in his chair with a kerosene lantern on his small table. He was the station incharge.

He told us that the station was Trawri near Karnal and the time was around 11:00 P.M. It was a small place and had one bazaar, just opposite the station entrance. He did not know how long the train would stop there. We went out and walked around in the bazaar, but could not find any living being there. We returned to our wagon as hungry as we had left. Balwant had informed me at Jalandhar station that the Government of India was not allowing any more refugees in Delhi as it had already received people much beyond her capacity. The trains going from the North terminated at Panipat or Sonipat. But we did not care and decided that we shall find other ways to reach Delhi when we arrived at the terminal.

It appeared that the lady luck was in our favour. The goods trains had no restriction and as our train jerked to a halt again, it was day time and we heard from the *hookah* smoking companions that it was the Subzi Mandi Station in Delhi. Without a second thought we jumped out of the bogie with our shoulder bags and approached a few *tongas* parked outside, waiting for customers. I had the address of Shiv Kumar's sister on a chit in my pant's pocket. But on my searching both my pockets, I could not find the chit there. Shiv Kumar was staying with his sister and we had to go there as decided. It was embarrassing standing before the *tongas* and not being able to tell them where we wanted to go. After thoroughly searching all pockets, I suddenly remembered that the name of the locality was Karol Bagh. I then told one *tongawalla* that we had lost the address but we wanted to go to Karol Bagh. The man replied that we were very near Karol Bagh but that it was a big locality. I told him that the person to whose house we needed to go was a Government of India employee and his name was Dewan Banwari Lal. He replied that he could take us to the government quarters in Karol Bagh and, if we were lucky, we might find our acquaintance living there. We agreed to his suggestion, and he took us to Tibbia College.

With the help of the *tongawalla*, we found the Estate Office, and enquired if Dewan Banwari Lal was an allottee there. But his name was not there on the list of the residents. We were disappointed and stood transfixed in the Estate Officer's office not knowing what to do next.

Seeing our helpless condition, the Estate Officer was kind enough to tell us that some government officers had been allotted vacant plots near Pusa Road and Arya Samaj Road and we could try our luck there. The sympathetic *tongawalla* agreed to try those areas and drove us to Arya Samaj Road. There we enquired from a gentleman about the location of the houses built for the government officers. He replied that the government officers' houses were spread over quite a wide area and that we should tell him the name of the person and some address to enable him to help us. We told him that the person was Dewan Banwari Lal. He enquired how did we know the man. We told him that he was the brother-in-law of our friend, who was staying with him. He then asked us the name of our friend. At his third question I felt what type of person had we contacted. He questioned like an intelligence man who considered us suspects. Balwant having noted little nervousness on my face, came forward and answered the gentleman that our friend was Shiv Kumar Sharma. Hearing this, the man asked us to follow him. Walking about 100 steps, he stopped and knocked at the door of a house. The door opened and there appeared the face of Champa *behn*, the sister of Shiv Kumar. She instantly recognized me and with a broad smile, invited us in. I was almost stumped by her unexpected appearance and our reaching the right address that way. I went in followed by Balwant and saw Shiv Kumar standing with a broad smile in the compound. We had forgotten about the person who guided us and the poor *tongawalla* who had all through served us so sympathetically. But the good *tongawalla,* without our knowledge, had followed us. Seeing that we had succeeded in finding our address, he congratulated us. It was then that we realized his existence and we duly paid his wage. Champa *behn* led us to the dining table and served us tea and biscuits. While having our tea, we narrated to Shiv the story of our goods train travel and the miracle of arriving there after having lost his address. We expressed our gratitude for a strange person who met us by chance in the bazaar and quietly lead us to their place. It was then that we were told that our guide was none other than the younger brother of Dewan Banwari Lal.

We were almost famished, and in our dirty clothes, looked like ghosts. We therefore hurried up in taking bath and changing into fresh clothes to feel like humans. Having a lunch-sized breakfast, we stretched on the matting in Shiv's room and in no time were dead asleep.

At about 5:30 P.M., as we were getting ready, Dewan Banwari Lal, arrived home from his office and came to our room to meet us. Although I had been very close to Shiv's family and had met his sister Champa once in Sialkot, it was the first time that we were meeting her husband. He had been a prey to smallpox during his childhood, which had very seriously effected his whole body, more so his face, which had turned dark and somewhat distorted. It was the act of Providence, but I was somewhat staggered to note the contrast in the physical looks of the couple. Champa was very fair, tall and slim. However, both of them were very kind to us and gave us a perfect and affectionate treatment.

We had a very comfortable time during the day as well as the night. Next day, on September 31, 1947, three of us got ourselves registered as refugees at the refugee registration office in Tibbia College, Delhi. With that registration slip we went to the office of Mr. Lobo Prabhu, an ICS officer, appointed as the Refugee Commissioner, to request for allotment of housing accommodation from the Muslim evacuees' properties. Only

Balwant was allotted a house at Faiz Road, Karol Bagh, New Delhi, whereas Shiv and I came home empty handed. When all of us went to see the allotted house, it was fully occupied by some refugee families. We showed them our allotment letter but they told us that they would vacate that house only when they got another place to shift. Balwant did not consider the place fit for his family and he handed over the permit to two of us to make use of it if we so liked. But we were also in no mood to enter into any dispute with the occupants of the house.

We then started looking for some vacant place, which we might occupy and then apply for allotment. We could not find any place in Karol Bagh and Paharganj, but could find a vacant flat on the G.B. Road near Ajmeri Gate. The flat was recently vacated by a well to do family as the bedrooms and the drawing rooms were fully furnished. We considered the matter of occupation but were not satisfied because of the G.B. Road neighbourhood.

There was a large size Philips radio, among other items, lying there. Forgetting occupation, Balwant lifted the radio, wrapped it in a bed sheet, put it under his arms and left the flat calmly telling us to follow him downstairs. This was the first and the last act of plunder, which we committed. The radio was sold in the market to a dealer and that money sustained us for quite sometime. We must have stayed for more than a month with Shiv's sister. Although all the members of Shiv's sister's family were very nice and she herself was looking after all of us very well, we were feeling embarrassed in continuing to stay with them.

Balwant was desperate to bring his wife and children from Dhariwal. He wanted some place in Delhi even for a short period. I thought that I might be able to help him. Two of my father's sisters were living in Delhi and as their husbands were serving with Central Government they had shifted with their families to Shimla, along with the whole Secretariat, for the summer. The elder aunt had a three room government quarter at Gole Market Lane which was lying vacant. The government offices would be shifted back to Delhi by the third week of January. I told Balwant that I could get that quarter for his family for nearly one month. For this I would have to go to Shimla to bring the keys. Balwant saw the quarter from outside and requested me to get the keys. I therefore left for Shimla by train with promise to be back in a week. Balwant also left for Dhariwal to bring his family to Delhi.

On the fifteenth December, the very day I was born 25 years ago, I took a train to Shimla. It was my first journey to Shimla and the first ever visit to my *Bhuaji* after more than 22 year of their marriage. Both my *Bhuajis,* who were in Shimla, were married in 1925 with a gap of 6 months. For me it was an occasion of great sentimental value. I had a lot of stories of both the *Bhuajis'* love for me when I was about 2 years old. These stories were passing like films in my mind during my journey from Kalka on a small gauge hill train. Except that I was quite low spirited, everything else about that journey had its special charm for me. My cousin Surinder Chopra was at the Shimla railway station to receive me and take me to their big bungalow perched on a hill side. My uncle, Rai Sahib Tara Chand Chopra, husband of my Shanti *Bhuaji*, was a Deputy Secretary in the Government of India and had been allotted a large bungalow. I was received warmly by all. Almost half the members of our joint family were already there and I was exactly the nineth member from the family at *Bhuaji's* house. *Bhuaji's* own family was large enough but she was a grand lady with her physical and mental qualities fit for being a queen. I saw her in her own house for the first time and I found her possessing a heart most generous and graceful beyond my imagination. Her household was very well organized and the children, all finely disciplined. I felt like having stepped into a wonderland.

But I had gone to Shimla with a mission and the first thing I told my *Bhuaji* was that I had to get the keys of the government quarter in Delhi allotted to my other *Bhuaji* at Shimla. The very next day I visited my other *Bhuaji* and after getting the same type of reception there, I received from them the keys of their vacant quarter in Delhi. She explained that my friend could use the place for a month and, when the offices from Shimla were shifted to Delhi, they would need the place for themselves.

My work in Shimla done, I expressed my desire to return to Delhi, but I was not allowed to leave. I had to prolong my stay for more than a week and I must say that my visit had been so enjoyable as to be remembered like a first romance of my life?

Those days, due to the influx of many refugees and the problem of war with Pakistan in Kashmir, Shimla was put under the military control. The commandant incharge there, happened to be Major Krishan Kumar who had been my class fellow in school and college. I fixed up a meeting with him on phone and went to his office to see him. He did not possess a good physical personality, being short in stature and lean in body, but as a commandant of Shimla, I found him a totally changed person. I was amazed to see the transformation in his voice and tone which fully displayed his authority as a commandant. He got up from his seat and received me with a broad smile and open arms.

After having a good time in Shimla, I left for Delhi with the keys of the quarter for my friend. He had already reached Delhi and was staying in a hotel in Connaught Circus. He shifted the same day and I helped him and his wife in cleaning the place which had remained shut for several months. Balwant insisted that I might shift with him in that quarter. His wife had learnt

Indian cooking and so it was fine for me. Living separately, we kept regular contact with Shiv Kumar. We were meeting daily and planning our future. After giving a lot of consideration to several proposals for earning, we decided that we may buy powder milk and sweetened Milkmaid tins from Bombay and sell them in the verandas of Connaught Place.

As there was acute shortage of fresh milk in Delhi, powder milk was very much in demand. Those days we were going to Connaught Place daily and saw many refugees selling the items of daily consumption, displaying those on the floors of ve[illegible]las. I was entrusted with the job of purchasing those tins f[illegible] Bombay, bring them with me to Delhi and then Balw[illegible] would manage to sell them in the Connaught Place vera[illegible] with the help of Shiv Kumar. I made two or three trips[illegible] found that transport in sacks in a train caused denting of s[illegible] tins which were difficult to sell. We abandoned this plan[illegible] then Shiv Kumar suggested that we might go to Madras whe[illegible]is elder brother was serving as a captain in the Defence Ve[illegible]ary Department. He had a large house allotted to him and[illegible]v felt that we could stay with his brother, and with his hel[illegible]d influence, we might be able to get a contract of a mi[illegible] canteen there. I supported him but it did not suit Balwant be[illegible]e of his wife and children. Shiv proposed that we two sh[illegible] prepare to leave Delhi in the beginning of February ar[illegible] was already the third week of January. My *Bhuaji's* fa[illegible] had come back to Delhi from Shimla and had occupied a[illegible]ms except one for Balwant and his family.

[illegible]heir spirit of helpfulness, they considered that they could [illegible]ge to live in two rooms for a few more days, till Balwant [illegible]ble to find another place for his family. They also knew [illegible] was living with Balwant and this was a major factor in [illegible]decision. But Balwant's wife proved very unsociable and [illegible]ehaviour with my *Bhuaji's* family was not proper. She

the Bhangi Colony to the Birla House. There, on the lawns of the Birla House, he delivered his daily lectures in the evening. Birla House was not very far from my *Bhuaji's* house where I was staying. One evening I could not understand why, I thought of going there to see and hear him in person and if possible speak to him about my views about his unreasonableness. I reached there about half an hour before his standard time to start the *Prarthana Sabha*, as his lectures were called. I walked in to find the Birla House compound empty. I moved ahead to see on the side of the open compound a raised ground, where the *Prarthana Sabhas* were held. The house building on the other side had rooms with glass doors and windows. Moving near the building, I looked inside from one of the doors and saw Gandhiji sitting on the floor wearing his loincloth and one person was massaging his back with oil. Gandhiji was sitting with his legs stretched forward and hands resting on the ground on both sides. On a chair near him sat Maulana Azad explaining something to him in a very serious mood. The scene was quite unexpected and I riveted my attention on it. I was seeing both those renowned leaders for the first time. I was very much absorbed by that unexpected scene before my eyes. Suddenly, I saw the Maulana getting up from his seat to leave. Next minute that chair was occupied by Sardar Patel. I was so full of excitement that I totally forgot the purpose of my visit there. After a few more minutes the Sardar left and the masseur stopped. Gandhiji was preparing to get up. A small time piece lying before him on the ground showed 3–4 minutes for the *sabha* to start. At that moment I saw Acharya Kriplani rushing inside from the door. Gandhiji was getting up from the floor and the Acharya was trying to speak hurriedly to him. The Mahatma stood up and two young khadi wearing girls came along to his sides on whose shoulders, he placed his arms while moving out of the door towards the place for the

Prarthana Sabha. The Acharya walked with him talking and stopped when Gandhiji started walking hurriedly and took his seat on a wooden bench. I had moved and stood at the other end of raised ground.

After taking his seat, Gandhiji closed his eyes and silently recited some *mantras* as a prayer. Everyone sat there silently while I stood still where I was. There were about 50–60 men and women. He opened his eyes, said, "*Hare Ram*", and started addressing the public. He spoke in a very low voice in a broken Hindi like a child. Very simple things like "love has a great power and we must love all people irrespective of their colour or creed. We are not to judge men as it is for the Almighty God to do so. We must go on doing our duty irrespective of the results as ordained in the *Bhagwad Geeta*. I am very sad for the division of the country and the uprooting of people and their suffering on both sides. I know how people suffered while leaving their homes and hearths in Pakistan. I also know that many Muslims from this side of the border were made to suffer because they had to leave their homes. It is not good. Those who had indulged in carnage in Pakistan on the innocent Hindus and Sikhs were evil persons and those who did the same thing on this side were also evil. Retaliation of evil by evil is bad and cannot be justified. The division of the country happened in spite of my best efforts to avoid it. Let us now consider that it has happened as God's will. The effect of partition has been seen by all; how the people on both sides are suffering? I fully realise the hardships the people are going through and have been telling the leaders on both sides to care for their people who are suffering for no fault of theirs. But what can I do? It seems that nobody listens to me. They have started considering that I am of no use for the country any more. I could never expect that my own people would start treating me like a counterfeit coin *Khota Paisa*. But it does not bother me. I have done my duty and will continue doing it until I live. You people who have come to hear me, take my words to heart that all of you, Hindus or Muslims are brothers, coming from the same stock, having the same blood in your veins. Do not get agitated or be violent. It is a great sin to hurt people, to kill them even in retaliation. What will you gain out of such evil acts?"

He then said, "when you are upset or worried over anything, take *Ram Nam*. You will get solace. God sees everything. He is the merciful and He will surely help you". He then started singing the *Ram Dhun* with those girls, taking the lead. And all who were present there, followed. The meeting dispersed after a few minutes. I stood totally mystified all through. I have tried to write Gandhiji's words as best as I could remember after lapse of nearly 55 years.

As I returned, I was thinking about the man, very small and lean but he appeared to me as one made of steel. The colour of his body also looked like the wrought steel. He spoke like a very ordinary man in a language meant for children. But he had some magnetism. Through all the simple words, said in a very simple manner, he entered the souls of the audience. At least it had that effect on me. For a moment all my scepticism about his policies and advice to the Government of India to pay 55 crores to Pakistan, was gone. And I was amazed as I saw all those stalwarts of the Congress Party going to him for his advice on all complicated political matters? How could that little and simple man make all the big leaders dance to his tune. He had full control on them although he said that no one cared for him at that time.

I was essaying what I saw and what I heard, but could not make out where I stood? Next day, I went again and witnessed and heard the same things. I concluded that the person was a superhuman, was much higher and beyond the caliber of ordinary people like me to understand.

A day or two after I came back from Panipat, my Sikh friend again met me and showed his annoyance at my failure to deliver him the revolver. I regretted that I had forgotten about it due to my pre-occupation with preparations to leave for Madras. At this he felt very angry and holding me by one of my arms, he said that I must fulfil my promise to him before I left Delhi. It was January 28, and I counted the number of days left for our departure. I had to tell him that I would try to leave for Ludhiana and deliver the revolver to him before our departure. But I could not manage to go to Ludhiana although I was trying to leave every day. On the thirtieth after spending the whole day with Shiv Kumar, I reached the house of my *Bhuaji*. It was dinner time and as I sat in the kitchen with a plate full of food, my uncle came from his office and gave the news that Gandhiji had been shot dead at the Birla House *Prarthana Sabha* that afternoon. I was startled and could not take the morsel of food in my hand to my mouth. I left it on my plate, got up from my seat and ran out. My uncle shouted after me as to where I was going? All roads were closed by the police and army men. I heard it but I did not care. I soon faced what uncle told me as I reached Gole Dak Khana. I tried many ways and many routes, spoke to many people on the road who were trying to reach there like me but nothing could be achieved. I returned to my uncle's house in a sullen mood. How strange! I felt an ache similar to what one feels at the loss of a very dear one. Every one in the family was commenting on the news but I was not listening. Uncle switched on the radio. It gave this news every fifteen minutes and all the channels were transmitting his favourite *bhajans* from all over the country. One thing which was repeated again and again was, that the assassin was a Hindu.

Next morning, all the newspapers gave the news in thick black types with black borders. The front pages gave only that news with details of how it happened and the inner pages contained his life, his policies, and his life's important landmarks, condolence messages from all heads of states and important leaders of the countries of the world. Those condolence messages continued for several days. Some of those messages were very emotional, some very philosophical and some offering tributes to the man in words which could not be matched. One such message from Albert Einstein said: "Generations to come will scarcely believe that such a one as this, ever in flesh and blood, walked upon this earth".

The government offices in the centre and states were closed till the cremation was over. All markets and all business establishments remained closed. Every religious place was offering prayers for his soul. It was a national mourning like which the history of India might have never witnessed.

The cremation was attended by all the Central Government ministers, ministers of all states, leaders of all the political parties, heads of several foreign governments, prominent leaders of all religions, almost every one from Delhi plus thousands from other states around Delhi. It was an unending procession which left on its passage tons of flowers. A special place was chosen on the bank of the Jamuna and a platform was erected where his body was cremated with sandalwood, scores of kilograms of *samagri* and *ghee*. That cremation place was given the name of *Raj Ghat*, which has become a place of pilgrimage and a national memorial. All foreign dignitaries who visit India have to pay their homage there before they start on their business.

After the cremation, the government made special efforts to bring themselves and the country out of this shock as they could not afford to remain in that state any longer. Offices opened and the government resumed their official work and responsibilities. The railway and communication departments started working and were coming to a state of normality. I controlled my emotions and realized that the date of our departure for Madras was drawing near. Before that I had to deliver the revolver to the *sardar,* whom I had promised. Considering this, I caught a Ludhiana-bound train on February 3, 1948 and reached there at night. I told Kapur Chand about the deal and in the morning, I caught the first train to Delhi with the revolver in my handbag. Reaching my *Bhuaji's* quarter I placed my bag at a safe place, under my eye, till the next morning. After breakfast, I wrapped the revolver in a newspaper in my room, placed the paper in the basket hung in front of my cycle and rode straight to my *sardar* friend at the shop in Chandni Chawk where he worked. I put my cycle on its stand on the footpath and called out my friend. He came out and wished me. I told him that I had done his work. He asked me, what work? And when I told him that I had brought the revolver for him and it was ready with me in my cycle basket, his face turned pale. For a moment he looked towards me in disbelief and then said, "Have you gone mad to bring it to my shop in such a congested bazaar? Gandhi was shot a few days back and the government is making arrests. Please go away immediately from here". Saying this he turned to enter his shop but I caught him by his arm and told him that I had gone to Ludhiana specially for his work as he was after me for a long time. Now that I had done the job, he could not run away. He listened to me very carefully and saw that I was very serious. He then hurriedly told me that I might deliver it to him at his house, in Darya Ganj, late in the evening.

In the evening, I reached at the address given to me. I delivered the piece to him in his room and received the money.

Six months had passed since we were forced to leave Sialkot, the place, which had become synonymous with our being. We were called Sialkoti. There were folk songs like "*Ve Mundiya Sialkotiya...*" sung during the Hindu marriage festivities by the girls in praise of the young boys of Sialkot. How securely settled did we consider ourselves in that city of our ancestors. The city of our heroes. The city which was as old as our country.

All was lost to us with no hope of return. It pained to think of it and the pain continues. I was then twenty-five and without a shelter of my own or any worthwhile job to do. A day before my departure for a long journey to Madras, I slipped into a reverie. My life with my family since my birth started passing like a motion picture before my unblinking and unseeing eyes.

PART - II

—5—

MY LIFE, MY FAMILY

I was born in a large joint family headed by my grandfather, Gokal Chand Sekhri, *trunkanwale,* who was a well known steel trunk manufacturer in Sialkot city, the district headquarter of the Punjab, now in Pakistan. He lived there in *mohalla wadehrian* in their ancestral house in a large *haveli* with his two younger brothers and their families. The suffix of '*trunkanwale*' after his name was earned by him for being the first manufacturer of steel trunks in the whole of the province, in the beginning of the twentieth century.

He had three sons and four daughters. It was to his eldest son Durga Dass Sekhri and daughter-in-law Dayawanti that I was born in that house on December 15, 1922. This date corresponded with the *Vikram Samwat* date of the first day of *Paush.* The month of *Paush* is considered as '*Kaneter*' meaning inauspicious when no functions like marriages, *mundans* inaugurations and other sacred ceremonies can be performed. But births being out of the domain of the humans my grandfather gave news of the birth of his first grandson to the other family members by announcing in his unadulterated exhilaration that a "*Pow Shah*" had arrived.

But, it was the time when the Punjab and the country as a whole were passing through a great turbulent period. The British government, who ruled the country, had perpetrated a ruthless massacre of innocent people on the day of *Baishakhi* in April 1919, at Jalianwala Bagh, Amritsar. As a result, the whole country was seething with anguished unrest. When I grew up to understand such things, some signs of the effect of that unrest were also seen by me in my family in the form of lot of discarded English dresses, neckties and bows.

As a child, I was suppressed being always in the fear of my father. By some special family equation, my father was allowed to act as an autocrat. He had many qualities, but he had enough anger to be swayed by it, and that shadowed all his other good qualities. Unfortunately, the worst targets of his anger were members of his own family among whom I was destined to be at the top. This was probably the main reason of my having a very low period of the first ten years of my life of which I have a very hazy recollection.

A few things are still there in my memory. At five, I was sent to the primary school branch of Ganda Singh High School. The four classes of the primary school were held in a five-room building. All the four teachers belonged to the Soni subcaste and the same village as that of my maternal grandparents. My mother being from a Soni family, told me that all my teachers were my maternal uncles.

We were taught Urdu language, arithmetic and the digits in the Arabic script, plus the geography of our district. All the boys in the school sat on the floor on hessian mats which collected dust for the full month after which the class teacher ordered all the boys to take their mats out to shake-off all dust from the mats in the central compound. I remained in that school for four years, getting promotion every year. Of all the teachers of that school I only recollect the figure of the Headmaster, Ram Rakha Mal Soni.

He was a tall, well-built man, wearing *salwar kameez* and a Peshawari turban on a *kulla*. He had very prominent pockmarks on his face which combined with his other physical attributes, instilled fear among all the students.

By the end of my first year in school, our family shifted from the old *haveli* house to our newly-built house in *mohalla* Ram Talai. The *mohalla* Ram Talai got its name from a small dry water tank around which it had been developed. That dry tank had steps on its three sides and the fourth side was a high wall. It had a permanent platform at its centre which was built from its backside wall up to the middle and was one and a half feet high from the ground level. Ram Talai was the only place for holding public meetings and for some important public events. It was also used as a playground for the children, for wrestling and *kabaddi* matches, for cock and ram fights. It was situated very near to the Sialkot junction railway station.

Our family occupied the accommodation on the first and second floors and a shop-cum-showroom of steel trunks was opened on the ground floor. The showroom was the extension of the family business, which was also then run through a shop in Trunk Bazaar, by my second uncle, Dwarka Das. Both the shop and the showroom were run in the name of 'Gokal Chand and Sons'.

Uncle Brij Lal, the third son of my grandfather, ran another trunk shop in Jammu, where he also lived with his family. That shop was named Madan Trunk House, and was run in partnership with a near relative, Kedar Nath Sekhri, the youngest son of my grandfather's blind uncle, Tarachand Sekhri. Madan Lal was the name of the son of uncle Brij Lal.

I have only very hazy memories about the time that I passed in the old *haveli*. Our family lived in the rooms on all the three floors in the north side of the *haveli*. My parents occupied two rooms on the ground floor and the other family lived on the first and second floors with my grand parents. A strange looking man, wearing all white, with his mouth covered by a piece of white cloth, shaven head and bare feet, used to come to our house daily. Without speaking to anyone, he went upstairs to the first floor kitchen, picked up one or two *roties* from the basket there and went out. I asked my grandmother about that person and his strange act. She told me that he was a Jain priest called *Pooj* from the *Upasra* opposite our *mohalla*. He collected *bhiksha* from our home as he was convinced of our being a pure vegetarian family, and because of the special request of my grandfather for that favour (Jain priests live like that and take *bhiksha* in that way).

The marriages of uncle Brij Lal, of my two *bhuas*, Vidya Devi and Shanti Devi, and the completion of schooling of two uncles Baldev Raj and Vas Dev, the motherless first cousins of my father, took place at the *haveli* after my birth. Being too young, however, I don't remember anything about them.

At the time of shifting to the new house in Ram Talai, our joint family consisted of 15 members (My grandparents, their two younger daughters; my parents with their two daughters and myself; uncle and auntie Dwarka Dass, with their daughter; uncle and auntie Brij Lal and their one son who lived in Jammu).

One of the two younger brothers of my grandfather, Brindaban Sekhri, had stopped living in the *haveli* after the death of his wife Roop Kaur in 1920. Uncle Baldev Raj and uncle Vas Dev were his sons, whom he entrusted to the care of my grandparents, and went to live in the hills of Kulu Manali. The second brother, Labhu Ram Sekhri, had shifted to Jammu along with his family, when the Jammu trunk shop was opened. He had since also been helping Madan Trunk House in Jammu.

For me the years in the new house were the time of dawning of awareness of my surroundings and happenings inside the family and outside. I remember the marriage of my third *bhua*, Leela Devi and her crying aloud when she was being seated in her *Doli*. I also recollect that I accompanied two marriage parties.

The one was the marriage party of my maternal uncle Mool Raj Soni in a village called Ghartal and the other was that of the second marriage of uncle Dwarka Das in the village Doojowal near Amritsar.

I saw the first movie, *Laila Majnu* with my grandfather in a big hall in Sialkot. I was awestruck to see the huge hall full of wooden benches, chairs, sofas all arranged meticulously. It was so different from the place where we used to see *Ram Lilas* while living in the old *mohalla*. I was further confused when the hall darkened and the large white screen before me became alive with full size photos of houses, streets, men and women who actually talked and moved. When I had asked my grandfather how it was happening, he told me to sit silently and continue seeing. It was that new thing for which he took me along to see.

After some time when I heard from my friends the story of another movie *Raja Harish Chandra*, I craved to see it but I was not allowed to see it as my father was strictly against seeing films. During my summer vacation when I had gone to Jammu, I got the opportunity to see it there in the company of my auntie and cousin Madan Lal.

I went to Jammu twice again. Once I went with uncle Brij Lal and with other family children from Sialkot, especially to watch from his road side house windows, the resplendent procession of baby Karan Singh, the only son of Maharaja Hari Singh of the state of Jammu and Kashmir. The second time I accompanied my grandfather to attend the marriage of a relative, where I saw an unbelievably fat man whose volume and face frightened me out of my wits. I was sitting on the carpet and near me, a very big special chair was placed where that man sat stretching his legs towards me. I was cold with fear that if that elephantine figure had by accident placed his foot on me, I was sure to get crushed.

I saw in one of the rooms of our new house, the bedridden mother of my grandmother who had come to live with our family in her old age, as she had no son to look after her. When she died in 1931, my parents went to Haridwar with her ashes to immerse them in the Ganga at *Har-Ki-Pauri*. I also accompanied my parents along with two of my younger sisters, Prakash and Kamla. The Ganga water was very cold but all of us had to have a dip in it. Kamla, who was only a few months old and had sore eyes, cried very loud when my father, holding her in his two hands, dipped her in the cold water. There were many monkeys who were very mischievous and troublesome. My father kept a long stick to ward them off while eating. From Haridwar the family visited Rishikesh in a *tonga*. On the way there was a thick jungle on both sides of the road. From his seat in the *tonga*, my father threw roasted grams to scores of monkeys coming out of the forest. At Rishikesh, we crossed the holy Ganga walking over a hanging bridge called *Lakhshman Jhoola* which swung slightly under our feet when we reached its centre.

Crossing over to the other side of the Ganga, we had to traverse back on foot, a distance of about a mile through the jungle to reach the various *ashrams*, the most famous of them being the *Kali Kamli Wala Ashram*. We stayed there and had our food from the free *langar* of the *ashram*. The next day we followed the same route to go back to Haridwar and from there back to Sialkot by train.

I can recollect the ground floor showroom of steel trunks managed by my father. The office work for the showroom was done sitting on a large cushioned *dewan* called *gaddi*, placed against the sidewall of the showroom. My father sat there assisted by my young uncle Chuni Lal who was 12 or 13 years old. Uncle Chuni Lal was the son of my maternal grandmother's sister. She had been married to a Sekhri and lived in our old *mohalla wadehrian*. She had great regard for my father and had brought her young son to him for learning business and good manners.

I remember a scene witnessed by me in the showroom for its unsavoury nature. It was evening, and uncle Chuni Lal, who had been taught to write the daybook in Urdu, was summing up the day's cash transactions.

After completing totals, he passed on the book to my father. My father checked the totals and detected some discrepancy. He asked uncle Chuni Lal to recheck the totals, as there appeared to be a mistake. Uncle rechecked but could not find anything wrong. My father then told him to do the additions by speaking out each figure. While he was speaking out, at one point he uttered "85+5 is 100". As he spoke this, my father's right hand struck his face which threw his turban off his head on to the road through the door. I stood transfixed at my place with my heart beating fast. Uncle Chuni Lal realised the mistake, corrected the total and moved from his seat to collect his turban from the road. That incident was the first in which I had seen before my eyes the quick temper of my father and his autocratic act of unsparing punishment for a mistake. The fear of my father, carried on through my infancy in my subconscious mind, became real for me that day.

The showroom where I witnessed the above incident, was full of trunks of various sizes, painted in different shades. One special trunk was called 'uniform case' in which the uniforms of a military officer could be packed without folding. This trunk had other special features like being airtight, having leather lining inside its lid on all the four sides. That lining sat squarely on the lower part of the trunk in such a way that when closed, it needed hard pressure to lock. Its paint was oven baked to become scratch proof. These uniform cases were supplied to the military officers in all Indian cantonments, in the tea estates of Assam and Bengal and to British officers in Calcutta, Madras, Bangalore, Rangoon and Colombo. I used to see large posters printed in thick Urdu letters all over on the road sides when I went to my high school. The poster read, "Always Remember—Gokal Chand & Sons—for all your requirements of steel trunks for your summer and winter clothes, your cushioned winter beddings, for storing wheat and wheat flour, steel cases for sewing machines, Sola Hats, etc. Visit our showroom and shops at Ram Talai and at Trunk Bazaar." My father told me that he got orders from the far-off places as a result of the advertisements in the newspapers like *The Statesman* of Calcutta and *The Hindu* of Madras. I used to see him typing letters on his portable typewriter for which he had not paid in cash but by depositing some small tickets that were found in some type of cigarette boxes. My father collected or purchased those tickets in thousands and deposited them in his friend's cigarette agency shop and received the typewriter against them.

I might have been about eight years old, when on my way to Ram Talai, to play there with my friends, I heard someone saying that Bhagat Singh, Raj Guru and Sukhdev were hanged in the Lahore Jail and their bodies were not handed over to their parents. The bodies were secretly taken out of the jail and burnt on the bank of the river Satluj with kerosene oil thrown on them. We all felt sad on hearing the news. We had seen many pictures of young Bhagat Singh with impressive moustaches and a tilted felt hat on his head. At that time I did not know much about Bhagat Singh's life, but after we shifted to our old *mohalla*, there were persons who told me a lot about his family and many astonishing details of his life. I used to sit transfixed while hearing his story and it moved my heart so much that hot tears would flow from my eyes, several times during the narration. He was a hero for the children of my generation in the schools.

Another episode that comes to my mind of those days—a big crowd of people throwing their clothes made from imported fabrics, into a bonfire in the centre of Ram Talai. When I saw my father throwing his English dresses in the fire, I too took from my mother, my favourite silk shirt with green stripes and ran to Ram Talai and threw it in the big fire. This happened sometime before the hanging of Bhagat Singh and his comrades.

BURNING OF HOUSE—THE FAMILY ON THE ROAD

Our family had hardly lived in the new house for about four years when in June 1932, our building was completely destroyed by a big fire and we had to go back to the old *haveli*. That terrible happening reduced the family to a state of total indigence.

It was hot summer night in June, 1932. All the members of our joint family living in our new house, were sleeping on the terrace, when a loud noise aroused the elder members of the family to find that the big building opposite ours was on fire. Seeing the flames rising high and also advancing towards our building, they shouted to the other members in panic, telling them of the fire. Almost everyone was up from their beds and ran to see the fire from the sidewall of the roof. I was out of my bed when my father shook me and told me to get up and run down the stairs following my mother and other elder members of the family. Very soon all the elders went out of the house with babies in their arms, followed by their young ones. When all were out of the house, the ladies collected their children, grouped together and finding a safe place on the side of the footpath, sat on the bare ground, away from the flaming house. Their eyes were fixed towards the fire hoping against hope that their house may not catch fire. Soon, some of the wooden planks protruding out on the road from our showroom, had also caught fire. Seeing that everyone was helplessly dejected.

It was then that the ladies realised that they had very paltry clothes on them. That realisation added embarrassment to their sadness. But when they realised that their own house was fully exposed to catch the fire, and get engulfed in it, all their sense of modesty vanished from their minds. They huddled together in a group and a few of them started crying in a subdued manner.

Both my father and uncle stood looking dejectedly towards their building fully in the grasp of the frighteningly fast-spreading fire due to the store of oils and paints in the showroom. My grandfather stood at their backside, counting his family members, especially making note of the children. All of a sudden, he flew away from there and reached before the big gate of his own house. The gate being at one end of the building, was still out of the reach of the big flames. He entered it and rushed upstairs. Reaching the top, he went straight to the section of the roof where my father's family used to sleep. Looking hurriedly but carefully at every cot and finding that all of them were empty, he rushed down the stairs. At that point of time there was smoke in the staircase. He somehow could get down but to his utter fright found the main gate fully on fire. He could not go out from there. Deciding something in his mind, he rushed up again through the smoke filled stairs and with great effort reached the top floor. There he looked for some escape first to the backside of our building, which was out of the reach of the flames. On that side of our house, deep down there was an open sarai, and he found no way to escape. He then went up to the '*mounty*', from its back wall, he found the connecting house-top which was a storey lower. Faced with death and thinking fast he caught hold of a *charpoy* and threw it on the roof of the connecting house. Luckily it fell flat on its legs. Then he hung himself down from the wall, and sprang to fall down on the *charpoy*. He at once got up, went down the stairs and reached his family sitting on the roadside.

Seeing him, the family members heaved a sigh of great relief. My father, who was greatly disturbed, asked him where he had been moving about? The entire family had been in a sort of hell for more than half an hour. My grandfather slowly replied that he had gone to the terrace of the house to check if Vishwanath had been left there sleeping, as he could not see him sitting behind his mother. My father was very deeply touched by his reply but told him politely that before taking such a big risk, he should have asked any of the family members about it.

After sometime, a group of small trolleys manned by uniformed men arrived and everybody was told to make room for them to let them go to the burning buildings. Their small trolleys with water tanks were quickly connected with municipal water pipes, their labourers started pumping the water and the firemen threw that as best as they could on the fiercely burning buildings. That small quantity of water was like a joke before the conflagration and by the dawn of the next day, both the buildings were reduced to big dumps of debris and smouldering fire.

Our relatives and friends, having heard about the big fire, visited us at dawn, to sympathise with our family. I noted two persons, Mr. M.S. Phillips, a very close friend and comrade of my father who brought clothes for my father and Lala Tara Chand Sekhri, the blind uncle of my grandfather, who arranged some *dhotis* for the ladies. When he arrived in the morning with an escort, who might have told him of the condition of the family sitting on the road side, he cried loudly embracing my grandfather. Later, he took the entire family to his house where we all stayed and had our meals for fifteen days. My uncle and aunt from Jammu also arrived the next day of the fire to stay with the family in the house of Lala Tara Chand. During these fifteen days, the elders of our families could jointly plan for their future.

My maternal grandmother and her family then occupied our part of the house in the *haveli* in the old *mohalla*. Our family had to manage to take on rent a small vacant building owned by the only daughter of late Babu Nathu Mal Sekhri, which was adjacent to the *haveli*. The whole family shifted there till my maternal grandmother could arrange another place for her family. My uncle from Jammu, after helping the family to settle, went back to attend to his business in Jammu.

A new life, in a new environment had begun—a life of virtual destitution, depression, confusion and anxiety. It caused very crucial changes in the life of the family, at all levels. The house and the showroom destroyed in fire, had been the joint property of all sons of my grandfather, including my uncle living in Jammu. The showroom, run under the management of my father, was considered as the prestigious part of the family business. Naturally, my father who had worked very hard to develop that showroom business felt its loss very seriously.

But he was a courageous man with a lot of self-confidence. He faced the situation stoically and considered it as the Will of the Almighty. He restarted his life boldly. He began attending the shop in the Trunk Bazaar. On the advice of some family friends, he filed a civil suit in the district court against the municipal committee for compensation on the ground that they had not provided proper facilities to control and extinguish the fire. The topmost civil advocate of the city was engaged. All the family members, young and old, were told that the tragedy was of God's making and must be borne with fortitude. Simultaneously, they were told that they must also learn to live according to the prevailing circumstances and resources. He himself was the first to set an example for others. He made his wife and children live a life of abstinence.

However, fate had some more curses in store for the family. The next three years were the darkest period of our life. Soon after the family shifted to our old *mohalla*, I fell ill. The high fever that I had was diagnosed as malaria but the medicine given did not show its effect. Then the doctors said that the fever had developed into typhoid. The treatment was changed but in vain. My maternal grandmother took charge of my health. When the high fever persisted, the old lady, half dead with worry over the prolonged illness of the only son of her only daughter, used to sit beside my bed all day long. With the allopathic treatment failing, some ayurvedic doctors were called. Their medicine too did not work. Then some *hakeems* tried their treatment. The fever had lasted more than forty days, Moreover, another ailment had also surfaced. My legs and some other parts of the body developed many abscesses. These were very painful especially when I had to move my legs and body. I was reduced to a skeleton and total helplessness was writ large on the faces of all the family members. In the meantime, my uncle and aunt had also arrived from Jammu.

One of the Muslim *hakeems*, after carefully examining me, concluded that an overdose of same drug led to an infection which had caused swelling in my body. In his opinion a crude treatment was needed for which the family must give their consent. He suggested that we may seek the help of leeches to suck the foul blood from each swelling.

Hearing this everyone was shocked and horrified but the *hakeem* calmly assured the family members that no harm would come to the patient. He was positive that after the bad blood was removed, both the abscesses and the fever would start receding. Ultimately, seeing no alternative, my father decided to give the *hakeem* a chance. Next day he came with another person who carried a round earthen pot with lot of inert leeches in it. All the ladies were asked to leave the room. The pot was placed by my bedside and was filled with water. An empty pot was also placed beside my bed and the treatment started. The other man began his work under the directions of the *hakeem*. One leech was picked up and it was touched to the head of one of the growths on my leg. I felt a sharp prick of a pin and shuddered. A cloth was placed on my eyes and my father was asked to sit on my bed to control my movements. The leech firmly dug its small teeth into the abscess and started getting inflated. When the leech was full and all red, it automatically fell from my leg into the pot placed on the floor beside my bed. The man picked up the red leech from the pot and crushed it in his grip squeezing thereby all the blood out through his fingers into the empty pot.

The swelling where the leech was stuck, vanished. The *hakeem* then asked his companion to apply leeches one-by-one on every growth. In just an hour or so, all the abscesses were treated and subsided. A lot of dark red blood was collected in the pot. After the initial discomfort of the pricks, I felt a lot of relief. The *hakeem* assured that the fever would start going down. To everybody's pleasant surprise, the fever started going down from the next day. I recovered fully in one week and started walking in my room. Soon I was allowed to go out and play.

—6—

MY SUPPRESSED AND TROUBLESOME CHILDHOOD

After my father was relieved from my side (because of my prolonged illness), he started giving all his time and attention to the court case. He daily went to the shop, planned his day's work and was busy doing it till evening. He had to contact his advocate, collect documents required for the case, meet various influential persons to seek their sympathies and moral support and do all the typing. The families' sustenance was looked after by the income of Sialkot and Jammu shops. The expenses, though very much controlled, were increasing as the families were growing larger.

My fifth sister, Daman, was born in mid 1933. A few months earlier, the first girl child was born to the second wife of uncle Dwarka Dass. In 1934, my elder sister passed her eighth class. She wanted to study further but my father did not permit it, to her great disappointment.

One of these days my father was driven to meet two gentlemen who had newly come to our *mohalla* as tenants in a house in our backstreet. They served in the railways and had been transferred to Sialkot station. They were both *Arya Samajis* and used to go together for a morning walk. While passing through the street, they sang *bhajans*. My father who was also an early riser heard these songs and had an urge to meet the people who sang those *bhajans*. One of those days he contacted them and came to know that they were *Arya Samajis*, and the *bhajans* they sang, were those sung after the *agni hotra* in the *Arya Samaj*. They go for walk to the Babe-Di-Ber water tank which was about two miles away from our *mohalla* and bathed there, came home and then went to the *Arya Samaj Mandir* for daily *satsang*.

My father was instantly impressed by these two gentlemen and offered to accompany them for the morning walk and to the *Arya Samaj Mandir* and was welcomed by them.

These two persons had very deep rooted and a life-long effect on my father. In a short time he became a staunch *Arya Samaji*. His interest in the study of the Vedas was next to follow. He bought all the *Vedas* and started studying them with full devotion. After a few months he also started holding *satsangs* in the open compound of our *haveli* and invited all the residents to join him every evening.

In the summer vacation, I used to accompany my father for morning walks and learnt swimming from him. He was a master swimmer not only in breaststroke swimming but also had the talent to float on the water surface like a log of wood for as long as he liked. He swam from one end to the other of the tank several times in one stretch, then relaxed by floating motionless on the water surface.

A close relation of my age came to spend his vacation with our family and started accompanying us for the morning walks. One morning, I got up very early and found everybody sleeping. I thought that I might go for the walk along with my friend without waiting for my father to get up. I woke up my friend and as per my plan, both of us walked to the water tank at Babe-Di-Ber. There was nobody there. We knew that it was too early and sat on the first step of the tank and started chatting. We felt proud that we had beaten our elders in arriving there ahead of everyone. After a long time we heard footsteps and as we turned to see, we found that it was my father. My father, distraught with worry and anger, started scolding and beating us. My friend remembered that day's thrashing all his life and often mentioned that incident gleefully. That was my first harsh punishment at the hands of my father.

Then came the turn of the family to get another severe jolt. Our court case against the municipality was decided against us with payment of damages to the defendants (municipality) for their expenses. It caused gloom in the family as lot of hopes had been pinned on a favourable outcome. The already bad financial position of the family got worse.

Soon followed another stunning blow to my father. He was the one who had handled the court case and devoted his entire attention to it on behalf of the family. After the court case was lost, he started giving all his attention to the trunk shop, taking some measures to expand and improve the existing business. Those measures included bringing to the shop the salvaged stocks from the debris of the showroom for their repair and sale, re-organization of production methods to improve the quality of our product and maintenance of proper accounts. With hard work, he could improve the financial position of the business very soon. My uncle, who had been running the shop independently in his own way, felt insecure and dominated. He complained to my grandfather against the new steps taken by my father, saying that all those years he had been running the shop well, independently. Introduction of new methods and other changes showed that he had been incapable. To add insult to injury, he told, he had now been asked to keep proper accounts of the purchases and sales. When my grandfather tried to console him by telling him that all those steps were for the improvement of the business and for the good of the family, he wasn't convinced and stopped going to the shop. On enquiry from my father, my uncle replied that he might ask the reason from his father. It was a rude shock to my father when my grandfather told him the story. My father thought over the matter and after recovering from the shock, he made his decision.

Here a little about my father's qualifications:

Being eldest in the family of my grandfather, he was the only one among all his children, who had passed the matriculation examination. He was the healthiest, had been the class monitor throughout his schooling and was the captain of his school football team. Although he passed his matriculation examination in high first division in 1918, he did not go to college because of the family's tight financial position. He started helping his father in the trunk business, in which he was having difficulties in dealing with his younger brother. He promoted the business, improved it on all sides, separated from his uncle who was creating difficulties for his father and placed the business on a very strong foundation by his hard work and honest dealings. He was a workaholic.

He told his father "If Dwarka Das feels that way, I will stop taking interest in the shop and stop drawing any money from the family pool. I will consider doing something independently. In the trunk business, I have earned much fame. I can as well start another shop in the bazaar. I am sure that I will attract all our old and regular customers. Dwarka Dass will have to face it and then he would have no right to complain". My grandfather replied that he knew who was the real builder of the business and who was the most intelligent and hardworking of all his sons. Even then, he requested my father to act in such a manner so as to keep the family united till he was alive. My father, who was a fine human being, replied in a spirit of extreme self-confidence that he would neither do the trunk business nor ask for any share in the profit from his brother, Dwarka Das. He would try to sustain his family without any assistance from the joint family business. The decision he took showed his magnanimity and courage.

After assuring his father, he reconsidered his position. Next day he took his disciple Chunni Lal with him and went round the city's inner *mohallas* where sports goods were manufactured on a very small scale by the skilled carpenters in their homes. He studied those items and made his final decision to go into the purchase and sale of these sports items. But he had no money and he would never go to his father or brothers for help. He remembered that Chuni Lal's mother had offered to deposit some cash in his showroom business. He borrowed from her 500 rupees on interest and bought some quantity of children's sport goods. Getting a corner of wooden board of the trunk shop cleared, he displayed the goods there for sale. Customers started coming and in a few days, as the number of customers increased, he was encouraged to buy and sell more. From that new business he gave my mother one rupee daily to meet her family needs and told her to manage within that amount for some time. Hardly a month or two had passed when the building adjacent to the trunk shop fell vacant and was available on a very reasonable rent. My father at once took it, got the premises cleaned and shifted his sports goods from the trunk shop to his newly acquired premises. It was a two storied corner building with a two door shop, which offered my father good facility to expand and develop his new business according to his taste and capacity. He planned to have a proper showroom in the new shop and also to include goods for adults. From the loan of five hundred rupees, he had not invested more than two hundred. He could have more goods and improve his sales at the new spacious shop. He knew a fine carpenter, a young Muslim boy, Mohammad Shareef. He was a small apprentice carpenter at the time of the building of our new house in the mid twenties. My father called him to make furniture for the new shop. The man was ready and started the job the next day. My father earmarked 250 rupees for furniture and thought that it would be enough. In the mid thirty's there was deep economic depression in the country and things were very cheap.

Mohammad Shareef started working with total dedication and finished the job within the specified time. The earmarked money was spent and my father decided that the polishing and glass fitting could wait till his earnings increased. The shop looked impressive, had ample space for storage and display as also for an office table and a few chairs. My father felt that he could keep in the shop a stock worth a few thousand rupees. He retained the name of Gokal Chand & Sons for the sports shop as a gesture of respect to his father. The small manufacturers, after supplying their goods to my father for a few months, were convinced of his fair dealings and volunteered to supply their product on credit. With expansion of the range of goods and their fine display in the showroom, the business assumed a proper form. My father worked very hard and used all his management skills to improve his sales. He got the glasses fitted to the showcases and very soon his shop came to be known as one of the best sports goods shops in the city.

Coinciding with the development of the newly started sports business, my mother gave birth to her second son, Satya Paul, on December 2, 1935, thirteen years after my birth. It was also the time when my father had become more devoted to the *Arya Samaj* and started following its ten principles as best as he could. He started holding daily evening *satsangs* at home.

After twenty-one days of her delivery, when my mother was free from her ceremonial bath etc., she remembered an incident that had taken place four years earlier. She sat on her cot with the baby in her lap and called me. She made me sit on her bed and then reminded me of the incident thus:

In our Ram Talai house one day she found me crying all alone. When she asked me why I was crying, I told her that many of my friends came to play in the *mohalla* with their brothers and I went alone because I had no brother. Telling me that, she lifted the baby from her lap and placed it on mine saying, "Look, your brother has also arrived". The contact of that little baby gave me a thrill which I had never experienced before. I only touched its closed hand with my finger and told my mother, "the baby is very soft, please take it back".

Having fully recovered and recouped after my long illness, I started going to school again. My school was the farthest from our old house. For a few weeks, my father arranged a *tonga* for me to and from the school, lest I should fall ill again. At that time I was in the fifth class. Our school was run in a huge plot of land with many class-rooms, playing grounds, a big hostel and many shaded trees on grassy grounds where classes were held when the weather was found to be favourable. The big entrance gate opened to the roads leading to the classrooms, the boarding house buildings and the playgrounds. It was known as Ganda Singh High School. Ganda Singh was the proprietor of the world famous sports manufacturing company, Uberoi Limited. He was a top most industrialist, president of the Sialkot Municipal Committee, a philanthropist and an aristocratic philanderer. The best attraction for that school for our family was that its headmaster was Lala Jagannath Sekhri, the grand old saintly person respected all over the town.

I was feeling the return of my old vigour in my walking, in the games at school and in our *mohalla*. But I also noted for the first time that I was not good in studies for which I had a little aptitude. I was more interested in sports and had developed a new habit of quarrelling at home with my sisters and in school with my classmates. The fear of my father in me had found an outlet in the form of my fracas with those whom I found weaker, whether at home or in school. A new characteristic came to light one day in my school, which later in life developed in me a talent of great social advantage.

I was being considered as a bad student both in studies and in behaviour at the school. The episode given here will show the type of mischief I created:

It was the geography period and the teacher was master Sohan Lal. He was very old with a very weak eyesight. He wore very thick glasses. Even then, when he read the names for the roll-call, he brought the attendance register so near his face so that his nose rubbed against it. When the students found his face fully hidden by the register, spontaneous mischief started in the class. On one such occasion, in a quarrel with my deskmate, I hit him on his face and he shrieked loudly. The *masterji* moved the register away from his face to enquire about the yell. Somebody shouted my name saying that I had struck my deskmate. He called me and picked up a wicket from the corner where the cricket game accessories for the fifth grade students were placed. He said that he would teach me a lesson of my life that day by caning me at least six times on my palms. He asked me to extend my right hand in front of him. He then hit my stretched palm hard. Exactly at the same moment. I involuntarily shouted "*Barkat*". On hearing it, *masterji* let out a loud guffaw. Seeing him the whole class laughed. I stood where I was, enjoying the reaction of my remark with amused looks. *Masterji* slowly moved near me still laughing, thumped my back and tenderly ordered me to go back and resume my seat, adding that I was an impossible lad. Incidentally, the word *Barkat* is popular with the Punjabi business community. *Barkat* portends that the bargain would be blessed with profits.

I was selected in the junior hockey team of our school and as such had to stay back after school to practice for half an hour. One day while playing I got hurt in my stomach and fell unconscious on the ground. After some time when I regained consciousness I found myself lying on a *tonga* seat with the headmaster, Lala Jagannath Sekhri, sitting by my side supporting me. At our trunk bazaar shop, he made me get down and escorted me to my grandfather who was sitting there. My grandfather stood up, paid his respect to *masterji*, who told him that I was hurt in my stomach while playing hockey. My grandfather immediately arranged a glass of hot milk, mixed it with a spoonful of *haldi* and made me drink it. After that he told me to go inside the shop and rest there for sometime. After about half an hour, he came in, checked my condition and finding that I was feeling better, he made me walk home with him. Next day, I felt quite normal and went to school.

My father's coaching at home, after my illness, though did not show any improvement in my class room, did show its effect in my final examination. I passed and was promoted to the sixth class. My father felt relieved and as a reward bought me a cycle to ride to school. That made me the centre of attraction in the school and many of my class fellows gathered around me after the school was over, requesting me for a lift.

My happiness for promotion and pride of owning a cycle were soon negated by the demonic treatment towards me of our Urdu teacher. I could not understand why he got berserk on seeing me and started speaking nasty Urdu words for me. It happened the very first day he saw me in his class. His attitude made me look towards him with awe and surprise. I got totally nervous and lost all my confidence the moment he entered the class and looked at me. He found some way to curse and condemn me with such bombastic Urdu words that made me shudder and my heart started beating faster. It seemed to me that the only business that he had in the class was to target and humiliate me for one reason or the other. One day I forgot my

Urdu homework copy at home and as I went to him empty handed and told him the truth, he lost his temper and looking at me like a ferocious animal went out of the classroom. The whole class was watching tensely and wondering where the teacher had gone? I stood motionless where I was like a mannequin, when he suddenly burst into the classroom with a freshly torn branch of a *sheesham* tree from the school compound outside our class. Coming straight for me he told me to stretch my palm forward. I did that and he struck it with that stick. The strike left a stinging red mark on the palm, and he ordered for the other hand. I did as he commanded and at the third stroke I cried so loud that he seemed to shudder a little, but he continued striking me and I lost my bearings. He rudely pushed me towards my seat and one of the class boys guided me to my seat.

After the school I did not talk to any of my friends and quietly cycled home. On my way home, I kept thinking, what type of teacher was that master Chunni Lal? During my five years in that school I had never seen such a man who always wore a stern face. He instilled such fear in me that my heart started beating fast in his presence and I could not speak to him in my normal way.

By the time I reached home I forgot about the anguish of the severe punishment and also about my aching hands and went to play in the *mohalla* with other boys. But when in the evening I sat in the kitchen alongside my father for eating supper, my father's eyes noted the awkwardness in which I was eating. He asked me why I was not eating properly. I told him that I had hurt my hands while playing. He insisted on seeing my hands, and when he saw the red lines on both of them, he looked at me and asked me in a troubled tone why I was not telling him the truth? I had to tell him about the episode at school. He felt very upset, but said nothing except asking me the name of the teacher and the timing of his class.

Next day my father reached the school and went straight to master Chunni Lal's class. He confirmed that he was master Chunni Lal and after giving him his introduction, directly asked him why he had punished me so severely the previous day. The teacher replied that I had not done my homework. My father told him that for a day's neglect of homework, he punished a child of eleven so mercilessly that his hands still showed the red lines of his strikes. Did he think that he was dealing with a criminal? The teacher replied arrogantly that being a teacher he knew what punishment was due to a negligent student. This enraged my father and he told him in loud voice that it was criminal on his part to have given such a punishment and for this he could drag him in the presence of the headmaster. But he would not do that. He simply warned him that if in future he touched me, he would teach him a lesson for the rest of his life. Saying that my father left the classroom and went back to his work. The teacher appeared nervous and for rest of the period he could not attend to the class properly. But from the next day he adopted a different course to demoralise me. At every chance he used taunting words for me to downgrade me in the class and continued in that manner till the final examination. When I was promoted to the seventh class, I told my father that I did not want to continue in that school. He considered it and agreed to get me migrated to K.C. Arya High School, which was nearer to our home.

In the new school, it took me a few weeks to get acclimatised. A new building, new teachers, new classmates and a different environment. What remained the same was my shallow interest in studies, my friends of *mohalla* and my involvement with the games played in the *mohalla*. It was then almost two years of our living in that *mohalla*. During this time in the *haveli* itself, I formed some close friendships with four boys of my age group. Two of these friends were brothers and from a

Sekhri family, and two from a Chopra family. The two Sekhris were not going to school, but working somewhere and were learning some handicraft. The other two boys went to the same school as mine. One boy was one year senior and the other was a year junior to me. Every evening five of us used to meet at the central platform of the *mohalla* to play.

During the summer holidays, my father would wake me up early and take me along for a morning walk. His destination then was a place called Dalowali, about four miles from our house in the direction of Jammu City. This place was on the side of the railway track leading towards Jammu. A few friends of my father gathered there, did physical exercises on the bank of a water stream called *Nala Aik*. They also swam in the water stream and had their bath. This was the time when they cracked jokes, laughed heartily and relaxed. Being the only child, I got bored. My father also noticed and told me to call upon my friends in the *haveli* to join the morning walk. I at once called my friends and asked them if they could join me for the morning walk. All of them agreed and started accompanying me from the next day.

Our group was supposed to be ready early in the morning to walk along with my father and follow him to the place where he met his friends. After reaching there, the two groups separated. In our children's group we talked and did our physical exercises. On Sundays, when the elders had also a holiday, they spent more time at the same spot. My father called my friends and me to the bank of the stream to teach us swimming. He took us, one at a time, in the stream and instructed us. He also firmly told us not to enter the stream without his permission. After a few days of learning, I felt confident that I had learnt enough. One day, in a foolhardy attempt to test my swimming skills, I jumped into the stream but could not come out. When my friends saw that I was not able to come out, they started shouting for help. My father and some of his friends jumped into the rivulet and brought me out from its bed where I was lying in a semi-conscious state. I was laid down on the ground on my stomach. My father thumped my back and I threw out water from my mouth two or three times in a painful condition. My whole body became absolutely cold for quite a while and my eyes turned red. When I regained my full consciousness, my father admonished me for my foolhardy act. That day I had to come back home holding my father's hand all the way.

From that very day, we were not allowed to go near the water stream. We were told to take bath at the Persian wheeled wells run by bullocks. There were a few of those wells on our way and they were operated in the morning for irrigation of the fields. After the drowning incident, we did not stop where the elders did and continued walking ahead on the railway track upto the cantonment railway station. On Sundays the elders spent more time at their meeting point. We too spent more time in gossips while sitting at the railway track or while bathing in the well water. On one Sunday morning, all the children decided not to spend our time sitting and gossiping at the cantonment station but to continue walking ahead on the track. The elders spent more time in body massaging, exercising, joking, laughing and bathing in the rivulet. We thought that we might spend that much time by walking more. As we walked laughing, talking, competing with each other in walking on the track, we got so much involved that we lost all sense of time and distance. In that abandoned spirit, we went on and on till some one out of us pointed out that the sun was up quite high and we might get late to meet our elders at the *Aik Nala*. We also felt that we were very hungry. All of us sat down on the track and the first thought that came to us was that we had walked a long distance. Looking at the position of the sun in the sky, we felt that the elders must have left for home long back. When we thought of turning back, we felt that we were not left with enough energy to go back home on empty stomachs. However we felt totally exhausted. Sitting and thinking about fatigue and hunger, we looked at each other silently. One of us pointed out the mud hutment at a small distance from us, which appeared to be a living quarter of one of the villagers. Our hungry minds decided that we could get some help from the people living in that hutment. The youngest boy from our group volunteered to go and find out. He went and knocked at the door. A rustic lady opened the door and showed surprise to see a city boy standing at her door. On her inquiry, the boy pointing to all of us told her that we were from Sialkot and had left our homes in the morning for a walk with our elders. While the elders stopped at Dalowali canal, we walked ahead and stopped there when we started feeling the pangs of hunger. She looked very confused on hearing our childish tale; but she hurried in and returned with a big *roti* which she gave to the boy. Without having a second thought, he ran with the *roti* to where we all were waiting. The eldest among us took the *roti* from him and divided it in five parts, one for each of us. Every one gobbled his portion while walking ahead to find a well. It did not take us long to find one where we drank the freshly drawn water to our fills. We felt that our hungry stomachs were somewhat satisfied.

Then sitting in the shade of a big tree near the well, we considered in which direction to move? The two older boys realized that we had gone too far from our homes, and in that situation going back would be more arduous than going towards Jammu City. The devils brains found a thrill in visiting Jammu and we resumed our journey after coming down from the railway track to the road going parallel to it for Jammu city. By taking the road instead of the rail track, we found it more comfortable to walk in the shade of the trees. As we were walking, we saw a man ahead riding his cycle. He stopped on one side of the road, parked his cycle on the stand, and sat facing the fields to urinate. Having finished he came back to his cycle and rode ahead. In the process of climbing his bike, something fell from his cycle on the road. We saw that and looked at each other, as if in a conspiracy to remain silent. Reaching the place we found a small cloth bag full with its contents. One of us pounced on the bag, sat there on the road, untied the bag, and overturned it on the ground. All of us sat there anxious to see if the contents of the bag had something useful to mitigate our hunger. However, we were disgusted to find that the bag contained the bones of a human body collected after cremation. We inferred that the man might be taking the ashes of someone dear to him to immerse in some water stream. Four of us stood up with repulsion and despair, but the fifth boy did not seem much affected. He started searching the bones with the hope of finding something for use. Soon he raised his right hand clutching *do-paisa* coin. Seeing the coin, all the feeling of repulsion disappeared and a new spirit was awakened in all of us. Leaving the bones scattered on the road, we ran in search for something eatable that could be purchased with that coin in our possession. Soon we saw the signs of some habitation. It increased our speed to reach there as soon as possible. Luck favoured us in the form of a vendor carrying several edibles in his two baskets slinging from his shoulder. We stopped him and ordered roasted grams for *two paisas.* The quantity of grams handed over to us was enough for our famished stomachs.

Apportioning the grams among us we all started munching our share while walking ahead in search of water. An open village tank with standing water came in our way and we pounced on it unconcerned about hygiene and drank to our fill, cupping the water in our hands. That put some life in our bodies, and energised our brains. We saw that the town where we stood was Nawa Shehar and Jammu City was not too far-off from there. I suggested that I knew the place where my uncle lived in Jammu and if we managed to reach there I could guide the way to my uncle's house, which was in Raghunath bazaar.

Everyone listened but none had the strength left to walk any further. We were all sitting on the side of the road munching the grams left with us. At a little distance from us, was a *tonga* stand from where we heard the *tongawallas* calling passengers for going to destinations up to Jammu. Seeing those *tongas*, a solution came to my head for our problem. I proposed that we should hire a *tonga* to take us to Jammu where I would manage to pay him by getting the money from my uncle. It suited all and we hired one to carry us to Jammu. Around noon the *tonga* stopped in front of my uncle's house. Telling the *tongawala* to wait, I got down and went into the lane to find the stairs going upto the flat of my uncle. I ascended the stairs and reaching the entrance door, I knocked and my aunt opened the door. For a moment, she stood there like a statue. After recognising me, she spoke my name with some doubt and when I folded my hands and said "*Namaste*", she shifted her gaze from my face to my dirty clothes and said in a broken sentence from where and how did I reach Jammu?

I answered her briefly and requested for a rupee so that I could pay the *tongawalla* who was waiting down there. She hurried in and came back in a second with some money in her hand. She followed me downstairs and was more shocked to see four more rustic looking boys getting down from the *tonga*. After she paid the *tongawalla*, we all followed her upstairs. She stood at the doorstep of her flat and tried to recognize the other boys who stood behind me. She asked me whether anyone in Sialkot knew that we had gone to Jammu? I told her in nutshell the story about how we got there. After listening, she at once sent her daughter to their shop to call home my uncle immediately.

Hearing that we had not eaten anything since morning, she asked us to wash our hands and faces and sit in the room for eating. Whatever she had from the lunch menu, she placed before us. That was the time of the *Behi Baras*, the ritual on which *Mathies* and *Khamiras* were cooked. These items were cooked to last for a week or so and were stored in a tin container. These were duly served. We ate whatever was served but still felt hungry.

She started cooking fresh chapattis when my uncle arrived. He had heard the story from my cousin sister and was seriously considering the situation that might be prevailing at Sialkot. After seeing that we were being fed, he went by a *tonga* to Jammu railway station. There he knew the railway telegraph clerk whom he requested to pass on a word to Sialkot station about our arrival in Jammu. He requested the clerk to convey the message through a porter to our shop in the Trunk Bazaar. After being assured of the transmission of the message, he came back home and reprimanded us for our foolishness. Next morning, he caught the first train to Sialkot with five of us. As we reached outside our *haveli*, my grandmother shot down from her first storey residence of the rented building, caught me by my arm and dragged me upstairs to her room. She made me sit on a cot and without uttering a single word reached in and came out with a morsel of bread, topped with a spoon full of fresh butter. She thrust that into my mouth and then spoke with definitive immediacy telling me to munch and swallow that quickly. When she saw that done, she again caught me by the same arm and accompanied me to the *haveli* where all were anxiously waiting for me. My father stood in the compound. My grandmother, with her arm round me and holding me tight with her body addressed my father entreatingly, "Durga Dass, the child is repenting, and is perspiring with fear. Please forgive him this time with a stern reprimand". My father did not appear to listen and dragging me from her body, gave me such a strong blow that it threw me on the ground. I cried aloud but my father continued hitting me till I lost my senses. My grandmother continued to shout her entreaties to stop and he continued beating me. At last she jumped in and when she got a blow she shouted very hoarsely calling him a cruel butcher. Seeing his mother being hit, he relented and went in his room without uttering a word. My mother who sat silently in her doorless kitchen came out and with the help of my grandmother dragged me in and made me lie down on a cot in the inner room. My father sat in the outer room on a cot with his two hands placed on his forehead. That was how my romance of travelling to Jammu on foot in the year 1934 ended. All the other four boys who accompanied me were only scolded by their parents except the older Chopra boy who was slapped by his elder brother to make him run to their stairs to go up. All the children with their family members stood silently outside their quarters to watch the scene. The elder Chopra stood watching it from the terrace of their house.

My grandmother left after my mother escorted me in but went on rebuking my father in words and tone that expressed her great agony.

My friendship with the other boys of our *haveli* continued. Soon after, the two Sekhri boys, who were not going to the school, started working somewhere, learning as well as earning a little. They became busy and were out of the circle of my friends. The two Chopra boys came closer to me. Both of them were very clever as compared to me but the elder one was a real devil. He had very prominent pockmarks covering his entire dark face. He was quite eloquent and a good storyteller. He therefore influenced me a lot with his clever conversations and tried to mislead me in many ways. I was a simple boy but it was the family influence as well as God's grace that saved me from his crooked and evil designs.

Although this boy could not drag me to his immoral acts but his close company and the stories of his misdeeds did affect my mind. The result was further neglect of studies and bad performance in the class. The teachers were unhappy with me and punished me for ignoring my lessons. My mischiefs and fights with my class fellows continued unabated. Despite all this, I could pass the class tests and also the final examination and was promoted to the eighth class.

Near the end of my seventh class, one day before the arrival of our class teacher, I had a fight with a class fellow. Both of us were embroiled bodily with each other and fell on the desks. Opposite to our classroom was the tenth class wherein our headmaster was teaching. Due to the noise of the other boys of my class who were watching and shouting, the headmaster's attention was drawn to our side. He sent his class boy to call the fighters before him. Before we reached there he had already sent for the peon to bring his cane from his office. He made us stand together on one side and continued his lecture to the class. After a few minutes the peon arrived and handed over the cane to the headmaster. The headmaster then addressed us that by fighting in the class we had broken the school discipline. Falling on the desks could damage the furniture and the noise caused hindrance in his teaching the class. He then very calmly caned our palms. After three strokes on each palm, I started crying and then lost the count. I was in a semi-conscious state when I was told to go back to my class. After the school when I reached home with hands still hurting, I went straight to my bed instead of eating in the kitchen. I told my mother briefly that the headmaster punished me. I was sleeping when my father awoke me after reaching home from his shop. My mother had told him of my punishment and my father seeing my hands was quite upset. But I told him about my fight in the class. Next day, it was Sunday and in the *Arya Samaj Satsang Hall*, my father met my headmaster after the end of the prayers. I had no idea of the talk my father had with my headmaster but he was told clearly that I was very poor in studies but outstanding in making mischiefs. However, the headmaster felt sorry that he had to administer disciplinary punishment. But he proved to be a perfect gentleman. He never made any mention of my father's protest meeting. But from that day I was careful in the school and tried to concentrate on games. My interest in studies remained as shallow as before.

The elder Chopra boy had stopped going to school a few months back. He kept himself close to me and I found him attractive in his very friendly and sympathetic talks. A few months before my examination for the seventh class, he accompanied me to see the *Basant* fair. I wore my best dress with a multi-coloured Rajasthani turban on my head. While we were going round in the *mela*, we noted that a tall Muslim boy was following us. We became conscious and tried to get rid of him by swiftly moving from one place to another. But he did not leave us. We got afraid and decided to leave the fair. As we hurried out of the fair ground and turned for our home, he left us but before that I felt the touch of his hand on my turban. Reaching far away from the fair ground, my friend stopped me to look at the top of my turban. He found there a small chit mentioning only that boy's name and address where he had invited me. From that day on my friend changed his style. He started telling me that I was very healthy, good looking and the only son of my parents. However, my own father who dealt with me severely did not appreciate my qualities. Why should a father treat so harshly, his only son who had so many good qualities? I heard him, thought over it and found it true. When he saw that I had digested all his statements, he was encouraged to repeat that whenever he found the right time. Living in the same *haveli*, there was little privacy and every single happening in one family was known to the others. After a few months when he was sure that I was fully convinced of the truth of his statements, he took the next step.

It was the second month of my eighth class. He took me to see a film, *Devdas*. Although I could hardly understand, the film, he said it was the best picture of the time. The hero was K.L. Sehgal who was considered as the best singer-actor and the company, which had produced that picture, was New Theatres of Calcutta, the topmost film company in the country. I heard attentively what he said and believed him. He continued with his theme on another day and told me that those film companies were always on the look out for good looking young boys. Then he added that I was by far the best looking boy he had ever seen in any of the films or in the *Ram Lilas*. Finally, one day he said that he had conceived a good plan, which would save me from the harsh treatment of my father. The plan he explained was that he would escort me to Calcutta and get me a job of a child actor in New Theatres with handsome salary. I heard all what he said and believed him. That was the state of my development, ignorance and foolishness at the age of thirteen. It also showed the extent of that boy's hold on me. I followed the rest of his full plan. I collected my monthly school fee from home but did not deposit it in the school. I started absenting myself from the school. From home, every day I left with my school bag exactly at school going time to meet my friend half way from school. Then on, I remained at his disposal but away from the school. From the school fee in my pocket, he got me stitched two shirts and two pyjamas, and fixed a date for escorting me to Lahore in a bus and from there to Calcutta in a train. A few days before the date fixed for departure, he suggested that the money left with me would not be sufficient and I should add to it by stealing some of my mother's jewellery. This was his first suggestion made during previous two or three weeks of his unfolding of his plan (trap) which I refused to execute. I told him clearly that I could not do such a thing to my mother. He at once retraced and told me not to bother about it, as he would himself arrange the required funds.

At last, the day of the planned departure arrived and both of us reached the Nanda bus station. The bus for Lahore was parking and the hawkers were loudly calling passengers for Lahore. When we were in the line to buy tickets, my friend remembered that he had left some important things at home and rushed back asking me to sit in the waiting room till he returned. For more than an hour I kept waiting for him, but he did not show up, and the bus for Lahore left without us. The next bus was scheduled to leave in 2 to 3 hours. When I got tired of waiting, I left the waiting room and stood on the road to look for him. It had been two hours since he left, and I started worrying about the delay. In this state of restlessness, I walked towards home avoiding the road which passed via my father's sports shop. I was walking slowly, but looking attentively ahead to find my friend coming back from home. Suddenly, a strong hand clutched my left arm from behind which made me turn around. Terrified and my heart beating fast, I saw it was uncle Chunni Lal, my father's assistant. Keeping a strong grip on my wrist he asked me, where I had been roaming? I turned pale and replied that I was not roaming about but had been sent on an errand by my teacher. He laughed loudly and said, "Come on, you naughty boy. Your teacher has sent someone from the school to inform your father that you have been missing classes for more than a week and have not deposited the fees for this month". I was caught red handed, dragged to our shop and then as directed by my father, to my home.

My mother was surprised to see me with uncle Chunni Lal holding me like a culprit and asked him why he had brought me home like that at that time when I should be in my school? He told my mother the whole story of my not going to school for about ten days and not having deposited the school fee. My uncle also conveyed to my mother the message of my father that I should not be allowed to move out till he came back home. My mother pushed me inside the room and sitting there on a cot asked me angrily what was all that she had heard? Where had I been wandering? Completely stunned I looked at her unhappy face but could not speak. She started crying and I too joined her. I had decided not to disclose the plan and the name of my companion. My mother was grieved and much hurt that I being her only son was not proving worthy of my father who was so much respected by all for his admirable character. She was also worried to anticipate the punishment I would get from my unsparing father. Then she saw my bulging school bag. When she opened it and saw my newly stitched shirts and trousers in that, she felt awfully alarmed. I was watching her like a dummy now, not knowing what to say or do. Showing me the clothes from my satchel, she looked into my eyes and asked me, what was that and where was I going to? Full of pain and in a hushed voice, she asked me if I was running away from home!

She sensed something very sinister happening to me and started crying again, silently but more intensely, cursing her fate. I sat totally stupefied. She got up from the cot, took me to the inner room, washed my face and hands and made me sit in the corner cot. She washed her face and brought me something to eat. She then went out to arrange for the night cooking. As she was busy outside, I lied down on the cot and went to sleep. Late in the evening, I woke up and heard the voice of my father outside. He had enquired about me and my mother had told him that I had not spoken anything but she felt that I had been possessed by some evil spirit, which was guiding me to act in that manner. My father then asked where I was? She did not speak but indicated inside by her hand's gesture. He came in and found me sitting on the cot. After one or two stern questions that I did not answer, he gave me the second hard beating with anguished reproaches. He was badly hurt inside and was uncontrollably angry. My mother did not leave the kitchen where she sat crying. All my sisters were crying loudly. Some elderly ladies including my grandmother intervened to make my father calm. He was badly upset and appeared totally exhausted, physically and emotionally. He sat down on the cot in the outer room with his hands on his forehead. When the ladies left, my mother came to my father and told him to get up and wash to take his meals. He did not speak but went in and washed. He came back to the same cot again and when my mother brought him food, he refused to eat anything and started shedding tears. I again slept after the hard punishment and remembered only that my mother made me drink a glass of milk in my sleep. Both my parents went to bed without eating but my mother made my sisters eat their meals.

From the next day my father took me along for the morning walk. When we returned, he told my mother to give me my breakfast. To me he addressed thus, "You have no interest in studies. It is your fate that you remain illiterate. So let it be. You will not be going to the school anymore to waste your time and life. From today, you start going to the shop along with Chunni Lal. Carry the keys with you and he will teach you, how to open the shop, clean it and prepare it for the day".

Thus, my schooling was interrupted and I started doing as directed from the next day. After coming back from the morning walk in the company of my father, I had to get ready soon, collect keys and reach the sports shop with uncle Chunni Lal.

My training started from opening the shop. There was a standard regimen of bringing water from the municipal tap on the road, sprinkling it on the shop floor and some area outside our shop, sweeping it with a broom, dusting the tables, chairs and the show cases, putting every article at its right place. After my father arrived, he taught me how to write the rough day book in Urdu. Everyday, I was given a new lesson in one or the other aspect of business. It was only then that I realised that when I was serious I was a sharp learner.

Within six months I could do all work relating to banks, post office and the railways. I was writing accounts both in Urdu and English. I maintained proper cashbook and the ledger. I learnt to draft as well as type general letters for our outstation customers. I learnt the name of every article of sports equipment that we sold. Not only this, I understood the difference in the quality of each item. I knew that the hockey stick is made in two parts—the blade of mulberry timber and the handle of cane. Similarly I learnt that the cricket bat is made of Kashmir willow and cane. Tennis, badminton and squash rackets, football, volleyball and rugby ball, different types and styles of nets for every game, different treatments given to every net, the balls used for hockey and cricket. In short, I grasped full knowledge about the ins and outs of all the sports equipment in only 6 months.

But it all happened without any interest and in a sort of captivity. Along with whatever I learnt in business, I also learnt a good lesson for being a wayward boy indifferent to my education. The lesson which I considered the most important of all was the realization that I was uneducated while all our customers were educated, well dressed and gentlemen. I developed an inferiority complex and a craving for getting educated. Most of our customers helped me in my transformation as they occasionally argued with my father as to why he did not send me to a school when he could easily afford? To my father's argument that I had no interest in studies and often ran away from the school, they replied that it must be due to my bad company. Otherwise, they said that I was intelligent, well-behaved and hardworking. I on my part, started telling my mother that I wanted to go to school and gave her assurance that I would study properly, would never miss school and show good results. My mother duly conveyed it to my father. At last, one day, my father told me that my mother and many customers had recommended my rejoining the school, but he feared that I might again go back to my bad habits. I took courage to reply that I would study hard and show good results and there would be no complaint from my teachers. My father agreed to send me to school with the condition that he would watch till the first quarterly examination result. If I performed well, I would continue, otherwise I would be back to the shop. I agreed and the very next day, he sent me to my school to see the headmaster for my re-admission.

When I went to see the headmaster in his office and requested for re-admission, he told me bluntly that I was the most mischievous boy in his school, always fighting and then one of the worst in studies. He did not want to land himself in trouble again by re-admitting me to his school. He was quite happy without a nuisance like me. I meekly replied, "Sir, I will not repeat those old bad acts of mine; I will attend to studies properly and show good results." I requested for being given one chance, as I did not want to remain illiterate. The headmaster chuckled and said that he could see that I had at least learnt to speak well but he feared that I had forgotten everything of what little I knew of the subjects. I promptly told him, "Sir, I was being taught English by my father from my class book, Nelson Reader". The headmaster replied that Nelson Reader did not constitute all the subjects. But I was prompt with my reply and said, "Sir, I was doing all accounts of our shop. I was doing correspondence with our outside customers, I can type also. I have learnt the tables up to 16 thoroughly. He gestured with his hand to me to stop and said that he could understand my anxiety to join the school and he would not discourage me but my admission would be subject to my showing good results in the first quarterly examination. I promptly accepted the condition whereby he sent me with the peon to school office for issue of admission form and for fulfilling other requirements.

I rejoined school. This is the event, which marked the first good turn in my life. My rejoining the school with zeal and craving made a major difference in my position in the school as well as at home.

On the first day of going to school, I was ready much before time. The younger Chopra boy, who was one class junior to me when I left school last year, was now my class fellow. For a short while, I had some feeling of hesitation mixed with a little humiliation of my demoted position but I shoved that feeling away. I waited for that boy to be ready so that I might accompany him to school. From the first day onward, I accompanied him to school and came back home with him. In the class I listened to every lesson with keen interest. This continued till the quarterly examination. In the class, I sat very quietly, did not talk to anyone except my friend and was very humble and obedient to all my teachers. I strictly followed the routine of finishing my homework first and then doing something else.

When the dates of the first quarterly examination were announced, I was filled with apprehension, that I might not be able to do my papers well. I started working harder. At last the examination started and I tried to do as best as I could. But I was not confident of the result and was scared till the results were actually declared. Sometimes I could not sleep at night for a long time thinking about the consequences in case my result was not good. At last the day arrived when the result was declared. Every teacher announced the result of the subject he taught before handing over the answer papers to the concerned student. I heard the first teacher announcing my name and my marks in the mathematics. I was completely nervous, and came back to real life when my friend thumped my back saying "Congratulations, you did better than me". Similarly, I scored well in English and other subjects. A big load was off my mind. After the school, I went straight to my father and showed him my result. He looked at my face and guessed about my satisfactory result. He shuffled my papers, and his face showed his satisfaction. He then said, "Ok, in the next examination you must show further improvement. Do not relax after this result. You have to consistently work hard. Now go home and tell your mother that you have qualified to continue in the school." My mother was very happy. She hugged me, telling me to continue to be a good boy. She further said, "You should follow your father's footsteps who had such a good record in his school." I stuck to my mother's body savouring its warmth and affection and detached myself from her when I felt something warm dropping on my head. I looked at her tearful eyes and cried to her "no mom" and ran to find my neighbour friend to compare my marks with his marks in each of the subjects. I had performed better in English and Maths and he in other subjects. Both of us were happy. That evening I accompanied him to the centre of the *mohalla* and we played with other boys after proudly announcing our success in the examination.

I was now confident of my position in the class. The period of three months had passed and I was no more embarrassed of sitting with junior boys in the school. I also made some new friends in the class. On the family front, I found sympathy in the dealings of every member.

During my work in sports shop, I saw my father solving crossword puzzles from the *Illustrated Weekly of India*, with one of his friends. He subscribed to that magazine and I too found time to go through it, but only for seeing pictures. On one of its pages I found pictures of various types of postal stamps of different countries. I could not understand why the pictures of postal stamps were included in the magazine? I asked my father about it but it was his friend who replied that the stamp collection was a popular hobby and some of the old and rare stamps were auctioned every year in London to fetch heavy bids for their owners.

One day, while sitting in the central room of the rented house of my grandparents, I noticed one room which always remained closed; it was not being used by our family either. Out of sheer curiosity, I opened it's door and found it all dark, full of stacks of papers all covered with layers of dust. Not being discouraged by the darkness and dust, I picked up one dusty bundle and brought it out. After dusting the bundle I opened it and found that there were letters from foreign countries and some other papers with the name of Babu Nathu Mal Sekhri on all of them. The envelopes had postal stamps of varied colours and designs. Seeing those I remembered the *Illustrated Weekly* pictures of stamps and the information given to me by my father's friend. I was wonder stuck to read the names of various countries about which I had never heard till then. The stamps belonged to countries of the British Empire and dated back to the nineteenth century and a few to the beginning of the twentieth century. I tied that bundle and went again to peep into that dark room. I saw a treasure hidden in that room, full of bundles of a similar type as the one picked up by me.

When my father came home in the evening, I showed him that bundle and told him that I had picked it from the dark room in my grandparent's house. He looked at the envelopes and the addresses they bore. He told me those letters belonged to Babu Nathu Mal Sekhri, the owner of that house. He said that on some holiday, he would narrate to me the story of that noble ancestor of ours.

While I waited to hear the story of Babu Nathu Mal Sekhri, on the next day, I started separating the stamps from the envelopes carefully without spoiling them. Then I bought an album and pasted the stamps in that. One by one I took the bundles from the room and followed the same routine upto pasting the stamps in the album till it was full. I bought another one and filled it also. Around that time, the family vacated the house and all of us shifted to Ram Talai where the burnt down house had been rebuilt.

My collection of stamps stopped but I continued reading the *Illustrated Weekly* for the latest information about old stamps. I regularly compared stamps from my collection with the valuable ones given in the weekly and this kept my interest in the hobby alive. As an additional benefit, I became a regular reader of the Weekly, and continued it till its publication was stopped in the 1980s.

One day, as promised, my father told me about Babu Nathu Mal Sekhri. He was the first cousin of his grandfather. He worked as a cashier in the Imperial Bank of India in Rawalpindi during the last quarter of the nineteenth century. As he was a very congenial person, he earned much popularity among the British army officers who had their accounts in his branch of the bank. He also lent money to the needy British officers. He charged them interest, which he collected from them on their pay-day. Thus, he became their banker friend. This activity also gave him some additional income. He remained in service upto 1901. After his retirement he came back to Sialkot and built that small but beautiful house. His family consisted of a wife and a daughter.

Coming back to Sialkot after retirement, Babu Nathu Mal Sekhri continued money lending to British military officers in Sialkot contonment. He could establish money lending as his full-time business. Though the British military officers got fat salaries, yet because of their spendthrift habits, they were always short of money. And Babu Nathu Mal Sekhri's generous nature and wise way of investment made him both popular and rich. His money transactions had long innings. Like a shrewd banker, he adapted a lending system. When he lent money to an officer, he made him sign a *hundi*. On the due date, the officer was required to pay back the principal amount as well as the interest due thereon. I then remembered that the papers other than the envelope in the bundles were the *hundies*.

Most of the officers could not pay back the principal even when they were transferred to some other British colonies. In such cases those unpaid *hundies* were revalidated, authenticated and guaranteed by the superior officers of the regiment, extending their time and liabilities to the places of the transfer of the concerned officers. *Babuji* thus used to get the interest from the British officers from all the British colonies, which in those days were spread to all the corners of the world. The understanding was that at their next transfer, the borrowers must arrange to pay-off the principal amount as well as the interest thereon.

As time passed, Babu Nathu Mal Sekhri's clientele increased, resulting in more and more profits. In the sphere of the military establishment, he was virtually a single man bank. The nature of his business brought him bulky foreign post daily. The postman of the area had to spend almost half of his time delivering all the foreign money orders, registered letters and other post, at *Babuji's* house.

Babu Nathu Mal Sekhri, had passed away before my birth. He was described as an endearing aristocrat and a philanthropist. He possessed a balanced body with a robust and red face. He wore a milky-white and starched turban, white shirt and *chooridar pajama* and local Indian style golden footwear. He owned a horse driven carriage in which he moved out in the city with a liveried coachman and a *sais*. His three-storey house, adjacent to our *haveli*, had palatial features. It had white and black square-tiled floors, walls and ceilings all painted with prominent episodes from our epics, viz., *The Ramayana* and *The Mahabharata*. It had been kept in a trim condition even when he was no more. Our family had the pleasure of living in that house for a few years after our own house in Ram Talai was destroyed by fire in 1932.

Babu Nathu Mal Sekhri had only one child, a daughter. She was of my father's age and was one of the most beautiful women I had ever seen. She had a divine face, very tender, reddish fair in complexion and round like a full moon. She wore beautiful silk attire and carried herself like a queen. Her physical attributes were fully matched by her human qualities. When she opened her mouth to speak, the words sounded like a sweet music and fell out of her mouth like pearls. For me in my teenage years, there was nothing more adorable than to be in her company. Her presence used to create strange inner feelings, like the passing of vibrations inside me, which kept me under the spell of her charm for quite a long time. I used to feel proud to be near her and to address her as *Bhuaji*. Her name, as we knew it, was *Bhua* Labho. She was the owner of her father's properties.

She was married into an aristocratic Bhandari family of Lahore. She used to visit Sialkot once a year. We had heard, that the Bhandari family of Lahore had a very high social circle, which included high court judges and high government officials. *Bhua* Labho had two children, a daughter named Kunti and a son named Kavi. Her daughter, Kunti, was elder of the two and was highly educated. Her marriage was celebrated in Sialkot with a young public prosecutor belonging to a well to do Vadehra family in the year 1940. On the day of marriage, I was there the whole day at *barat bhawan*. The marriage party being from Sialkot itself, almost all its member were known to me or had familiar faces. What was new, were the guests from Lahore. They presented a real novelty for us. We had seen aristocratic families in Sialkot as well, but the guests from Lahore appeared to have landed there from a different world altogether. By saying 'Lahore guests', I mean the female guests. Their beautiful faces, glittering dresses, their gestures, movements and the way of speaking, all these combined to weave a spell around us and our young innocent minds were devastated. Our intensive desire to remain near them and enjoy their exquisiteness was rudely interrupted by the arrival of the marriage party. We had to reluctantly run to the service points of duty. Almost 60 years have passed since then but I still remember the magic of those celestial damsels.

But the curse of partition showed no regard for anything sublime. *Bhua* Labho's family had to migrate to Delhi in tragic circumstances. She lost her husband and became a dedicated devotee of Radha Swami cult's Agra branch. I met her twice in Delhi, once when she came to our Shanti *Bhuaji's* house and again at her residence in Darya Ganj. She mostly stayed at Agra. Her daughter and son-in-law lived in Delhi near Gole Dak Khana. Her son Kavi left for some East African country, settled there never to come back to India. Because of the loss of her husband and the conditions caused by the partition, *Bhua* Labho lost her regal geniality to a great extent. But I did find in her, traces of old nobility. She died some time during the fifties.

Babu Nathu Mal Sekhri used to financially support many of his Sekhri relatives. He had built a *sarai* in the centre of the city providing facilities to those who came to the city from distant places. The *sarai* was a large building. One side was a stable for his carriage and horses and the other had rooms for the outside visitors. He kept a good stock of sweet soda water bottles in an ice filled tub as a normal daily routine to serve the small Sekhri children of his *mohalla*. Little children joyfully visited the *sarai* in the summer days after they had finished their classes in the schools, to be served with those sweet cold drinks and among those children, were my father and uncles. Babu Nathu Mal Sekhri loved children and was in turn loved and respected by them.

—7—

RESCUED AND REFORMED BY A HIDDEN HAND

In my school, I had unintentionally gained prominence as one having a bicycle. Not only did I own it but I was also considered as a very proficient cyclist. Many of my class fellows were obliged to me for having been taught cycling by me on my bicycle.

Some time in 1935, I accompanied my grandfather, along with my cousin Madan Lal to Lahore to attend the marriage of uncle Vas Dev Sekhri. In Lahore, we visited a zoo for the first time in our life and moved there from one cage to another with extreme excitement. So many animals—docile and ferocious, so many birds of various pedigrees, forms and colours and reptiles of fearful figures. The bad smell from the cages of tigers and lions and their restless walking therein kept us at a distance from them. But we remembered them the most. We went to see the Anarkali Bazaar where we had sweet soda water from Kesari Soda Water Shop, the best in the whole of the Punjab. We then visited Bhalla Shoe Company, a big shoe shop, where my grandfather bought a pair of shoes for Madan Lal, making me sulk for not being considered for that favour.

It was a very popular saying in the Punjab; "a person who has not seen Lahore is not born yet". Back in Sialkot, I felt that I possessed an additional quality to impress my *mohalla* friends and class fellows. Slowly I was gaining popularity with my class fellows and teachers. The first boy who was attracted to me and developed a close friendship was my classmate Onkar Pandit. He was very fond of seeing films. Till that time I did not have much interest in them. I had seen only *Laila Majnu* with my grandfather, *Raja Harish Chandra* in Jammu with my uncle's family, *Devdas* and *Amrit Manthan* with my rascal friend. When Onkar talked about movies, he appeared to have good knowledge about them and also the film companies. I was quite impressed by his knowledge. He exhorted me to see *Achhut Kanya* with him. By that time my mental faculties had developed as much as to be able not only to understand that film but also appreciate the theme and the acting of the main characters. Onkar added further details for my knowledge by telling me that the heroine Devika Rani was the wife of the producer of the film, Himansu Ray who had started his studio after studying this art in Germany. He also told me that she was related to Rabindranath Tagore's family and the company that made the film was called Bombay Talkies, which had many German technicians working in it.

This was about the time when we were preparing to shift from our old *mohalla*. My friendship with Onkar grew fast. He was also good in studies and had very clean habits. Our further diversion towards cinema was cut short when our final exams came near. We started giving more time to studies. In my final examination, I was promoted to the ninth class with good marks. By the year 1937, we had shifted to Ram Talai *mohalla* where our house had been rebuilt. In rebuilding the house, my father and his two brothers contributed almost equal money but the actual construction was mostly attended to by my father with good help from uncle Brij Lal. The family shifted to the new house after living for more than four years in our old *mohalla*. In those four years, most of the family members had formed new friends, from whom we had to part. I had spent my formative years living in that *mohalla*, cultivating new friends and playing new games. The only source of satisfaction, my old stamp-collecting hobby, was lost.

While living in the old *mohalla*, I observed for the first time a community ritual which we performed before every marriage and *mundan* in our family. It was called the Seva Mata *Puja*. I had learned about that ritual and had known the story of Seva Mata who was the progenitor of the Sekhri community. It was an interesting tale, which I must record, in a separate chapter entitled 'Origin of our Clan'.

In the new *mohalla*, in our immediate neighbourhood, there lived two brothers, Arjan Singh and Nirvair Singh who were both in the tenth class. We came to know each other quickly. Their father had been transferred to Sialkot exactly at that time and so his sons needed friends in the new place. During my talks with those Sikh brothers, I asked them how they found the ninth class studies. Nirvair the younger and more clever of the brothers cautioned me about Geometry, the new subject that started from the ninth class. He said I must pay special attention to it as he found it the toughest.

When it came to the selection of subjects, I opted for science subjects. Unfortunately when the classes started, I fell ill and could not attend the school for the first two days. When I went to the school on the third day, the first two periods were for Physics and Chemistry. The teacher taught the lessons of the third day, which I could not understand and felt confused as the basic scientific terms and names of the laboratory glassware and other equipment, had been taught on the first two days. I sat like a dumb-doll, hesitating to seek assistance from other class fellows or ask the teacher for help. Rather, I started thinking that the science subjects were too difficult for me and decided on my own that they were not my cup of tea. I also faced the same difficulty in other classes but I did not feel so nervous, as in the science periods.

After the school I reached home in a confused state and did not talk to anybody. Before going to bed at night, I made up my mind to give up the Science subjects and go for the Arts subjects. Next day I got up early in the morning and found myself still drowned in my anxiety. I decided to see the headmaster and explain to him everything. I did so and the headmaster, looking at me guessed my difficulty and allowed me to change the subjects. Science books were returned and in exchange I bought Sanskrit, History and Geography books, which I thought I could understand better.

I faced the same problem in Geometry, but as this subject could not be changed, I decided to face the situation with courage and hard work. I handled this problem in a peculiar way. I took up the Geometry book and started reading the first theorem and its solution from beginning to the end. I could not understand anything in first reading. I read it again and went on over and over till I could repeat the whole theorem without looking at the book. But I did not leave it there. Sitting, standing, or walking, I kept on repeating the theorem. I must have repeated it at least one hundred times. Then, I started understanding it. I wrote the first theorem in my notebook again and again. The same technique was adopted for the second and third theorems. In just two days, I was able to follow the teacher when he taught the subsequent theorems. Not only could I understand the lessons in the class, I also started to find the subject exciting and stimulating. Strangely, as the lessons progressed, I automatically remembered all the previous theorems and their solutions. After every theorem in the textbook, there were about a dozen exercises, which were not taught in the class. Naturally, I had never paid any attention to these exercises. The teacher only referred to these and said that when the basic theorems were properly understood, then these exercises could be easily solved.

Our class had about sixty students. Two among them were considered to be the top students. After the start of the class, another boy migrating from a school in Gujranwala was admitted in our class. His name was Ram Prakash Bombah. He was a real genius and he surpassed everyone including those two bright boys. In fact this new boy created a sensation in the whole school. Every lesson of each and every subject, when taught in the class, was quickly understood and grasped by the boy. Otherwise too, our class was considered to be the best that our school had ever had. This was the general opinion of the teachers and our headmaster. The headmaster, who taught Maths to our class, liberally uttered these words of acclaim in the class. He was so fond of our class that when he entered our classroom, he was a totally changed person. He used to teach our class in a very friendly manner.

In the first quarterly examination, I did well in English and Mathematics. The Geometry paper was considered to be very tough as the questions therein included the exercises too, which had not been taught in the class. Unexpectedly, with my mastery over the theorems, I could easily do the full paper including the exercises. The same teachers who taught the subjects were grading the papers. As the result was declared, and the answer papers were being distributed in the class, the peon came to our class and told the teacher that the headmaster had sent for three boys. Two of them were Ram Prakash Bombah, the genius newcomer, and Maharaj Krishan Khanna, who was the next best. The third name was mine. My heart started beating fast as I accompanied the peon along with the other two boys. I was wondering why was I included in the call. The headmaster who was teaching the tenth class, made us stand by the side of his chair. He then held out one answer paper done by Ram Prakash. He announced that in his Geometry paper, he had done all the questions correctly and had scored 95 marks out of 100. The second paper was that of Maharaj Krishan Khanna. He had also done all the questions correctly and had scored 94 out of 100. The third paper was mine with 93 marks. After handing over the answer papers to us, the headmaster told the tenth class saying that in geometry this was an unusual result. After declaring this he asked me, "But, Vishwa Nath! How could you do it?" I silently stood there holding my answer paper with a creeping sense of pride. There was a loud applause of appreciation from the tenth class students.

The result of the quarterly examination showed that I was good in Mathematics, English and Hindi but below average in Sanskrit, History and Geography. But I did not try to improve my weak subjects; instead I felt satisfied with my proficiency in the other three subjects. I paid more attention to sports like *hockey*, *gatka*, *lathi*, etc. As a result, of my interest in sports, I was selected in the first hockey team; and I was also considered as one of the best in the self-defence sports.

In 1937, the DAV Schools, Lahore organized a mini-Olympics in their city on the occasion of Golden Jubilee of the DAV Schools. Different teams from all Arya Samaj Schools of Punjab were invited to participate in that mini-Olympics. Our school decided to participate in three events—*hockey*, *wrestling* and *gatka*. All the selected players, accompanied by the headmaster and our games teacher, reached Lahore in a special bus and stayed in accommodation reserved by the hosts, the DAV School, Lahore. I was one of the three boys selected for the *gatka* team. The Olympics was to go on for six or seven days. After the opening ceremony of the games, the matches started. Both our hockey and wrestling teams were out of the competition after losing the first two matches. However, the *gatka* team reached the final. This was the only team on which our school could pin their hopes. Our headmaster himself took care of the three *gatka* players and at meal times, he started making them sit near his chair; they were served the dishes under his supervision. More *ghee* was added to the dishes served to them. I, being the youngest in the *gatka* team, received special attention from the headmaster. I remember that he would specially come to my bed at night with his peon and woke me up and made me drink a glass of milk.

On the day of the final match, we were showered with lots of praise and encouragement. The headmaster specially told us to fight courageously without being nervous and enter the arena with determination to win. Our final match was with the team of DAV School, Jalandhar. As the match started, the tallest member of our team went into the ring, but was defeated. The second boy from our team, fought very well and won. The game came to a draw and the third match in which I was to fight had become very crucial. The headmaster came to me, and encouraged me a lot but I was not listening to anything as I was in a state of excitement. I heard the announcement of my name and entered the ring with my *gatka*. The match started with loud shouts from the audience cheering up their respective players. We both started fighting with equal skill and the match lingered on. I felt that my confidence was increasing with every passing minute. Simultaneously, I had discovered the weakness in my opponent's movements. This made me still more forceful in my attacks and shortly, to my pleasant surprise, my opponent failed to withstand the force of my strike and his *gatka* fell out of his hand on the ground. I was declared the winner and with me our team won the gold medal. Our headmaster hugged me most warmly. The game teacher patted me affectionately. Two days later, at the closing function, our team members received individual trophies and the school a gold medal. My stature at home and at school increased additionally.

From the beginning of the ninth class, I was experiencing a rapid change in me. It was like the flowering of my latent qualities, which had been suppressed so far. I gained a new confidence, which resulted in my communicating more freely with my classmates. I came into the good books of the headmaster and other teachers. Many of my classmates seemed to be impressed by my new deportment. I made many new friends. Onkar Pandit, being my steadfast companion and friend, two other boys Brahm Dev Bahl and Sukh Dev Bahl came very close to me. With these three friends, I had a life long friendship. Brahm Dev and Sukh Dev, two real brothers and sons of the district income tax officer, were very good singers and the best dressed boys in the whole school.

In the free classes, I was surrounded by many classmates to hear from me humorous stories, and jokes which I had learnt during our stay in the old *mohalla*. Many of these were dirty. Paradoxically, those vulgar narrations made me still more popular in the class.

My new exploits lead to a lopsided development, which resulted in my ignoring the studies and taking keener interest in extra-curricular activities. Most of my after school time was given to the sport of hockey and watching films. Onkar Pandit introduced me to another group of friends who organized picnics in the summer. Mohammed Sharief, the only Muslim boy in the group and a non-student was the leader. These picnics were arranged to go to one of the cold water canals, one in Jammu Tawi and another near Sambrewal, a small town in the Sialkot district. Both those places were within 20 miles from the city and we could easily reach there by train or bus. We carried food, mangoes and milk with us. Reaching the canals, we would hang the mango basket and milk bottles in the canal so that they got cold. We enjoyed bathing, swimming and joking. Many a time we would share a small part of our meals with the monkeys. Spending the day there to our full satisfaction, we reached back home in the evening.

These diversions made me further indifferent to the subjects in which I needed special efforts to improve. The teachers for these subjects tried to make me serious but when they found me incorrigible, they gave up. After my rejoining the school, and my initial good result in the eighth class, my father stopped paying any attention to my progress. He was under the impression that the interest once created in me for studies was still prevalent. Curiously, I passed in my weak subjects in my examination and finally got promoted.

When the final result for the ninth class was declared and promotions made, our headmaster chose the top eighteen boys out of 66 who had passed. He made this selection for his class on the basis of marks in English and Mathematics, the two subjects he taught to the tenth class. As I was the ninth in that list, I was placed in his section. Besides he admitted two more students in his class.

In my tenth class, I could somehow maintain my position in the two subjects taught by our headmaster. Rather I did very well in Mathematics, which happened to be the headmaster's favourite subject. He was therefore, very happy with me. By his administrative acumen he could see that all the best boys in his section were my close friends. My popularity in the class was mainly due to my congenial behaviour and my narrating of folk tales to my class fellows during recess and in the free classes. I also became captain of our school hockey team, which won all the friendly matches with teams of other schools of the city. After the first quarterly examination, the headmaster noticed my indifferent result in Sanskrit, History and Geography. He called me to his office and showed his concern about it. Because of his love for me he told me that he would speak to my Sanskrit and History teachers to give me extra time after school hours without any payment and I should try to make up in these subjects. I had little or no sense to think that the final result of the tenth class carried a big importance. In spite of the headmaster's personal interest and initiative, I remained indifferent and negligent in those subjects.

The Hindi teacher considered my presence in his class as a problem and nuisance. So immediately on his entry in the class he would address me, from the door of the classroom itself, "Vishwa Nath, my dear, you would like to go for the call of nature or drinking water etc., you are most welcome to do so". This provided me the liberty to leave his class. After his class was the recess and therefore I had double time of leisure. Strangely, as in English and Maths, my result in Hindi used to be good.

I consider my year in the tenth class as the best time of my school. In studies I had a reputation of being good; in games, I was the captain of the prestigious hockey team, I was good in *lathi* and *gatka* fights; and a master cyclist. Besides that, I was the undeclared group leader of the cream of the class and was the most favourite student of our headmaster. The teaching time of the headmaster was a real treat for the entire class. He spent more than half the time in telling different experiences of his life. And the time when he did teach, he interspersed it with several convivial anecdotes keeping complete communion with the students. When teaching Geometry, he used to draw figures on the blackboard. He possessed a very good hand in drawing straight lines, and different geometrical figures like triangles and circles. The circles, which were the most difficult to draw correctly, were always his challenge and he really possessed a talent to draw them right.

His clothes were always snow-white and well starched. Naturally we thought that he changed daily but to our utter surprise he said that he changed his shirt and trousers only twice a week. When the class expressed their doubt in chorus, he confirmed his statement by explaining the way he could preserve their neatness and right crease. He wore these clothes only for school hours and after reaching back home, he took them off and wore his *dhoti-kurta*. The school shirt was hung on a peg in his room but the *pyjama* was treated differently. He took out the chord from the *pyjama* and folded it exactly at the creases and then put it under a pillow. The *pyjama* rested under the pillow day and night and got the treatment somewhat similar to being ironed.

About his shoes, which were always shining bright, he explained that he was very particular that they were comfortable to wear and were neat both inside and outside. Then he added another astonishing statement about his shoes. He said that old shoes in which his feet had adjusted well were retained by him, as long as they looked good.

Then came the point of his good health and ruddy face. He was a pure vegetarian, ate on time and did a lot of walking. In his diet, milk and it's products were the main ingredients. He stressed that simple vegetarian diet and milk and it's products are the best diet.

He emphasized that besides food, the other things necessary for good health were good moral character and simple living. The head should be covered during daytime to protect it from heat and dust. In addition, once a week, if not daily, the body should be massaged before taking a bath. The hair on the head should be trimmed, well oiled and mildly combed.

Nobody was allowed to come to school bare headed. Once in our own class, Sukhdev and Brahmdev came bare headed and explained to the headmaster that their old caps had become dirty and new ones could not be purchased. But he would not listen to any excuse in the matter of school discipline. He sent both of them home with an order to come back soon with heads duly covered. The headmaster himself narrated the story of a boy from the school hostel who came to school after summer holidays with long uncut hair finely combed and shining. He was very angry when he saw the boy. He asked him why he had come without turban and with uncut hair. The boy explained that during vacation he had gone out of station and could not get time to get the hair cut and his turban was not clean. He heard the explanation of the boy, called him to his side and made him sit on the floor there. Then he called the peon, instructed him for some quick action and attended to his class. After a few minutes, the peon came back followed by a barber. The headmaster instructed the barber to shave the boy's head. The boy had thought that sitting on the floor was the only punishment. When he saw the barber and heard the headmaster's instructions to him, he stood up swiftly with a loud cry. He requested the headmaster with folded hands that he might be spared for only one day. The headmaster slapped him hard and ordered him to sit down quietly. Terrified, the boy sat down but did not stop crying while the barber did his job. The headmaster instructed the barber to show the boy his face in his mirror; this made the boy cry more hoarsely. Another boy of the class was told to accompany him to the hand pump in the school to wash his head. In the meantime the peon bought a new turban for the boy. Only after he had put on the turban, he was allowed to attend his class. The expenses both for the turban and the barber's job were debited to the boy's account in the hostel bill.

A similar episode occured in my class when my deskmate Ram Saran, a well-behaved boy, above average in studies and a member of the school hockey team came to the class without a turban and with hair well oiled and combed. His seat was on the other end of the aisle and was not visible from the headmaster's chair. The poor fellow was conscious of his breach of rules and therefore kept his head low. In the normal course of his teaching, the headmaster could not notice him.

But to Ram Saran's misfortune, while teaching a new lesson from the text, the headmaster started walking. As he arrived near our desk, his eyes slipped towards poor Ram Saran. He abruptly stopped, brought his hand holding the open book down, and looked a bit puzzled. Then he uttered, "Is it Ram Saran? Why with bare head and no turban? Stand up" Ram Saran stood up with his face pale with terror. Having a full look at his head, the headmaster was more surprised. Ram Saran's hair being wavy, looked beautiful, falling slightly down on his forehead. All that made the headmaster go berserk.

He asked him how he had come to the class bare-headed with his hair combed like that of prostitutes? The whole class looked stunned and turned towards Ram Saran who stood in his seat with folded hands pleading for forgiveness. To the relief of the whole class the headmaster took pity on the beseeching boy and only told him angrily to get out of the class and come back only after a hair cut and wearing a turban.

The above incidents showed his strict attitude in maintaining school discipline. But he was a very fair minded person. We had never found him lacking in fairness whenever there was any incident in which his eldest son, who was in our class, tried to show his privilege as his son. He used to reprimand him in the class strongly whenever his son ever tried to do so. But somehow he openly favoured me to allow me to make humorous and witty remarks in his class, which made the whole class laugh heartily.

Unfortunately, such exceptioned position in the class gave me only thrills, and did nothing to help me in my weak subjects. No one could bring home to me the awareness of a balanced attitude towards all subjects. I continued with my own egoistic life style. The vacation time for preparation of final examination arrived. Then I started reading the text-books of the subjects in which I was weak and was shocked to find that I knew very little. I could not even read through the whole books. That situation made me nervous. In that condition I could not think of going for the class photograph, on my own.

Preparatory holidays were too brief a period for me to make any improvement in my weak subjects. On the first day it was the History paper and I could not decide what to study and what to leave. I was holding the book in my hand from 4:00 A.M., totally confused. At last I had to leave the book, get ready and reach the examination hall. Now I faced another serious problem. Nobody was to be seen outside the examination hall and I wondered whether I had arrived at a wrong place? Then, from the verandah, I saw all the boys sitting inside the hall and writing. The doors of the hall were closed. My heart started beating fast when the clerk told me that I was late by twenty minutes. One of our school teachers, who was an invigilator in the hall, saw my vacant seat and got worried. He had been looking towards the door all the time and as he saw me from the glass door standing outside, he requested the door keepers to open the door for me. When I was in, he reprimanded me. But he had no authority to allow me to take my seat. He hurriedly took me to the head invigilator and told him that I got late as I had an accident while riding my cycle to the examination centre. He requested that as a special case I might be allowed to sit in the exam. The head invigilator was a kind-hearted man. He took pity on me and gave me permission to do so. As feared, that paper was a disaster.

Only English, Mathematics and Hindi papers were done well and in others I fared badly. But I hoped to scrape through. I was only doubtful about the History paper.

After the examinations were over, I was required to attend the sports shop. Since I had left the shop to rejoin school, it had extended its business and was then supplying goods to the outstation shopkeepers. Uncle Chuni Lal was going on tour for securing orders. That was the time when he undertook his tour and I was asked to help him to prepare for it and also accompany him to get training as a travelling businessman.

Uncle had already got ready a steel trunk, as a sample case, to accommodate all items of sports; both for lower and higher class students. I helped him in collecting and packing those in that case. Uncle also instructed me about the type of clothes and bedding that were to be carried by me for the tour. The programme was finalised by my father in consultation with my uncle. The first station of the tour was Rawalpindi, which was a big city near the borders of the North-west Frontier Province and the princely state of Jammu and Kashmir. By virtue of its strategic situation, it had a big cantonment and an ordinance depot.

We caught the train from Sialkot in the morning and reached Rawalpindi in the evening with a change at Wazirabad station. Coming out, we hired a *tonga* and reached a *sarai* which was uncle's favourite lodge in that town. The innkeeper allotted us a room of our choice.

Rawalpindi city centre was a shopping market, sprawled round a large square. It dazzled me with its glittering lights and loud mixture of various film songs. The whole scene in the bazaar was fascinating for me but my uncle did not appear to be affected at all. He lead me straight to a *dhaba*, where we had our vegetarian meals. While returning to our *sarai*, we had a glass each of hot milk from a shop.

Next morning, we hired a *tonga* for the full day and went to the cantonment. As we reached there, we started visiting the sports shops one by one. Uncle appeared well known to every shop-owner, who after seeing our samples placed their orders with us. To every shopkeeper uncle had introduced me as the son of the proprietor accompanying him as a learner. We then rode to the other side of the city where there were more shops but smaller ones. Many of them had enough stocks and did not want to place any order. Only two or three customers obliged us and placed small orders. Finishing the days work, we went to our *sarai*. The first day of my initiation in travelling with its experiences was thus over. Next day, we headed for the Murree Hills, the best and perhaps the only summer resort on the western side of the Punjab.

This was my first journey to a hill station and uncle warned me that the bus journey through the zigzag hilly roads could cause me dizziness. He advised me to avoid looking out of the windows. He handed over some sweet and sour candies and instructed me to chew them as soon as I felt nauseated. Uncle, who sat next to me, seemed relaxed while I had some feeling of anticipation growing in my stomach. The road got narrower from the foot of the hill and the bus slowed down. It could be just psychological, but I had some queasy feeling in my stomach. I immediately put one candy in my mouth and sucked on it rapidly to extract more juice. I then tried to feel normal and looked straight ahead of me. The sound of the bus engine was changing according to the steepness or the flatness of the road; and after a few minutes, I got used to the sounds. The road was getting more serpentine and we were now surrounded by green hills on all sides. Uncle carried a small bottle of *chooran* which he gave me to swallow as a precaution.

The journey was coming to the end and I did not feel any more dizziness. Uncle was very relaxed because he had travelled a lot. Reaching Murree, uncle hired a coolie and gave him directions to go to his known *sarai*. Our room was very clean and spacious with almirahs, two beds, two wooden chairs, and a centre table. The city through which we walked from the bus stand to the *sarai* was also very neat and clean. The air was pleasantly cool. We went out after arranging our luggage in our room. The place was quite small and very peaceful. Everything appeared to me to be novel and pleasant. We visited a few sport goods shops that were our old customers and told them that we would be visiting them the next day with our samples. After the meals, we went to the main road for a stroll. I was very much impressed by the calm and orderly atmosphere. Looking down from the ridge side, it seemed to me a type of Diwali in the hills, greenish dark spots interspersed with trickles of light. After a short walk, we went back to our *sarai*. We had a very sound sleep because we were tired from the tight seated bus ride. Next morning after our breakfast, we went out to visit different sports shops. Uncle impressed me as a good and successful salesperson. I remember that he booked orders from over 90 per cent of the shops he visited. He approached the customers with full confidence and a genial face like that of an old friend. He was well experienced, knowledgeable and a respected person. The shopkeepers appeared very comfortable and happy to do business with him.

In the morning, uncle told me that there was an old historical place in these hills. It was said that *Pandavas* of the *Mahabharata* had spent sometime there in the year of their hiding during exile. We went to see the place and could not find any significant sign of that old historical event except a small cave like shelter. From there we made a move to the City Mall Road. As we reached there, I heard a newspaper hawker shouting that the matriculation result of the Punjab University was in the paper he was selling. I purchased the paper from the man and stood on one side of the road to go through it. I found my roll number in the pass list and instantly felt a strange upheaval in my body. I told my uncle that I had passed and would like to go back to Sialkot. He was happy to learn about my result, congratulated me but told me in clear words that it was not possible for me to go back without completing our full tour. But I was overpowered with an unexplainable emotion and insisted on going back home. He tried to convince me that he had been given a tour schedule by *babuji*, which must be followed by him. But I was adamant and decided to go back alone. He was really in a fix and worried.

He decided to go back to Rawalpindi by the afternoon bus. In the *sarai* in Rawalpindi he sat on my cot and very sweetly asked me why was I insisting on going back so soon? He told me that since I had passed my examination, it was all the more reason for me to work harder and learn touring and canvassing etc., to be more successful in business. All his coaxing had just no effect on me and in the end he decided to send me back. He wrote a long letter to my father and handed it to me with clear instructions that it should be delivered to him as soon as I reached home. He then escorted me to the railway station, bought me a ticket for Sialkot and gave me some money for food and drinks during the journey. When I reached back home, everyone in the family was surprised to see me back so soon from my tour.

My mother anxiously enquired the reason for my early return. I told her that I had passed my tenth examination and wanted to join my college. My mother admonished me that I had again done something which would upset my father and thereby create unpleasantness in the family. My father came home in the evening and as he saw me, he angrily told me that I had caused another loss to his meagre income by my foolhardy act. He made it clear that he could not afford to pay for my college education. He also added that he had a large family to support, my elder sister was to be married, and he had other family responsibilities to meet. Controlling his anger, he told me to forget about college and start helping him in the shop from the next day.

With regard to my father's responsibility to support his family, another member had been added to it by the birth of a third son, Raj Paul, to my parents.

It was repetition of the situation that prevailed three years ago when I wanted to rejoin the school in my eighth class. The main difference this time was that I was a mature person and the shop was doing much better. There were two more employees in the shop. But there was a very little change in my father's mindset about the burden of his large family. With all his energy, courage and efforts, there was a continued and deep sense of insecurity in him. So the tussle between my father and me simmered. I wanted to make my carrier in my own way and he was forcing me to follow his directions. Time was passing rapidly for me. The admissions in the college had already started and I was nowhere near my destination. If my father remained firm in his opinion, I too did not let the idea of further studies leave my mind. I could sense that the general opinion in the family and among some family friends was in my favour, but nobody had the courage and confidence to plead my case with my father. I was a dejected young person, not interested in the work in which I was being forcibly pushed. I felt like a helpless caged animal.

Then, one day, the principal of the Montgomery College, who was a near relative, came to Sialkot unannounced to buy some sports goods for his college. He came straight to our shop, placed a good order for early delivery, and spent the night at our home.

After dinner, we went to the roof where all the beds had been laid for the whole family. My father's bed was placed next to that of the principal. They were talking on general issues of their interest and I was listening to them sitting nearby. The principal was a congenial person and I was very much impressed by his robust attitude to life. Seeing me listening to them attentively, he asked me in which class was I studying. I told him that I had passed my matriculation examination that year. "What division did you get", he asked? I replied that I had missed the first division by a few marks and it was a sheer bad luck as I reached the examination hall half an hour late on the first day. It was that day's paper which had done the damage. He was quite encouraging and told me that I should not continue to be depressed over what had happened. I should learn a lesson to be more attentive, alert, and serious in whatever I was doing. My father supported me by saying that I used to secure more than 90 per cent marks in Mathematics and was very good in English. In business, I was doing very well in accounts and correspondence, etc. After listening to all this, the principal asked my father, "if he is so smart and intelligent, why is he not going to college?" He then asked me why I was not interested in further studies, which was necessary for the development of a young boy with my capabilities? I told him that it was not me but *Pitaji* who did not want me to join the college. He asked my father why he had taken this decision. My father told him that he was alone in the business and he needed me there. He further added that he had a big family to support and daughters to be married. The principal said, *Lalaji!* You are a wise man. Once the time of getting education in life is gone, it is impossible to regain it. The boy has all his life ahead to work; regarding your responsibility towards your family, the children's education also has its important place among these responsibilities. I know that you are quite successful in your business and you also have an assistant who is very efficient and sincere. Let the boy attend the college. I guarantee you that I shall be giving you enough orders to meet the expense of the boy's education. The principal was a teacher and an educationist. His words carried a lot of weight and therefore, my father agreed to send me to college. With an indirect reply to the principal's argument, he addressed me, "Vishwa, look how providence has sent an advocate to plead your case? I declare you winner, go to the college tomorrow to fill the admission papers and take the money from me in the morning".

Everybody in the family heard what my father had told me and felt happy. I immediately went to see my mom and hugged her. My sisters came to me and congratulated me.

Next day, I walked to the college and happily covered the distance of about a mile. My school friends were surprised and happy to see me in the college because they had lost all hope of my joining and a few of them really missed me. I chose Mathematics, Economics, Philosophy, Sanskrit and Hindi as my subjects of study and then bought the books.

It was at that time that I felt again the presence of a force around me of which I had no knowledge. This force I realized, was helping me out in every situation that came to impair my future.

Out of my circle of friends, some had moved to other cities with their parents. Onkar, Braḥm Dev, Sukh Dev, Chander Prakash were there with whom I continued having close association. Academically, the first year of my college was not a good experience. I was comfortable in English among my old favourite subjects and Philosophy among the new; I also found the latter very interesting. My biggest frustration was Mathematics and I found it altogether different from what I had learned in the school. The real reason for this was again my joining college two weeks late. The lessons taught in two weeks contained the basics of the new Mathematics. As this was my favourite subject in the school, difficulty in it was a big disappointment for me and throughout the two years, I could not make up the deficiency. As for other subjects, I found Economics a bit boring and Sanskrit continued to be a problem. The quarterly exam results were not good and I was jolted out of my lethargy. I started paying more attention to my studies and was able to go over to the next class.

I made up in mathematics and economics by paying more attention. I made a different approach to Sanskrit. I had repeatedly read all the Sanskrit textbooks without a proper understanding of that language. Both the text and its translation in English were thus committed to memory. Having thus memorized my textbooks, even the bright students used to get my help for revision. I used to repeat to them both the text and translation of the entire book on the day of the examination. In this way, I overcame my Sanskrit problem. In the second year, I was much more comfortable in all the subjects. The restrictions imposed by my father on my expenses were lifted and I got a new cycle. My mother was a big help for my pocket money; it enabled me to see more films. I made some new friends and became more thick with some of my old ones. Onkar Pandit continued to be a steady comrade and Braham Dev and Sukh Dev developed further deeper relationship with me. Their life-style was distinctly different from that of other boys. Both were lovers of music. They wanted me to get my clothes stitched from their tailor. Once they dragged me to a shoemaker in the cantonment where we three got two types of shoes made for each of us. These shoes had similar designs.

As we were promoted to the second year, their father was transferred to Lahore. In order not to disturb his sons' education midway in intermediate, he arranged for them a two-room flat in a newly constructed building with a cook-cum-domestic servant. This new development provided them with a chance to further foster our intimacy. They started taking me for a daily walk in the evening. On one occasion, they made me visit their flat and this turned out to be a watershed event which changed my life altogether.

Sometime after my joining college, my elder sister, Shakuntla, was married to a young handsome boy who was employed as a storekeeper in the Army. My grandfather had been feeling unwell for sometime. On April 13, 1940 on the *Baisakhi* Day, my father and uncles decided to get our family's photograph with my grandfather. All of us, without the womenfolks, went to the shop of Nanak Chand, photographer, and got us photographed. It is considered today a very precious possession of the family as it happens to be the only record of our grandfather's family.

Shortly after this, my grandfather expired. With his death, the family lost its real builder, a sage who gave his family a good name and good culture.

The same year in November my mother gave birth to her last child, Govinder Paul. It was a difficult birth and the family had some anxious moments.

While I was in my second year in college, the environment at home started improving. My father voluntarily removed the restrictions he had imposed on me at the time of sending me to college. He bought me a cycle without my asking. There was no mystery about the improvement in his attitude. It so happened that my father and his brothers had hit a treasure trove in starting a new business of manufacturing shovels which were badly required by the government as a result of the start of the war in 1939. As the requirement of the product was huge, the factory started working 24 hours from its start and even then was unable to produce adequately to meet the requirement of their two customers. They were lifting the day's production daily by paying cash down. The earning of a lot of money made the whole difference.

The factory in the five shops on the ground floor of our house, found lot of money coming to it from the very start. As the war became more and more intense and wide-spread, the factory was pushed into producing more, adding more and more space for its working by renting whatever space was available in its neighbourhood. A very large open compound about a quarter mile away was rented, shed constructed in it and further extension was started there. As I was promoted to the second year, a lot of money was tingling daily into the cash chest of the firm. My father, who had been given the maximum credit for quickest implementation of the cash rich project, by way of better share in that business, found lot of money coming to him and that development removed his sense of insecurity. That also made him generous in his dealings with his family members.

The liberal attitude of my father naturally brought a major change in my personal and social attitude. A complex created in me by my father's restrictions at the time of my college admission started slowly and subtly getting erased. I became more outgoing, more confident in my talks and in general disposition. I had more access to pocket money, and I started spending more liberally. I started feeling the glow of my own transformation. The change in my lifestyle appeared to have a special effect on my friends, especially those from my school mates.

Brahm Dev and Sukh Dev had their well-furnished flat on the first floor of a newly constructed building on the road on which we three friends used to go for evening walk. One day they dragged me to their flat, and took me around their separate bedrooms with study tables, chairs and cupboards. Their kitchen had several racks to house its provisions and vegetables etc. There was a table with marble top with a stove. We took our seats in the drawing room. Their servant came and gave the elder brother the copy for laundry received from and given to the washerman. Both the brothers got up from their seats and sorted their clothes, went in their rooms and arranged their clothes in their cupboards. I was very much impressed by their aristocratic and orderly way of living. It was very different from the way and standard of our living.

As I was watching and savouring the manner, in which they lived and conducted their affairs, Brahm Dev came back from his room carrying a *khaki* shorts and a *khaki* shirt. I noticed their familiarity on the basis of similar clothes that I used in my scouting days. He told me that this uniform was called *ganvesh*, a Hindi word for military uniform, used in the RSS on the day of the rallies or the route marches. I could not understand what these occasions were. When he saw me paying attention to what he said, he told me that the RSS, was an abbreviation for the *Rashtriya Swayamsewak Sangh*. There were many branches of RSS in our city, called the *sangh shakhas*. These were held both in the morning and in the evening at different places. The evening *shakhas* were attended by school and college-going students and the morning *shakhas* by office going people and shopkeepers. In the daily *shakhas*, the programmes were of two types, the physical and the intellectual, called in the *sangh* language as *sharirik* and *boudik* respectively. The physical programmes were of many types viz., military drill, games, learning the defensive use of long baton, sword, spears etc. The wielding of long baton and other outfit was called *shastra vidya* meaning knowledge of the use of weapons. To avoid contravention of law, the swords were made of wooden blades. The intellectual programmes consisted of lectures and group discussions.

The intellectual programmes were the real thing in the organization, as they created awareness among the Hindus about the real cause of their present sad plight in their own motherland. That was all due to their disunity. The Hindus must be awakened to that reality and should be told that Hindustan was the only place belonging to them. Hindustan was their *Matri Bhoomi* and *Punya Bhoomi*.

He further said that the *Rashtriya Swayamsewak Sangh* was very different from all other organizations in our country. This was started by Dr. Hedgewar, in Nagpur on *Vijaya Dashmi* Day in 1925. From there it had spread all over the country. In 1937 three young students, all at the age of about eighteen, were sent to the Punjab. One boy was sent to Lahore, the second to Sialkot and the third to Rawalpindi. Since then, the RSS work was flourishing.

The young boy who was sent to Sialkot was K.D. Joshi. He started the *sangh* work in Sialkot with an introductory letter to Lala Charan Das Puri, advocate and president of the *Arya Samaj*. Joshi was made to stay in a room in the *Arya Samaj Mandir*. He joined Murray College in the third year and started the *sangh shakha* in K.C. Arya High School in the evening. It was announced in the school that a young man would be imparting training to the school boys of all classes in military drill, wielding of long baton, spear, sword etc., in the evening without any charges. Only a few boys attended the first day but as Joshi was a very talented person, he started attracting more and more students of all the schools as well as from the Murray College. He was intelligent, dedicated and a good organizer. In addition, he was proficient in the practical knowledge of all that he was to teach. He had left his home at such young age and came so far for the noble cause of uniting the Hindus through the medium of physical training. He was also a wonderful speaker with a good knowledge of our scriptures, history, and the current political situation. With a spirit of sacrifice, coupled with all other qualities, he attracted both young and old people. In two years time, he was able to start six evening *shakhas* for school and college boys, and as many morning *shakhas* for office people and businessmen. A total of about one thousand *swayamsewaks* attended these *shakhas*. Each *shakha* had one *mukhya shikshak*. Besides the daily programmes, there were special activities like celebration of national festivals like *Vijaya Dashmi*, *Holi*, *Lohri* and holding of winter camps and picnics. These camps were held in the month of December at a distance of few miles from the city in open areas. Tents were pitched for the *swayamsewaks* in which they had to sleep for three days in freezing cold.

Though very strict discipline was observed, everybody enjoyed the camp life. Drill, games, and lectures were held at fixed times within the premises of the camp. There was a camp commander whose word was a law for people attending the camp. At night there were four watchmen who spent the whole night standing outside the four corners of the area to watch that nobody from outside could come and create a mischief. If anybody was seen coming towards the camp at night, the watchmen would scream at the top of their voice, "Who is there? A friend or a foe?" If the person was an intruder the watchmen would immediately stop him. He was then taken under custody to be produced before the camp commandant, who took necessary action against him. If he was somebody from the camp, he would be allowed to come in after he told the watchman the correct 'watchword' of that day. The camp commander fixed the watchword for each day and told it to all the camp attendees. That was a secret word, not to be shared with any outside person.

Special arrangement for cooking meals for all the attendees was made. There was a mess incharge whose duty was to procure all the rations and fresh vegetables. Professional cooks were arranged for those three days. Morning tea, breakfast, lunch, evening tea and dinner were all served at the right time. The *swayamsewaks* who attended the camp had to pay for everything provided there.

Route marches were held every year, when all the *swayamsewaks* donned the military uniforms. The uniform consisted of a *khaki* shirt, a *khaki* nicker, leather belt, black boots, black *gurkha* hat, and a pair of *khaki* socks. The uniform was perfectly stitched by an approved tailor in the city and was well starched. A very senior and disciplined *swayamsewak* headed the route marches. In front of the marchers was a full brass band, constituted by the *swayamsewaks* who were specially trained to play bugles and other instruments. It was K.D. Joshi who organized all that. The commandant carried a military staff in hand and marched along side the *swayamsewaks* watching steps of everybody and shouting "left-right, left-right". Nobody from the public dared cut across the line or misbehave. It created such an awe that nobody, not even from any of the Muslim localities, could stir through the route march.

I was listening to all this like a man under some spell. I could understand much of it and was awestruck to hear that one boy, only eighteen years old, created so much in Sialkot. He must be a prodigy, a special person from heaven. His achievement was beyond my imagination. Watching me, my friends were totally surprised as they had never seen me like a dummy, so mute, overpowered, and conquered.

What had been achieved at Sialkot, was also done at the other two places of the Punjab and all that was made possible by the efforts and hard work of those young boys. They did not make use of any press or public platforms for their propaganda. The *sangh* did not rely on these methods. It believed in expansion by personal contact from man to man and from door to door, "*Deep se Deep Jalay*" as they called it. Within three years, two boys from Sialkot had gone out as *pracharaks*. One boy, named Raj Paul Puri, was sent to the Sindh province. He had a widowed mother, a younger brother and a sister to be married, but he left forever leaving behind his crying mother. Another boy named, Jagdish Abrol, was sent to Jammu. Raj Paul had passed B.A. and Jagdish Abrol, F.A. Both were handling their responsibilities pretty well in their respective territories. At this point there was a call from the kitchen that the dinner was ready. I was then lead to the kitchen to sit there in a chair at a small dining table.

They changed the subject and told me about the potato curry cooked in a different manner by their expert cook. As the dinner was served, they again talked about RSS. Every year a forty days camp was held at Nagpur where the *swayamsewaks* from all the *shakhas* of the country went for their training. The *swayamsewaks* who went to Nagpur to attend that training camp, had to pay all the expenses for their travel and food which was cooked in a community mess. At the time of eating, all the boys sat on the floor on long mats in rows without any distinction whatsoever. "Everybody is a Hindu" was and is the main principle of the *sangh*. This created a real sense of equality and individuality. Those camps were held every year in Nagpur where there were separate training programmes for the first, second and the third year. A *swayamsewak's* stature was assessed by the years of his training. The three-year training imparts every type of proficiency to the *swayamsewaks* to enable them to work anywhere and to meet any and every situation or emergency that they may face in their life as a *pracharak*.

Dr. K.B. Hedgewar, who started the RSS, was a medical doctor, who neither practised medicine nor got married. He dedicated his entire life for the *sangh* work and was called *Sar Sangh Chalak*. The few fundamental concepts of the RSS which every *swayamswewak* had to understand and believe in, are (i) The *Sar Sangh Chalak* is the supreme authority and his word was a law; (ii) *Bhagwa Dhwaj* is our guru, and before commencement of any programme at the *shakha*, the *dhwaj* is hoisted and everyone has to salute it; (iii) Service to your motherland is your prime duty. Before close of the *shakha*, devotion to the motherland is expressed in the form of a *prarthana*. Dr. Hedgewar died in 1940 at the age of 51. After his death, *Guruji*, whose full name was Madhav Rao Sada Shiv Golwalker was declared as the *Sar Sangh Sanchalak*.

The brothers continued their discourse further saying that in the real sense, the Hindus were the only *rashtravadis* or nationalists who treat this country as their motherland. As a matter of fact, it was a Hindu land as its name Hindustan denoted. As England is for the English, France for the French, and Germany for the Germans so is Hindustan the land of the Hindus. It was this consciousness, which the Hindus had lost and which the *sangh* tried to inculcate in them. The goal of the *sangh* was to create *sangathan* among the Hindus to face their traditional enemies, who had been bullying and harassing them collectively and individually for centuries. They had destroyed our temples, burnt our libraries converted our people to Islam by force, took away our women folk to auction them in the markets of Arab countries, raised to the dust all our centres of learning and seats of civilization. The Hindus were constantly suffering in their own country in which they were in majority. The Muslims were smaller in number and yet they were beating the Hindus whenever there were riots in the country. Why did it happen like that? The simple answer was that the Hindus were not united whereas Muslims were always sticking together. Union is strength. For example, you can break a single thread, but when several threads are joined together to make a rope, you can even drag an elephant with it. So the *sangh* took into account this truth and propagated it among the Hindus all over the country. With the *sangh's* coming into existence, things were changing and that we could see in our own city right before our eyes. Now, wherever a Hindu was found in trouble, all the *swayamsewaks* of the RSS immediately assembled and dealt with the other party unitedly.

My friends kept talking in turns. They continued this even while we were having our dinner. There was only one dish of potato curry and it was so tasty that I called the cook and asked for its recipe. I was told that it was made with yoghurt and crushed *warian* and there were no tomatoes or onions in it. When I was finished with my dinner, I was asked whether I would like to attend the *shakha*. I was so overawed that I considered myself inadequate for such a stupendous organization, but the brothers insisted that they would come to my house next day at 4:30 P.M. and call me from the road and escort me to the Arya High School *shakha* for the students. I told them that I did not have the proper uniform. They said, "Do not worry, the uniform will come later. You must attend the *shakha* first". That night I lay in my bed awake for a long time with my eyes open and head full of the things I had heard that evening. Sleep came to me very late. Next day they did exactly what they had planned for. It was my first day at the *shakha* conducted by Shri Ravinder Sachdev, the elder brother of my class fellow Charanjit Sachdev. There were thirty to forty boys in that *shakha*. Some of them were still going to school and the others to the college. The previous night's experience had left a very deep impact on me and what I saw at the *shakha* appeared unique. The faces of many of my class fellows attending that *shakha* appeared to me quite different and new. I listened to everybody but spoke very few words and that also when I was asked a question. When I was called to give my introduction, I spoke in such a low voice that it was hardly audible, and while I spoke those words, I was just in a semi-conscious state. I was not at all in control of myself. I could neither understand nor assess where destiny was guiding me. Something having a volcanic dimension was happening to me, and it transformed my physical and mental state.

At home, my family noted the abrupt change in my voice, language, my eating, sleeping, and walking habits. Similarly, my college friends were very much surprised to see the change in my attitude and behaviour. Some of my friends, with whom my relation was solely on the basis of our equal proficiency in the use of filthy and abusive language, felt rather defrauded by my new disposition. They tried their best to bring back my old self, but to no avail. Actually, they felt deprived of the inner satisfaction by my new image and attitude. They abused me profusely to ignite in me the little old spark, but all in vain.

After exhausting all their efforts they confronted me face-to-face and asked me as to what had gone wrong with me? At last they found from one of our common friends that I had started attending the RSS *shakha*. But in a few days, all my friends had come to know that I was a changed person. I started attending the *shakha* regularly, got my uniform made, and slowly opened up with the other *swayamsewaks*. The effect of the RSS ideology and the daily preaching of the *shakha* went deeper and deeper into my soul. I heard the *baudhik* given by a Sikh *swayamsewak* with rapt attention so that each word penetrated straight to my heart. I was amazed at the content and the language of each and every sentence that he spoke. It was in pure Hindi, the expressions and the theme were so mature that I felt transported to a different and new world of thought, never known, heard, or experienced before by me. An era of new education had started for me. Strangely, in the *shakha*, it appeared to me that somehow, I was the only attraction for all the *swayamsewaks* there. Such was the environment created around my person.

The *mukhya shikshak* conducted all the programmes in that *shakha*. I could easily sense his special attention towards me. From the very first day, as I entered the premises of the *shakha* and was introduced to him, he gave me an affectionate welcome and took charge of me. After the *shakha* was disbursed for the day, I was surrounded by several other friends who were also attending that *shakha*. As a new recruit, I got special attention from each *swayamsewak*. At the end of the day's programmes, the *mukhya shikshak* expressed his happiness that I had become a *swayamsewak*. Next day I reached the *sanghsthan* on my own. I got the same welcome and loving treatment from everybody. I was told to get my long baton, uniform, belt and boots from their known sources of supply of those things. As my interest in RSS grew day-by-day, my hesitance got erased and I started feeling at home with other boys. I also started shedding my shyness and was slowly coming to my natural self but with a marked difference. My old habit of speaking loud and using abusive language was totally gone and its place was taken by a low voice and a clean language. As I started talking in Hindi, it made me—utter my words slowly and thoughtfully. A new style of speaking was taking shape in me slow and smooth, and sensibly short. It was the magic of the method of grooming the newcomers in the RSS.

On Sundays, all the *shakhas* of the city—both morning and evening—gathered at one place. It was a huge gathering of young and old *swayamsewaks* in their everyday uniforms of white shirt and *khaki* nicker. For me it was a novel experience to be one of a large assemblage of nearly a thousand person wearing the same dress. As I arrived there for the first time, almost all my friends made a point to come to me. They introduced me to lots of important and senior *swayamsewaks*. For a short period of time, I was lost in the grandeur of that huge uniformed assembly. The programmes for that day were also special. The conductor of that day's gathering was a senior *swayamsewak* with a grand personality and a very forceful voice. With the blow of a whistle and a loud order, all stood in their respective lines according to their *shakhas*. After the hoisting of the flag in pin-drop silence, all were ordered to sit down. Everyone sat at the same place where they were standing. A patriotic song in praise of our motherland, worded emotionally and sung in a soulful tune, touched my heart as it had never touched before. After the song, the physical programme, the drills, the games were held and I could watch the best boys in the drills as well as in the games. In the end, there was a lecture explaining the merits of the RSS ideology and the way it was being practised to achieve its ideal. It all sounded so relevant, meaningful, thoughtful, and full of wisdom. I listened to it spellbound. Every programme that I saw and participated in went deep inside my self, and I made it my sacred duty to attend the daily *shakha*.

As I went deeper into the organization, I forgot everything else and gave it the first priority. I was particularly wonder-struck as to how Dr. Hedgewar conceived and started such a unique organization. I was told that he had been in the Indian National Congress. But as he found the loop-holes in that party's policy of appeasement towards Muslims and in the personal character of some well-known leaders, he left that party totally disillusioned. After he came out of the Congress, he had been thinking hard how best he could serve his motherland. What remained to be done was to find the best way in which he could serve his country. His going to Calcutta for his medical education was the Almighty's design to provide him with an opportunity to be in an intensely surcharged patriotic environment of Bengal. He could also have an easy access to the relevant literature, especially the works of Bankim Chandra and Swami Vivekanand. Most probably, he was guided by the divine words of Swami Vivekanand which gave a clear outline of an organization needed to guide and discipline his countrymen, mainly the weak and demoralized Hindu society. He decided not to marry as he considered himself already wedded to his country. When he made-up his mind to start a new organization as per the divine dictate, he talked to some of his close friends in Nagpur. He presented his views, arguments, and the future line of action. Those who agreed with his views, sat with him for several days and chalked out a detailed programme about the proposed organization including its scheme of daily assembly at one place etc. Dr. Sahib, who had conceived the whole scheme, became the central figure.

His few comrades were no less proficient and devoted to the cause. It speaks volumes about the honesty, sincerity, and self-sacrifice of Dr. Sahib and his comrades that none of them ever looked back though they had to face a lot of opposition and threats from their opponents. They were the young *sanyasis* without saffron robes who had consciously and voluntarily took oath to serve the motherland at all cost, till they lived.

Those wise men, with a sense of sacrifice and complete commitment to what they were doing, worked day and night with a clear vision and honesty of purpose. They could create many followers who were ready to do anything for the cause. Dr. Sahib was a *Sthitaprajna*, very affectionate and loving, self-sacrificing and with a capacity to work day and night without any rest. His only demand from the *swayamsewaks* was to attend the *shakha* daily. From among his followers, trained in each and every activity of that organization, he inspired many who were ready to work as *pracharaks* at any place in the country to start the *sangh* work. Those pioneers inspired by an intense love for their motherland, could create *swayamsewaks* with all the required qualities simply through their example and loving behaviour. Every *swayamsewak* is thus made to understand his duty towards his motherland, the aims and objectives of the RSS, and the importance of daily attendance in the *shakha*. Among those *swayamsevaks*, many young boys voluntarily came forward to leave their homes and families to go to far-off places in the country to do the work they were taught to do. It was the *sangh's* way of reawakening of the Hindu society. Starting in 1925 in Nagpur, the *sangh shakhas* were opened all over the country and at the time of independence, the organization was in full bloom.

Dr. K.B. Hedgewar, the founder of RSS, died in 1940 and Shri Madho Rao Sada Shiv Golwalker (*Guruji*) became the *Sar Sangh Chalak* of the organization. By that time the *sangh* work in Sialkot was very well established. When K.D. Joshi was fully satisfied that he had created several talented and dedicated *swayamsewaks* who could carry on the work independently, he left Sialkot for Nagpur.

When my F.A. university examination was over and vacations started, it was time for the 40 days camp at Nagpur. I had made up my mind to attend the camp along with several other *swayamsewaks* from Sialkot. My friends, Brahm Dev and Sukh Dev had also planned to attend. I had to seek permission and get money for the expenses from my father. When I sought his permission to go to Nagpur for 40 days training, he flatly refused saying that he could not understand why I should waste my time and money. Knowing that I would not get permission from my father, I thought of other ways and means to fulfil my goal. I started avoiding my father and decided not to mention the subject again at home. My mother instinctively understood that I had made up my mind to go even without the permission and support of my father. When she was free and alone, I sat with her and tried to explain that what I wanted to do was good for my soul. She advised me to do it with my father's blessings. I told her that it was not possible.

The day I was to leave, I silently packed my suitcase and bedding when my father was not at home. I knew my mother was very unhappy and was all the time watching me. I tried to muster inner strength to take leave from her. When I was finally ready and went to her with folded hands, she started crying. I immediately turned away my face but she swiftly got up from her seat and put one hand on my back and the other one on my hand. She gave me some currency notes and I turned towards her and embraced her. I quickly picked up my suitcase and holdall and ran down the stairs without uttering a word. I had to report at the RSS office where all the boys going to Nagpur had assembled. I registered my name and placed my baggage with the other boys' bags. Our seats were reserved from Sialkot to Nagpur. We had to take the train coming from Jammu Tawi and in that train the *swayamsewaks* from Jammu joined us. At Wazirabad, we changed to train going direct to Nagpur via Lahore and as we were ushered into our reserved seats, *swayamsewaks* from different cities of the western Punjab and those from NWFP (North West Frontier Province) had joined us. Again at Gujranwala many more boarded the train. At Lahore there was a flood of *swayamsewaks*. This way by the time our train reached Nagpur, it appeared as if it was a special RSS *swayamsewaks*' train. The expression of brotherhood among all was so contagious and profound, that I had forgotten my individual physical existence and was totally merged in the collective identity. I was sticking to my friends Brahm Dev and Sukh Dev ever since they joined me at Lahore. In the same fashion, we three got down at the Nagpur railway platform and were led to the place of our stay. We placed our bags side by side in one corner of a big hall and sat down for a little respite. I was feeling as if I was an inert pack of very strong emotions totally remote controlled by my two friends.

A local RSS *adhikari* was visiting all parts of the building, supervising and guiding the *swayamsevaks* in regard to their sleeping arrangements. After an hour or so, everyone was settled in their allotted place.

K.D. Joshi, who had started the RSS work in Sialkot, visited our hall specially to meet the Sialkot boys. I was introduced to him by some seniors who accompanied us. Madho Rao Mule, who held charge of the Punjab Province was also there. Raj Paul Puri, the first *pracharak* from Sialkot, who had been sent to organize the *sangh* work in the Sind Province, came to our hall to meet the *swayamsewaks* from his hometown. Jagdish Abrol, who went to Jammu as a *pracharak,* joined us with his boys at the Sialkot railway station. On meeting both of them,

I felt a sense of pride in me for being from the same birthplace. The spirit of welcome prevailed all around, but the state of my mind and body was something between suppressed joy, manifest nervousness, controlled activity, and being tongue-tied. I was simply looking around, moving mechanically, not by my own force but by the guidance of some unseen force in the surroundings. I could see that, unlike me everybody was enjoying the atmosphere and mixing with others. When I was dragged to somebody for introduction, I could feel the sense of satisfaction in him in having found a good recruit in me. After the first hour or two, I started unwinding and opening up little by little but only with my two friends and the boys from Sialkot. The written programme for the day was distributed among all to follow.

Our designated programme in Nagpur was to start at 4:00 A.M. from the next day. We had to get up and get ready in less than half an hour wearing our uniform and holding our *laathi*. The walk to the grounds, where *swayamsewaks* from all over India were pouring in like an endless stream, was about two miles. Though being a part of that multitude, I stuck to the group of my city comrades. At exactly 5:30 A.M., there was a sharp and loud whistle coming from the loud-speakers. Another whistle followed after a few moments, and with the third whistle, thundered an order for "fall in" at our designated lines marked by chalk powder. Simultaneously, the order for silence made the whole area hushed up with all the *swayamsewaks* taking up their respective places in an erect standing position. Nearly 1,500 *swayamsewaks,* in their variety, presented a miniature picture of our great country. All considered themselves *swayamsewaks*, Hindus of Hindustan and the only overpowering feeling was to listen to the next order and to follow it.

When everybody had taken their right position, the proceedings of the day started with the unfurling of the flag followed by flag salute and the day's programme step-by-step. The military drill, games, breakfast of raw water soaked salted grams, followed by the coaching in different weapons. The programme went on for two hours and then ended in the same fashion as it had began—first falling in line and then dispersal—after the *Prarthana, Dhwaj Pranam* and its dignified lowering.

It was time to go back to our respective places of stay to continue with the other programmes of the day. After taking bath and wearing our regular clothes, we were allowed to take rest, read, or discuss till noon, when everybody was ready to go to the special *shamiana* for lunch. Long mats were spread on the floor in perfect order to accommodate all the 1,500 *swayamsewaks*. We selected the place of our choice and placed our *thali*, tumbler, *katori*, and *chamach* before us. When everybody was seated, the food was served. There was a whistle for silence and the reciting of a mantra on the microphone, to be followed and recited by everyone, prior to the start of eating. Everyone had a full plate. After a few minutes, the supplementary service for every item started. When all had eaten to their full satisfaction, there was again a whistle for dispersal. There were several small tanks dug into the ground where the remnants of our *thalis* were to be thrown and water taps to wash the utensils. Everybody returned to their respective quarters after the meals. Then there was a break for two hours in which the boys were at liberty to do anything they wanted. They could sleep, read, or wash their clothes.

At about 3:00 P.M., we heard the same whistle to reach to the *shamiana* for *Baudhik Karyakram*. All the 1,500 *swayamsewaks* reached the *shamiana* and took their seats in rows meant for their provinces and cities after the flag hoisting. First a patriotic song and then a long lecture explaining the *sangh's* goals and objectives; the way it was to be conducted and the importance of attending the daily *shakha*. Inspiring incidents from the lives of our national heroes were included in the lecture. After the programme was over, we were ordered to disperse. In the late afternoon, we had to walk again to the grounds for the next physical programme. Thereafter, everybody was ordered to go to his rest house and get ready for the evening meals. It was the same routine everyday. This camp was called Officers Training Camp (OTC). For forty days everybody went through strenuous physical exercises, drills, games, and regular lectures on the basic ideology of the RSS. The *Baudhik Karyakram* was considered to be the most important part.

Training in the OTC for full forty days made a very significant difference both in the body and the mind of a *swayamsewak.* The body became rugged to face any hardships and the mind became stronger and bolder. Different speakers spoke on varied subjects in the daily lectures. All these discourses concluded with the same message, viz., that the Hindu society, which constituted the oldest and the best civilization in the world, disintegrated and was degraded because it became disunited. With that decline, the country was so much weakened as to be easily overpowered by foreigners who were smaller in number and far less civilized but united and better organized. The country became a slave and continued to remain under their political control for centuries. It was only under the foreign occupation that a big number of Hindus were converted to Islam and Christianity by use of force or seduction for which our degenerated and disunited society became an easy target principally because of our maltreatment of our own people.

For me and most of the other boys, the total impact was immense. Whereas before joining the RSS, I had no such ideas about my country and the Hindus, after joining RSS and attending the Nagpur camp, I started thinking about my people and my country all the time. A special feature about the RSS programmes was that all the games played in the *shakhas* were Indian involving no equipment. In only one military drill, participants used a *Lazium* drill. This drill with its multiple formations, is a treat both for the eyes and the ears. The other impressive part of the parade was the band, which was of a military fashion with the brass bugles, trumpets, drums and other musical instruments. This was headed by a tall and healthy 'band master' *swayamsewak,* holding and wielding a crowned staff.

After the closing of the OTC, I along with Brahm Dev and Sukh Dev joined a group of twelve *swayamsevaks* from different cities of Punjab and decided to go back stopping on our way at Bhopal, Jhansi, Gwalior, Agra, Mathura, Brindaban, Delhi, Haridwar, and Rishikesh. At Bhopal we saw the Lake considered as the biggest in the country. At Jhansi and Gwalior, we saw big forts. Rani Jhansi who fought with British forces valiantly from her fort, had to leave the fort along with her little adopted son and ride out with him on her horse. She died fighting in Gwalior where a small *samadhi* has been built in her memory.

From Gwalior, we reached Agra where we saw the Taj Mahal in the moonlight. We also visited to the Agra Fort where a guide led us to see the Darbar-i-Aam and the Darbar-i-Khas. The Mughal Emperors used to hold court there for the commoners and for their courtiers respectively. Leading us to the Darbar-i-Khas, the guide told us an episode of Raja Amar Singh Rathod's courage. Shah Jahan once called him to his court. As the *Raja* presented himself before the Emperor, his courtier Salabat Khan showed disrespect to the *Raja* who punished him swiftly by cutting his head there and then. Thinking that Salabat's act was under advice from the Emperor, he attacked him also but the later fled from his throne through the back door and saved his life.

Amar Singh Rathod then left the court immediately. He rode his horse and realizing that it would not be possible for him to go out through the closed gates, he directed his horse towards the rampart of the fort. The faithful horse, assessing the dangerous situation, instinctively raced towards the rampart of the fort. It jumped over with such force as to cross the 20 feet wide trench and land on its bank. After performing that extraordinary act, the horse did not survive. The statue of this horse has been built at that spot to perpetuate the memory of this brave act.

The guide then showed us the room in the fort where Aurangazeb imprisoned his old father Shah Jahan and the small hole in that room through which the imprisoned emperor, could see the Taj Mahal where his wife Mumtaz Mahal had been buried.

After seeing Fatehpur Sikri and the incomplete white marble temple of Radha Swami Dayal Bagh cult, we reached Mathura. We stayed there with a Panda who took us to see the famous temples in Mathura and Brindaban. After taking bath in the river Jamuna, we took leave from the Panda who demanded more money than what was settled with him. When we refused to pay him in excess, he poached Brahm Dev's new bedding. All our efforts to retrieve it from him failed and we had to leave without Brahm Dev's bedding. It was the most disgusting experience of our entire tour. From Mathura we reached Delhi and we saw Lal Quila, Sis Ganj Gurudwara, Jama Masjid, Birla Mandir, Jantar Mantar and the Qutab Minar. From there we went to Haridwar, took bath at Har-Ki-Pauri and left for Rishikesh. Crossing the river from Lachhman Jhoola Bridge, we saw several Ashrams and took our bath in much deeper and serener Ganga.

I moved with Brahm Dev and Sukh Dev as a team throughout our tour, never separating and even sleeping side-by-side at night. Brahm Dev and Sukh Dev wanted me to stay with them for a few days in Lahore. As the train stopped at the

Amritsar station, we heard the newspaper vendors shouting that the F.A. result of the Punjab University was out and was published in that day's paper. Since the three of us had appeared in that examination, we bought the paper to see our results. Then lightening struck on us as both my friends' roll numbers were missing from the list of successful candidates. The atmosphere turned glum and depressed. We did not even dare to look at each other and sat on our seats like statues. The train started moving and as it stopped at Lahore station, both my friends picked up their bags and left the train silently. I went with them up to the exit gate and let them depart after affectionate hugs but without anybody speaking a word. The whole game was lost and with it all our happiness of being together. For some time after they left, I continued looking out of the window. I felt so near them that their failure hit me as it were my own failure. I was totally crestfallen and could not speak to my other companions travelling with me till the time some other *swayamsewaks* came to me and expressed their sorrow at the result of Brahm and Sukhdev.

At every stop of the train thereafter, my farewell to our departing *swayamsewaks* was without warmth. Throughout the remaining journey, I sat listless and reached Sialkot and my home in the same condition.

As I reached home, I became more pensive. I knew that I had gone to Nagpur against the wishes of my father and he would not be pleased to see me back. But everybody else in my joint family were very happy to see me back and to know that I had passed. My mother though happy, was subdued in her expression. When we were alone, I told my mother that I wanted to join college for my further studies. She did not say anything but her face turned grave. Both of us knew that my joining the college was dependent on my father's permission. We had our apprehension that it was not going to be smooth for me to convince my father.

I stayed at home the first day of my arrival. All the men folks were at work and I shared my experiences with my sisters and other grown up members of the family. Everyone was happy to listen to the descriptions of the historical places I had visited.

Late in the evening, when my father came home, I went to him and paid my respects. He acknowledged it but did not look at me. I had expected something like that from him since I had gone for the RSS camp without his permission. But I had a small hope that the time being the best healer, the hurt that he felt at my disobedience, might have been healed by the passage of two months. My having passed F.A. examination was another reason, which could also serve as a balm. But nothing like that happened. He ignored me and even stopped talking to me.

The first night passed. Next day, it was exactly the same. He left home for work without caring whether I was at home or not. I was puzzled and could not find any way out of the impasse. I had the feeling that I might not be able to find a solution to amend my home situation. I, therefore, started thinking what would I do if I did not join the college. This time my mental attitude had changed a great deal. The *sangh* had touched every single nerve in my body. Telling my mother that I was going out and might not come back for lunch, I left for the RSS office.

Reaching there I met the person incharge of the city organization. He asked me, when was I joining the college? I told him I was not sure about that. He was surprised to hear my answer. I then frankly told him the position at home. He listened to me but could not assess that the situation could be so serious as to effect my future education. But I explained to him that my father was a man of his own views. And supposing that I could not join college, what would he suggest me to do so that I could prove useful for the promotion of the *sangh* work. He looked at me with most unbelieving eyes. It was only a few months back that I had joined RSS. Soon after, I had gone for the first year OTC. He knew my record of those few months. I was one of the most enthusiastic new members. I was also showing a quick grasp of the ideology and was developing very fast. But my life in the RSS had not been even one year.

After considering the matter for some time and gauging my seriousness, he told me that going out for the *sangh* work was not that easy. One had to be very proficient with a capacity to live a very rugged life full of hardships. Since, it had been only a few months that I had joined the RSS, he said he would have to give the matter a much deeper thought and would also have to consult those *adhikaris* with whom I had been in direct contact for all those months in the organization. He advised me to go home and try my best to clear the misunderstanding with my father and join the college.

I went back home in the evening and going straight to my room I sat in one corner pondering over the situation. I did not know what my father had planned and how he would punish me for my disobedience. But I had a strong desire to do something concrete for my country. If I could not join the college, then there was no purpose of my continuing to stay at home. I felt like searching for some mission in my life. As the hours passed, my restlessness increased. My mother looked into my room and seeing me sitting in one corner, silently came in and sat on my cot near me. I expected that she might say something to me but as she sat silently I looked up to her and saw that she was crying. I was shattered to see her suffering on my account. It was quite clear to me that she must have spoken to my father at least about my success in my college exams and that his reply must have caused her tremendous agony. But the poor thing was very helpless in dealing with her husband when he was angry. I too did not want her to speak to him about me any more. I was trying hard to control myself and kept within me whatever I was thinking. But she was a mother, a noble mother whose heart pined to see her son depressed.

At last she spoke in a weak voice, "Can't you make-up with your father? How long can this go on? We live in a joint family and your conflict with your father causes damage to his influence on the other members of the family. This is not good for anybody". I could not think of any response and sat quietly as before. She continued, "Why don't you go to him and ask for forgiveness? You know he is very strong, a man of principles, with a spotless character and sterling qualities. Everybody respects him and some of them even worship him. Only you have stood up against his wishes as no one else in the family has the courage to do so. Even his father and mother had never gone against his wishes. You must realize your duty as a good son. He has given you birth and groomed you to be a healthy boy. It is simply on his account that you have all that good in you and it is he only who injected all the good qualities in you. Do you hear me? Why don't you say something?"

I had nothing to say as I felt that my mother knew my point of view fully. She was sure that I had done no wrong and the cause, which I was pursuing, was good. All she wanted at that time was that I should bend a little, talk to my father and try to apply some balm to his wounded feelings. I felt that I must talk and say something to comfort her. I said, "*Mataji*, you know in your heart that I am not going astray. You have also seen how my joining the RSS has changed my life. Have I now uttered a single harsh word to anybody in the family? Have you not seen how well I have started behaving with everybody? I am no more abusive nor do I get angry with my sisters. All these good changes in my life have come only due to my association with the RSS. You, dad, and other members of the family may not realize how much I have gained by going to Nagpur. I am sure I have not done anything to hurt or harm *Pitaji*. I respect him as a good and noble father. What can I do if he does not like to look at my face as If I am a criminal? How can I ask for his forgiveness? I can apologize for disobeying him. Would you kindly convey that to him?"

My mom listened to me quietly but kept silent and tears rolled down her cheeks again. I knew she was helpless. She could tell me all those things but did not feel that her mediation at that juncture could help me. It was getting dark and she asked me to get up from that corner, wash and come to the kitchen for dinner. I took my meals early and went to bed, but sleep came quite late as I kept on thinking about my future. Next day, my father spoke to me indirectly. While I was having breakfast, he said to my mother, "Living in this house, he has not been obeying me. If this is the way he wants to carry on, then I don't have any place for him in this house." Both my mother and I were stunned to hear him say such harsh words but nobody could utter a word. After saying those words, he left and went downstairs. I looked at my mother. She was dazed, her face was pale and cold and she could not speak a word. I went inside my room and looked for something in my cupboard. My mother came inside my room and asked me why I was standing there and what was I trying to find in the cupboard. I did not reply and sat on my bed brooding. She could easily assess what my thoughts could be at that time. She spoke in a very compassionate voice, "My son, you know your father very well. You are not a child anymore. You are young and intelligent. Everybody in the family, including your father loves you. He had been a dominating person all his life. Everyone in the family obeys him because he has very good qualities—honest, spiritual, courageous and kind. He just has a bad temper, which should not be disturbed or ruffled. Why can't you do as Madan Lal, your cousin is doing? You see that boy; he is younger to you and not even a matriculate. How he has become close to him? Your father loves him, and always praises him. Madan Lal seems to have understood the nature of your father better but not you, his eldest son. It is for you to understand him and act intelligently. He will forgive you if you bend a little and I am sure, he will also agree to send you to the college."

I listened to her without speaking a word. She looked at my face and asked me, "Why do you sit like a dumb person? Do you hear what I am saying?" I was silent again as I did not know what to say. Whatever she said was true but somehow I could not do what she had advised me to do. I was thinking of something else and the pain caused by my father's words was not mitigated by my mother's compassion. I was not angry with my father anymore but I was pensive. I was trying, in my mind, to take a decision. I had some hazy idea what I wanted to do and I was trying to muster inner strength to act. The more she pleaded, the more rigid I became in my posture. When she found me in that state, she uttered something hoarsely and loudly. This shook my senses, and I instantly looked towards her. There was terror in her eyes and her hands, stretched towards me, were trembling vigorously.

I got up from the cot and took her in my arms. Her whole body was shaking and she was slipping down with weakness. She was cold, pale, and limp. I then felt instinctively to speak to her. I told her that she should not have any fear on my account. I was not thinking to do anything foolish. She clung to me without speaking. I told her further, "Mother you know I am not doing anything bad. By going to Nagpur, I have gained a lot and there has been an improvement in my old habits. Everybody feels that I have become a better person. It is only *Pitaji* who does not want to acknowledge this. I am sure that you also feel the same way. If *Pitaji* does not want me to join the college, I will bow to his wishes and not force my way into the college. He has told me that if I do not follow what he wants me to, then I have no place in his house, I know it is his house and he is running it. I have patiently thought over the situation and realized that he has the right to command".

At these words, she trembled violently, detached herself from my arms and coming face-to-face with me, asked me in a hoarse voice, "What have you decided to do?" I spoke to her in a very calm and tender voice, "*Mataji*, you do not have to worry or fear anymore. I will go for the *sangh* work, because it is very sacred to me; but I promise you that I will not act in any manner that may bring bad name to my family. I will be working in the spirit of a *sanyasi*." I consoled her, hugged her again and added, "and I will tell you the name of the place where I have to go."

I did not understand how it happened but my mother at once became calm on hearing my words. She was quite normal from the outside and spoke to me very softly, "Now, that you have decided to leave the house and go for the *sangh* work, my blessings are with you. You may soon bring good name to your father. I am certain he would be proud of you then. But when would you tell me where you are going?" I told her that I would go to the *sangh's* office and meet the people who would decide about this.

I went straight towards the RSS office. On the way, I stopped for a few minutes at the workshop of my two *swayamsewak* friends. One was a close relative and very dear to me. He was Lakshmi Chand Khanna who was my undeclared mentor and was a sage like supporter. I told him that I might not join the college here but go out as a *pracharak*. He was happily surprised and I proceeded to the RSS office. There I was engaged in long and serious discussions when I disclosed my intentions to the *sangh* seniors. I understood that I might be sent to a small place near Sialkot where they could easily watch and guide me whenever it was needed.

Finally it was decided that I go to Narowal, a tehsil town in Sialkot district. They gave me a letter of introduction to a school teacher in Narowal whom I had to contact for any type of help. I was told that Narowal had three or four high schools and an intermediate college. There was a Mandir, a Samaj, and a Gurdwara. I knew the Narowal station as we hired *tongas* from there, whenever we went to our maternal grand parents' village. I was given several important instructions by the district *pracharak* before I left the office.

It was a new place and the *sangh shakhas* had to be started there, both for evenings as well as mornings. I was told by my seniors that I had to be very careful about my conduct; The quality of the *sangh* work depended entirely on the attitude and the behaviour of the person who starts the work. The *pracharak* must exercise full control over his mind and body; his total personality must present an ideal for the *swayamsewaks* who were going to enlist. In view of the preceding instructions it was very important that I paid attention to my actions, language, and be very scrupulous in my dealings with people of different ages and professions with whom I might come in contact.

I listened to each and every word very attentively. The whole process of my orientation took many hours. It was past midnight when it was over and I slept in the RSS office itself.

Next morning, when I reached home, my father was not there, he had gone for his morning walk. My mother was waiting for me and met me with an eager face.

I then proceeded to my room. She followed me and asked me what had been decided? I told her that I had to go to Narowal that very day. She listened to me silently. I then picked up a shoulder bag, collected two half pants, uniform shirts, soap, two sets of civil shirts and trousers, a towel, couple of underwears and few other personal items and put them in my bag. Then, I requested my mother to give me a simple summer bedding. She asked me where was I going to stay in Narowal?

I told her that I had an introductory letter for a school teacher who would help me in finding a place for my permanent stay. It could be a room in the *Arya Samaj* or in some *Mandir*. I reassured my mother that I would be writing to her when I reached Narowal. She said that my maternal grand parents' place was about four miles from Narowal and if possible, I might go and stay there. I told her that it would not be possible because I had to conduct *shakhas* in the evenings as well as in the mornings. I assured her that I would be visiting my grandmother as often as I could.

She then handed the bedding to me and went to the kitchen. I think my mother informed my father about my decision the previous night. When my father left for the factory, my mother brought breakfast to my room. After finishing, I told my mother that I had to leave, as I had to report to the RSS office and from there, go to the station. She called our domestic servant to carry my bedding. I hung the bag on my shoulder, touched her feet and left the room hurriedly. The servant followed me with the bedding on his head. I had to pass my father's office to go to the railway station. I walked straight without looking on the sides and passed before the office quickly. Hardly had I walked a few yards, when a factory worker came running after me and told me that *Babuji* had called me to see him in his office. I turned back and followed the messenger. My father was sitting on a chair and seeing me before him, he said that what he had said to me the previous day was all in anger. He did not mean it. Anyway, he felt sorry for his harsh words and said that I should go back home. I stood before him, and could not utter a word. Tears came in my eyes at his words and as I looked up to him, he also had tears in his eyes. He turned his face back and wiped his tears with the tail of his turban. I left him in that state without saying a single word and went back towards our home gate. As I had made up my mind firmly and everything about my future programme was settled with the RSS *adhikaris*, it was not possible to change my mind even though I was momentarily moved by my father's words. When I reached the gate of our house, I made a quick decision to follow another route to the station. Directing the servant, I moved fast on the other route and before anyone knew, I was in the RSS office and few minutes later in the train for Narowal. My father could not gauge about the determined spirit with which I was working.

The events of that day made a permanent change in the nature of my relations with my father.

My train reached Narowal station in the afternoon. I called a coolie and gave him my bedding to carry. As I was giving him instructions about the address of the school teacher to whom I had to report, I heard someone calling my name and saw standing before me one of my college classmates. Both of us were equally surprised to find each other at the railway platform. I told him of my purpose of visit to Narowal and he told me that his father had been transfered there as a forest officer. When I told him that I had to report to the *Masterji*, he said that the teacher I had to go to lived near their bungalow and that I need not go to the teacher and might stay with him. We both walked to his house. He made me sit in his drawing room and told the coolie to place my bedding in one corner. He went in and brought me a glass of cold *sharbat*. He introduced me to his mother as his class-fellow from Sialkot. She very affectionately asked me about the purpose of my visit to Narowal and I told her everything.

After dinner, we were sitting in the drawing room when my friend's father came and shook hands with me. When I told him the purpose of my visit, he did not show any interest and left the room. After some time, a servant came and informed that our beds were made in the open yard of the bungalow. I was quite tired, and as soon as I stretched myself on the bed, I went to sleep. I got up early next morning but kept lying in my bed till somebody else in the family was also awake. My friend's mother was the first one to get up. I sat on my bed and as she got up from her bed, I greeted her with folded hands. She acknowledged silently. I was ready before anybody else and went to the drawing room, where my bag was placed. There I sat on the *dari* to say my prayers. I had a small *Geeta*, which I used to go through, a chapter a day, as my prayer. After I finished that, I took out the book on the life of Swami Vivekananda and started reading it. Breakfast was served to me there and as I was eating. I heard my friend's mother telling him that he might take me to the teacher's house as his father, being a government servant, would not like to be found associated with a person engaged in the RSS activities.

When my friend came to me, I requested him to take me to *Masterji's* house as my work could not be started without his help. He did so and left after I thanked him for his hospitality.

As I knocked the door of *Masterji's* house, it was opened by his wife who invited me in after I told her that I was from Sialkot and handed her the letter addressed to *Masterji.* She made me comfortable in her drawing room telling me that her husband would come from his school in the afternoon.

Lunch was served in the drawing room where I waited till *Masterji* arrived home and came to my room. He told me that he had read the introductory letter I had brought from Sialkot. He took me along to the *Arya Samaj*, just across the street. It was a simple compound with a *yagyashala* and a small room. Rest of the place was an open ground which I found good for my purpose. He then asked me to follow him to the adjacent house belonging to the *Arya Samaj* President, Lala Ram Rattan.

The President was a tall, well-built gentleman and a leading advocate in the town. He welcomed me and appreciating my purpose of visiting Narowal, offered the facility of *Arya Samaj* compound for holding *shakhas* and a small room for my stay. I then asked his permission to start the work from that day itself to which he had no objection. I went back with *Masterji* to his house, changed my clothes to the *khaki* nicker and white shirt and went back to *Arya Samaj*. A few young boys were playing there. I stood amongst them and asked each of them their names, the class they were studying in, and invited them to play some interesting games under my direction. They all agreed and I introduced them to *Kho-Kho*. In a few minutes they understood the game and found it very interesting. As it was quite late in the evening, I asked the boys to come at 5:00 P.M. the next day so that I could make them play again and also teach them another game. The boys accepted my offer. Both *Masterji* and advocate *sahib* came there to watch me and looked satisfied with whatever little I had done. I requested the advocate *sahib* to show me the room for my stay. He showed me the room.

From the Sialkot RSS office, I was given the cloth part of *Bhagwa Dhwaj*. With *Masterji's* help, I could buy the seven-feet long bamboo stick suitable for the flag. Next evening, a little before 5:00 P.M., I went to the *Arya Samaj* and with the help of the peon, I dug a hole in one end of the compound to accommodate the bamboo and keep it up and straight. When the young boys came there, I made them stand in a straight line, taught them how to stand "at ease" and "at attention" and their Sanskrit equivalents. Standing at attention, I told them to keep still and to watch what I did. I then took up the bamboo flag pole and the *Bhagwa Dhwaj*, carried those to the spot where I had earlier dug a hole, inserted the flag into the pole and put the pole with the flag into the ground hole so that it stood there erect with the flag. Withdrawing two steps back from the flag pole, I saluted it in the manner of the RSS. I then addressed the boys and told them that what I had done before them was called "*Dhwaj Arohan*", the Sanskrit words for flag hoisting. I spoke to them in simple Hindi, which they did not have any difficulty to understand. I then told them to disperse and play *Kho-Kho* and one or two other games. After those games, I made them sit in a straight line and spoke to them about the flag that I had just hoisted. I told them that it was the National flag of the Hindus of Hindustan. This flag was used by all our ancient Hindu Kingdoms from the times of the *Ramayana* and the *Mahabharata* till the times of the Marathas, the Rajputs, and the Sikhs. This flag deserved to be respected by us as a sacred symbol of our nation just as the English people respect their Union Jack. It must be saluted when hoisted and again when it was lowered. As they had assembled that day and the *Dhwaj* was hoisted and saluted, that assembly would be called an RSS *shakha.* RSS is the short form of the *Rashtriya Swayamsevak Sangh.* The salute to the *Dhwaj* is called *Dhwaj Pranam.* After my lecture was over we would recite RSS *prarthana.* I would recite first to be followed by all the boys in one voice, standing erect with eyes closed and the right hand raised to their chest like I did. I made them stand up at attention and asked them to follow me in words and actions when I recited the *prarthana.* After that, everybody was made to salute the flag. I then marched to the flag, saluted it again and then took the cloth piece out of pole and the boys were told to disperse. All the boys did what I told them and thus my first day's holding of a new *shakha* came to an end. There was enthusiasm among the boys. I myself had an unusual peace and satisfaction.

I was so completely involved in my first day's trial and test that except for the boys before me, I did not notice anybody else's presence in the *Arya Samaj.* When the *shakha* was dispersed, I saw that *Masterji,* his daughters and the advocate *sahib* standing there. Both of them looked very much impressed with what they saw me doing. Advocate *sahib* was highly appreciative and told me that the room for me in the *Arya Samaj* was ready and I could occupy it right away. *Masterji* told the advocate *sahib* that I was comfortable at their place and need not shift so soon. All the three little daughters of *Masterji* had already clung to me and were then dragging me to go home with them. I accompanied the girls and found their mother waiting for us in the sitting room. *Masterji* also arrived a little after. The dinner was served to both of us. The noble lady prepared and served as if I were someone very near and dear to the family.

On the fifth day, they entrusted me to advocate *sahib* with whom they had a close relationship. He assured them that he would take proper care of me and got my baggage carried to the room I was to stay in. *Masterji's* family left Narowal the same day as the schools were closed for vacation.

During those first five days, the *shakha* had grown bigger with several senior students joining it. I remember particularly, the two Jain brothers — Balbir, who was studying at Lahore for his B.A., and Dharambir who was an intermediate student in a local college. They were very intelligent, energetic, courageous and very sincere. The elder one was attracted to me more and was most helpful in establishing the *sangh* work in Narowal. They were the sons of a teacher. They developed into the best *swayamsewaks*. Balbir Jain took over most of the responsibility of my wellbeing. After two weeks or so, I felt that the evening *shakha* had started well. The elder Jain brother had taken over from me the responsibility of a *shikshak*. Thus encouraged I decided to start the morning *shakha* also. Several shopkeepers, businessmen and service men had already approached me to start the morning *shakha*, which I managed to do at the same place. It made a very good start and several sincere persons came to attend the very first day. A young man working in the fruit market, was particularly very enthusiastic and sincere. Within a few days, the morning *shakha* started running as smoothly as did the evening *shakha*.

All those days, I was not allowed to spend any money on my food. Advocate *sahib* consented to become the city *sangchalak*.

I stayed in Narowal for three months. The *sangh* work was well established there. *Adhikaris* from Sialkot visited me fortnightly for guidance and assessment of my progress. They also brought there some necessary requirements like laziums and wooden swords for the *shakhas*. After about one and a half months, some *swayamsewaks* were prepared to buy full uniforms. Both the *shakhas* had committed *mukhya shikshaks* and many patrons. During the last month, when the work of both the *shakhas* was on secure grounds, I went every alternate evening to visit my maternal grandmother in a village four miles from Narowal. I went there to make my widowed grandmother happy; she waited for me with my dinner ready. After finishing my dinner I would go to sleep, and before dawn, I left the place to be back in Narowal before the morning.

My stay at Narowal was a test for my capability, efficiency and endurance. I passed the test with compliments and received real training through *tapasya*. By the grace of the Almighty, I could make very good contacts to enable the *sangh* work to go on smoothly. Moreover, during my stay there, I did not face a single instance of discouragement. I visited Narowal several times after that, and was happy to find the *sangh shakha* prospering. But I did not meet *Masterji* or any of his family members there. He had probably left that town and got a job elsewhere. I still remember that family with immense gratitude.

After working in Narowal for three months, I was told to hand over the work to the most capable and sincere person and proceed to Pasrur, another '*tehsil*' town of Sialkot. The *sangh* work had already been started there earlier than at Narowal, but there were some problems. I was advised to look into these problems and make my report. I stayed there for fifteen days and reported the position to the Sialkot office. I was then asked to proceed to Gujrat, a district place, where the *sangh* work had been started a year earlier but had to be stopped for some reasons. I had to restart it. After studying the situation for a few days, and in consultation with one or two old *swayamsewaks*, I was successful in starting the *shakha* again. The evening *shakha* was started in the *Sanatan Dharma* High School. God showered His blessings on me again. I could get around several college and school students who were both intelligent and sincere. When the Gujrat *shakha* started working smoothly, I was told to visit Jalalpur Jattan, a very prosperous town in the Gujrat district, for an assessment of possibilities to start *sangh* work there. I had also to visit Bhimber, a *tehsil* town of Jammu and Kashmir state for the same purpose. Bhimber was accessible from Gujrat through a wild approach route. I stayed in Gujrat for nearly six months. Although I was able to do everything successfully there, I found that it was very tough to stay there because of the non-availability of proper boarding and lodging facilities for me in that city. I fell ill in my small rented room, which was outside the city and had no facilities of toilet, electricity and water. My *swayamsewakas* attended on me, called a doctor to examine me, and brought me the prescribed medicine. I refused to move to anyone's house. I had some relatives in Gujrat who came to know of my illness. They insisted that I move to their place, but I refused. My fever was not coming down and all the medicines had failed. The news reached my home in Sialkot. In that state of my health, and on the advice of the doctor, my relatives finally escorted me to Sialkot. There, my family received me with open arms. With the treatment and care at home, I recovered soon.

The time when I went back home was when admissions for the new-year in the college had started. I joined the college for my bachelor's degree, thereby terminating my *pracharak's* tenure. But my dedication to RSS never diminished. As the college closed for summer vacation, I went to Khandwa for the second-year training without the least hitch. From the day I started going to the *sangh shakha*, I never missed it. Attending the *shakha* daily, became my first priority. I improved my general knowledge by reading biographies of all the great people of our country in the last century. My special study was on Swami Vivekananda. The reading of such literature resulted in stabilising in me a nationalist and spiritual spirit. I became a staunch Hindu with a liberal outlook. Although I was firm in my own views, I was open to the opinions of others. I was as proud of Hinduism as I was ashamed of the society's shortcomings and weaknesses. My circle of friends changed, shifting towards the brightest of the *swayamsewaks*. These friendships became so strong that even after the partition of the country, I have continued with all of them.

—8—

COMPLETING EDUCATION AND ENTERING BUSINESS

With the ending of the war, the government had stopped its purchases for the defence. Our family firm which for more than four years was engaged only in the production of defence items, had to change its line of business. It started manufacturing pad locks, small hand tools and shovels for commercial use. After my graduation, I studied those items and was sent on a tour in India in the beginning of 1945. A class fellow, Charanjit Sachdev, accompanied me. He represented some other company, in Sialkot for some different products. Our tour started from Delhi. We went round all the big stores of Connaught Place. He could secure some orders and helped me visit some shops for my products. Though I did not succeed in booking any orders, but I was tremendously impressed by the grandeur of the buildings and the layout of the shopping centre. We spent only one night in Delhi and stayed with my friend's elder brother, Ravinder Sachdeva, employed in Government of India. I knew him well as the *mukhya shikshak* in the RSS *shakha,* I attended on the first day. From Delhi we went to Bombay. It was in the morning when we got down from the train at Victoria Terminus. There, we were received by one of our class fellows, Jagdish Khatri (Sareen). The multitude of people on the platform, the vastness of the station and the loftiness of its building, filled me with awe.

The taxis, trams and buses, both single and double deckers, plying on the roads, were total novelties, which, living in Sialkot

I had never imagined. As our taxi ploughed through that unique traffic and went through the large entrance of the Saint Xavier's College and Institute, I was totally awestruck with the lofty magnificence of my surroundings. Using a lift was also my first experience. We got free from our morning chores as soon as possible and left the hostel. It was a Sunday and Jagdish guided us to an Irani restaurant for breakfast. From there we walked to the Marine Drive. The sight of the large buildings in a curve on the shore of the Arabian Sea appeared to me like pearls strung in a garland. They had an altogether new architecture, a different finishing, rich in their appearance and were beautifully layed out. The Arabian Sea, with its bluish vastness was amazing. The sound of its tides and appearance of some ships far away on its surface were a wonder for me. I was lost in all that magnificence and walked with my friends like a villager.

We must have spent about two weeks in Bombay and Jagdish managed our stay with him in his hostel cubical, despite the fact that guests in the hostel were strictly prohibited.

I contacted our old customers of shovels in the Bombay hardware market. New parties were also visited and I was able to secure some orders from one or two parties for shovels. But no order could be secured for other items. I was totally disheartened.

In the evenings, when we met at the college, Jagdish was ready to take us around to show us every important tourist spot in the city. We travelled in the trains and buses and sat on upper decks. One day we visited Chaupati and on another day the Malabar Hills and the Hanging Gardens. Again a day for the Gate Way of India and the Church Gate Reclamation. He took us to the aquarium and the zoo. We also went to the sea beach at Santa Cruz and to the Elephanta Caves. He took us to the best cinema halls to see some English as well as Hindi films. By the time we reached the college hostel at midnight. Jagdish managed the gatekeepers who would promptly open the gate and receive a generous tip. We then moved to his room on tip toes and went to sleep. In short, our first visit to Bombay was one of the most exhilarating experiences of my life. Jagdish deserves full credit of making it so. That was also the time when I learnt to wear English dresses and speak the English language well. I also got some good trousers stitched for me from Jagdish's tailor there.

At last the day arrived when we had to return home. We reached the V.T. station to find the platform full of people waiting to board the train. As we travelled in third-class, it was again Jagdish who managed the coolies for getting us good seats. By the time the train moved all the coaches were crowded. I was wearing a shirt with two pockets. In one of these I had put some papers like purchase bills etc. and in the other, I had kept my purse. The purse contained money and the rail tickets, both for me and Charanjit. As the train stopped at Jalgaon station, I wanted to go to the toilet, but our coach was so full that it was not easy to reach there. I found it easy to jump out from the window and pass urine on the ground, than to find my way through the crowded coach to the toilet. I had to enter the coach through the same window, duly helped by Charanjit. The train started and as I touched my pocket, I found it empty. The purse with our tickets and money was gone. Charanjit and I searched it on and under our seats, felt the pockets of our pants nervously but it was nowhere. I then pulled the chain of the train to stop it. It did stop but after covering a good distance. I quickly jumped out of the window and ran back to the spot where I supposed I had first jumped out. It was dark and I could not find anything. As the train guard approached me and questioned me for the reason of my pulling the chain, I was quite nervous. I told him about my problem and requested for his help. He appeared a little annoyed but he did help with his hand lamp to search for my purse. However, we found nothing at that place.

I wanted to search more thoroughly, but the guard told me that he could not hold the train any longer for our sake. However, he allowed us to get down the train with our luggage at that spot.

We carried our bags to the station in darkness. Placing our bags on a bench near the stationmaster's room, we both went in and saw the stationmaster. We narrated our story to him and requested him to help us with one of his staff members with a lamp. He too appeared irritated to hear our strange story, but looking at our crestfallen faces, helped by providing us with a coolie and a lamp. We went with the coolie and searched the place thoroughly for half an hour, but could find nothing. We had to return empty handed to the station master's office. Hearing about our failure, the stationmaster suggested that my pocket must have been picked by some passenger. He advised us that we might file our complaint of loss or theft of our purse, money and two tickets for Delhi, with the railway police. We did that and got a copy of the report. With that document, we boarded the next train going to Delhi. It was a passenger train stopping at almost every station. In our coach, there were some *pathans* travelling in a group. As two of us sat on our seats quietly all the time, neither moving nor eating or drinking, one of the senior *pathans* among them spoke to us and asked us about our unusual behaviour and grim faces. We felt embarrassed at his query but the words of that man echoed sympathy. We told him all that we had gone through. He then forced us to eat some pieces of cake, which they were carrying with them for the journey. To our further embarrassment, they ordered tea for us. We felt beholden to the *pathans* for their graceful help.

Three ticket examiners came to our coach during our journey up to Delhi and we had to explain to each one of them our sad story and had to show them the police report. Our co-passengers in the compartment gave us full support and the ticket examiners did not take any action. The final test awaited us at Delhi where we were stopped at the gate and had to wait till all the other passengers had gone out. We had to tell our tragic tale to the station master, who finally allowed us to go out. Outside the station, we took a taxi and reached the residence of Charanjit's elder brother who paid the taxi fare. We were in a miserable state with famished faces and dirty clothes. Hearing all about the way we had to suffer, Charanjit's brother showed full sympathy and affection. He looked after us with the kindest care. After staying there for a day we left for Sialkot with monetary support from Ravinderji.

My tour was a failure and as such, quite disheartening. The suffering caused by the loss of my purse further added to my total disenchantment about doing that type of business. I also felt very small in the eyes of my uncles and my father. I told them that I did not want to continue working in their firm. Privately I told my father that I would like to start my own export business. Knowing my views, my father sent me to one of his friends Shri Bishan Das Mahajan for learning the preliminaries of export business. That gentleman had his office in our *mohalla* and was well known to me. He was an expert in export business and explained to me the basic things that were very essential to be a successful exporter. From the printing of the stationery to the conduct of working, he touched every detail. I heard everything with full attention like a devout pupil. When I actually started that business, I followed his instructions faithfully with very good results. Even today I remember those things and realise their value in business.

Before starting my exports venture, I had on several occasions been forced to do business. The first was in my eighth class when I spent nearly ten months working in my father's sports shop as an assistant. There I learnt some elementary things, which gave me a good foundation for use in my future business ventures. The second time it was for only two months after my matriculation examination. The third time was during my fourth year in college when I started the manufacture of hockey sticks in partnership with my close *swayamsewak* friend, Shiv Kumar Sharma.

Shiv Kumar had done his B.A. a year before me. He had been selected for a permanent King's commission in the Army. It was war time and hence his mother was apprehensive about him joining the service but he was adamant. The old lady was very unhappy at his decision. As the discussion over the issue took place in my presence more than once, I supported the mother and volunteered to dissuade Shiv Kumar from taking that step. I convinced Shiv Kumar not to go for the military job and to start sports goods manufacturing in partnership with me. As a partner, the investment and know-how was to be my responsibility and management of the business of manufacturing hockey sticks was to be Shiv Kumar's. That business ran in the name of Prabhat Sports and was managed by Shiv Kumar up to the time of partition of the country in 1947.

When I decided to do the export business, I had before me two serious offers for partnership. One was from a class fellow named Chaman Lal Aggarwal, a very close and affectionate friend. The other was from Kapur Chand Jain, a *swayamsewak* friend who was already running his business of handloom textiles in partnership with his brothers.

I thought over both the offers and opted in favour of the one from Kapur Chand. The decision of partnership having been made, we decided to work as merchant exporters of goods being manufactured and exported from Sialkot, such as sports goods, the EPNS wares and cutlery goods. A small room on the ground floor of our house, which had been used as my study, was converted into our firm's office. Several names were considered for the firm, out of which "Grounds & Meadows" was selected.

The first job of purchasing stationery, printing and moderate furnishing of our office took six months. The maximum time was taken by the printing of the three catalogues on art papers with full illustrations for all the items included in the range of the three types of goods.

Simultaneously with the work of catalogue printing, we compiled statements of the names and address of dealers in the three different lines from Kelleys World Directory in the countries of Africa, South America, Burma and Ceylon. Introductory letters for the three different lines were sent by book post on daily basis. I really enjoyed doing this work of getting the catalogues printed and letters posted. It gave us a real thrill when the first enquiry was received in our office by a cable asking for samples of some sports items and their prices. We celebrated the receipt of our first enquiry by a tea party among four or five friends who used to assemble in the evening in our office for a friendly chat.

We sent the samples against the cable enquiry by air-post and that party placed their trial order for a hundred sterling pounds with a promise to place their regular orders if that sample consignment camė upto their satisfaction. It was from an English firm of Kenya in East Africa and we supplied them the goods of the best quality and sent the shipping documents with our bill through their bankers.

We were very much encouraged by this single response and planned to undertake a more courageous step of sending a representative to the Gulf and African Countries. My class-fellow friend, Charanjit Sachdeva, was prepared to work with us on salary basis and was also ready to go on a foreign tour.

An application was submitted to the Passport Issuing Authority at Lahore, for Charanjit and all arrangements for his travel were got ready.

Two weeks had passed. We had collected all samples and arranged those in two boxes. Charanjit's personal things were ready but the passport was not received. We went to Lahore Secretariat the next day to collect our passport. While our passport were getting signed by the Chief, we were asked to wait in the veranda.

As we waited in the veranda, we heard some noise that slowly grew louder until it became impetuous. In our curiosity we moved to the front veranda of the building and there we saw a big crowd of Muslim League demonstrators shouting slogans outside the big steel gate of the secretariat. The Lahore Secretariat was combined with the Governor's office, which was at the back of the secretariat building. The gatekeepers had closed the gate before the arrival of the procession. There were about a dozen policemen and security guards inside the secretariat. We stood in the veranda watching and hearing the Muslim Leaguer's slogans, like 'Pakistan Zindabad, 'Qayad-I-Aazam Zindabad', 'Muslim League Zindabad', 'Khizar Hayat Murdabad', 'Unionist Government Murdabad'. That day they shouted a new slogan "Up Up the Muslim League flag" and "Down Down the Union Jack". The slogan shouting was as hoarse as it possibly could be. But that did not satisfy some of the demonstrators and they appeared restless facing the closed gate.

On the outerwing of the secretariat building the Union Jack was fluttering at one of its domes. The restlessness of the demonstrators found its first expression in some young demonstrators who climbed the high gate and jumped into the open compound of the secretariat. Curiously the security men stood watching all that quietly. Some more young boys were thus encouraged to jump into the compound following their companions. Very soon there were scores of them in the compound. They continued with their slogan shouting. The outerwing of the secretariat building on which the Union Jack had been hoisted was separated from the main building. The agitators advanced towards that office. Seeing the demonstrators' menacing advance, the staff hurried out of their office. When the boys reached there, they saw the office sans human being. They entered the vacant rooms and started throwing out whatever came to their hands. Stationery, trays, files started flying out of the rooms. Then came the turn of the chairs, tables, racks meeting the same fate. As some boys were thus venting their anger on the stationery and equipment in the rooms, a few of them climbed up the roof of the building. The boys who had climbed the roof had something specific in their minds. It became clear only when two boys could climb up the dome carrying the Muslim League flag. Riding up the Dome they pulled down the Union Jack off from its staff and, throwing it in the compound, installed the Muslim League flag in its place.

We stood watching the whole scene. A few minutes after the Union jack was pulled down and thrown down in the dust, there appeared in front of us from the back, three young English boys with wooden sticks in their hands. They advanced towards the agitators gathered in the compound and started hitting with their sticks whosoever came before them. Seeing the three white faces with sticks, the agitators started running to the gate to jump over it as fast as they could. In the meantime, the security police who had stood there as spectators so far, also became active. Thousands of agitators demonstrating outside the gate stopped their slogans, abruptly and seeing the three English boys, started running in all directions wherever they could find their way. The English boys seeing the agitators jumping out by climbing the gate ordered the gatekeepers to open the gate. As the gate was opened, all the agitators in the compound ran out as fast as they could. In a matter of minutes, the entire compound was cleared and there were no demonstrators near the gate also. Only a few boys who had climbed up to the dome and pulled down the Union jack were left there. They did not see any escape. The three English boys calmly waited for them and when those boys had to jump down reluctantly, they were ordered to be arrested and taken to the back of the secretariat.

Watching all that pathetic drama, I had completely forgotten our purpose for visiting the secretariat. Thereafter, we went to the passport section, which had also been emptied because of the scene outside. Nobody was in a proper state of mind to attend to work. Our passport was still lying unsigned. The section officer regretted that our work could not be done. He advised that we might go back to Sialkot and come back in a day or two. He assured that he would keep the passport ready for us to collect.

We returned to Sialkot without the passport. During my journey to Sialkot, I remained sitting in my seat silently thinking over all that had happened at the Lahore secretariat. I felt a strange pain inside.

What I could not comprehend easily was the total tolerance and indifference shown to the rowdy demonstrators. Why did the police remain as silent spectators? Then happened the most perplexing scene in the entire affair. Out of the thousands of the young Muslim demonstrators not a single person dared to stand before the three English boys with sticks. I had never known or seen in my life the Muslims to be such cowards. It actually hurt me inside to see all the thousands of young Muslim demonstrators fleeing away like a flock of sheep without raising even the sound of their bleats at the sight of three white boys with small sticks. There were no guns or pistols in their hands. My pain of seeing those poor Indians acting as dumb driven cattle was giving place to some other feeling. My thoughts shifted to our cunning rulers. I had already read in some newspaper and magazine that the scheme of Pakistan was in reality, the brain child of some British cabinet ministers of the thirtys who got that idea injected into some Muslim intelligent persons around them through their Intelligence Agency. My mind started thinking about that day's episode in the light of that information. The Governor of the Punjab at that time, Sir Francis Muddie, was a well known English conservative, totally against the Nationalist Indians.

Soon it became clear in my mind that it was all a made-up affair to record the strong Muslim protest in favour of early creation of Pakistan. What had been destroyed that day was the property of poor Indians. It was no loss to the British rulers.

Next time Charanjit went to Lahore alone and collected his passport. He then immediately left for Karachi from where he had to take the ship. Visas for the countries he was to visit, were also to be collected from Karachi. By that time the division of the country into India and Pakistan had become certain and Sindh was sure to go to Pakistan. Charanjit tried his best to obtain visas from the respective consulates, but due to the political situation he could not succeed, even though he spent almost one month in Karachi. At last, he had to come back to Sialkot leaving all his samples and literature with a friend there. He thought that after the political trouble was over, he would again go to Karachi, collect visas and proceed on his tour with the samples. But that was not to happen. However, we started receiving orders by post.

From the year 1946, political and social conditions in the country were deteriorating day-by-day. Muslim League leaders were giving inflammatory statements and speeches. When they felt that their provocative speeches and propaganda were not serving their purpose, they changed their tactics. They created disturbances in those parts in the country where they were either running state governments or were in a majority.

The first disturbance was created in Calcutta on 16th August 1946, under Chief Minister Sohrawardi, a Muslim Leaguer. He started bloodshed by organizing Muslims, and provoking them to attack the Hindus in the Muslim majority areas. A lot of blood was shed by killing innocent Hindus who were taken-in by total surprise. Later some Sikh taxi and bus drivers got together and retaliated. Mahatma Gandhi had to visit Calcutta and go on hunger strike to stop the bloodshed.

The above mentioned carnage in Calcutta affected my family directly as my younger sister, married only a year back, then lived in Calcutta. Her house was looted and she, along with her husband, had to save their lives by running to the railway station where my brother-in-law was a railway guard. Frightened, they reached Sialkot in the last week of August, in a miserable condition. My sister was then in an advanced state of pregnancy.

Next came the turn of Noakhali, where thousands of Bengali Hindus were massacred by the Muslim population. Gandhiji had to shift to Noakhali to sit on a hunger strike there. Most of the Hindus had to leave the district and take safe shelter in Bihar, which was a Hindu majority province. The bloodshed in Calcutta and Noakhali of the Hindus caused the ouster of all the Hindu labour force of Bihar back to their homes. When they narrated their tragic stories to their people, their arose a deep feeling of resentment which, when accumulated, turned into retaliation on the Bihari Muslims.

We in Punjab were hearing about what was happening in Bengal under the Mulsim League Chief Minister. Punjab had a Unionist Government since 1945. Chief Minister Khizar

Hayat Khan ran the coalition government with the support of Congress and the Akali Dal. The League leaders were intensifying their agitations for his resignation. The type of agitations being organized till then were not serving their purpose. Then they whipped up mass hysteria with the help of "Muslim National Guards", defying the ban imposed on them. But when Lord Atlee announced his plan of independence for India after the division of the country on the basis of religious majority in provinces, Khizar Hayat Khan resigned on February 20, 1947. Muslim League was thus encouraged to do a Bengal in the Punjab. When the new viceroy, Lord Mountbatten had taken over in March, 1947, Muslim League considered it the right time to put pressure on him by starting something sensational to attract his immediate attention.

—9—

ORIGIN OF THE SEKHRI COMMUNITY — MY ANCESTORS

While living in our old *haveli* during 1932 to 1936, I had observed a ritual called *Seva Mata Puja* performed before *mundans* or marriages in all Sekhri families.

I had seen the *purohit* of the clan coming to our house two days before the ceremony, and managing to place in one corner of our house, an earthen vessel full with laddoos, a lighted diya before it and leaving those things at the care of the family. He came again on the morning of ceremony, did a sort of puja at that place and made a call for all Sekhri male and female, young and old, to go to him and bow their heads before that lighted diya to receive five laddoos from the purohit as *Seva Mata's prasad.* This way *Seva Mata* was remembered by the entire Sekhri clan.

I had made its mention in the foregoing chapter and here I give the story of how *Seva Mata* became the originator of our family. Many centuries ago whenever the invading armies of Muslim hordes used to descend on the Indian soil from the hilly areas of the Northwest Himalayas, they caused lot of destruction to the human life, their properties, temples and the cultivated fields. They looted their wealth and molested their women who by their misfortune fell into their hands. Hearing of the coming down of such marauders the people of the Western Punjab, who happened to bear the first assault, used to run away from the cities and towns to some safe places, leaving their homes and hearths. The exodus of those frightened and panicky people used to be chaotic.

On one such occasion, a town known as Chiniot in the West Punjab, fell on the route of a marauding army and all its residents took flight from their homes. Among the fleecing mob, a young girl from a Kapur family got separated from her family members. Finding herself without her kith and kin, she shouted frantically some names of her family members but she could get no response. Nor could she see any known person to whom she could hinge herself. In sheer desperation, she started crying and like a semi-conscious person, had been pushed ahead by the crowd without her knowing where she was being driven to. In her desperate condition, she could not think of anything else but to walk on where her fate took her.

The fear had made her limbs numb and her cries became whispers of God's name. At dusk, she felt cold with fear and completely nervous. She was alone in a strange, desolate place with no movement and no living creature around. Then she saw a tree, and reaching it with determined steps she sat down, adjusting her body to rest her back against its big trunk. Her legs automatically stretched in her front, affording her a little more comfort. Within a few minutes her eyes closed and she completely forgot her bearings till the rays of sunshine fell on her face and her eyes opened. She again closed her eyes but shortly opened them again instinctively. This time she saw a tall hazy figure standing at some distance watching her. She was too tired and benumbed to make any movement. The human figure moved towards her and as it reached near her, she opened her eyes wide, withdrew her legs towards rest of her body as automatically as she stretched them. She timidly and prayerfully looked into the eyes of the man and at once felt calmness descending down her whole body, by the benign looks of the tall bearded man.

The man addressed her as a daughter and with his fatherly expression asked her as to who she was and how she had reached alone at such a lonely place? His curiosity and kindness further grew when he observed that the girl was in the family way. When she did not reply, he sat in front of her on his knees and comely put his hand on her head. He asked her again, more politely, assuring her to have no fear and to speak out. Instead of speaking she started crying and in a few seconds her cries became louder and louder and uncontrolled. The man understood and let her cry as much as she could, slowly putting his arms around her providing her parental shelter and security. She had a feeling of physical relaxation with the fatherly arms around her body and after she had exhausted all that was still left in her of the human energy, she could only utter "*Baba*, I am very unlucky". The old man consoled her saying sweetly, "No my child, you are not. The Almighty God had guided me to approach you. You need have no worries as I had been especially commanded by Him to help you". She felt more relaxed and on his bidding and with his support, made an effort to stand-up. With the movement to stand-up, she felt, after a long time, that she carried inside her, another small body solely depending on her. With that feeling and the overflowing kindness of the man supporting her, she made determined effort to walk along with him slowly but with sure steps.

The holy man guided her to his hermitage nearby, made some room in one of its corners, and gathered some dried grass to make the ground a little cosy for the girl to lie down on it. Giving her some water to drink from his hermitage, the *baba* introduced her with his name as *baba* Sheikh Farid. He then took leave of her for an hour or two, in which he would go out and manage to bring from the nearby market, something for her to eat and also make arrangement for some lady-help in whom she may find a companion in that secluded corner of the world. The *baba* came back having accomplished both the things he had mentioned to her. Giving her the food, he introduced the lady accompanying him, as *bibi* Fatima who, he added, was a capable person to take full care of her. The girl looked and found her also having a benign face. The lady spoke to her first addressing her as daughter and her sweet voice at once put the girl at ease. The *baba* then considered it the right moment to ask the girl her name and address of her family. She told him her name was Seva Dai and that she belonged to a Kapur family of Chiniot.

Seva Dai gave birth to a healthy son under the care of the two saintly persons in their hermitage. With the coming of her son and melting away of all her fears and apprehensions of the troubles at delivery, she started feeling the blessings of the Almighty. The infant boy grew up in the hermitage of the *baba* but no name was given to him as his mother wanted it to be ceremoniously done by her own people. After sometime when she felt normal, she requested *baba* to arrange for sending her to her people. *Baba* sagely advised her to wait till the marauders, who had passed Chiniot going South, might come back following the same route after finishing their loot, plunder and other nefarious deeds. It would then be the right time to arrange for her return. She instantly agreed being convinced of *baba's* good judgement. The infant boy in the meantime grew up to be a sweet child. He had some boys of his age, from the close-by habitation come to play with him. Finding the hermitage boy with no name, his playmates started calling him as Shekhra (tiny *sheikh*) and the name stuck to him. His mother, baba and *bibi* too addressed him as Shekhra. They all considered that name as pretty and appropriate.

Seva Dai passed her time in the hermitage, with her son, being looked after and helped by *baba* Farid and *bibi* Fatima. She got all the love, affection and care that she might have got from her own people, but she still always remained dejected, thinking all the time of her family in Chiniot. At last when the marauders returned after having their fill of the loot, the *baba* considered it a favourable time to make arrangements for sending back Seva Dai and her son to their home and their people. He considered it advisable to send someone to Chiniot to find her people, following the directions provided by Seva Dai. He did so and the man returned after a few days to give the report that Seva Dai's people were no more at Chiniot. From the neighbours, he came to know that the whole Kapur family had left Chiniot to settle at some other place, that was safe and out of the way of the occasional looters and raiders from the Northwest. However, before leaving they left a word with their neighbours and relatives in Chiniot that they would inform them about the new place of their settlement.

At this news, Seva Dai's dejection turned into painful disappointment. *Baba* and *bibi*, though worried, gave her more attention with additional care and love. *Bibi* tried to remain by her side all the time. She even fed her with her own hands and lovingly told her to have courage as she had to look after her little one, who was her only hope. This way the time passed. *Baba* on his part did not fail to send his followers at regular intervals to Chiniot to find if any news had been received there about the new resort of the Seva Dai's people.

As the good times have a cyclic end, so have the bad times. At last one day the messenger brought the good news from Chiniot that the new place of settlement of Seva Dai's people was Sialkot. It was nearly 120 miles from Chiniot towards south and was situated near Jammu city. When Seva Dai heard from the messenger that her family's new address, she felt a new spirit infused in her inert body. All the hopes of her joining her own people were revived. Both *baba* and *bibi* too felt a great relief. They at once began to plan for the journey with all necessary details. After a few days, the starting date of the journey was fixed. On the day of departure, *baba* and *bibi*, felt such painful wrench in their hearts to bid farewell to the girl and her child that they had never experienced in their lives.

They consoled themselves with the thought that it was all God ordained and was inevitable. Seva Dai, who had been waiting so anxiously for the day, felt the sting of separation from *baba* and *bibi*. Emotions had to be controlled and for this *baba* and *bibi* took it on themselves to console Seva Dai. They promised that once she was safely transported to her people, they would be visiting her off and on. The journey was covered within the stipulated time. Reaching Sialkot, they reached Seva Dai's people. At her home, the rapturous scenes followed at the rejoining of a lost member with the family.

When the household got back their daughter-in-law along with the beautiful boy, their happiness had no bounds. After a long period of black disappointment, they had got back the full principal with its compound interest. It was a celebration in which all the people who escorted Seva Dai were requested to join. Shekhra with his beautiful face and a peculiar name attracted the maximum attention with the accompaniment of kissing and hugging in such an abundant measure as to make the little creature totally confounded and embarrassed. He had not received that type of experience before.

The family had given a new ceremonial name to Shekhra but continued to call him by his old name. The family continued to live together happily. They remembered the suffering and hardships of Seva Dai and the providential help she got from the two saintly persons, *baba* Farid and *bibi* Fatima. After passage of sometime, the progeny of shekhra had probably made it obligatory for their family to remember their ancestor, Seva Mata and her travails, on the important functions. In our time the progeny of Shekhra had grown into a small community which had faithfully stuck to their ancestor's name.

After Shekhra, his sons started adding Shekhra to their names instead of Kapur and with the passage of time Shekhra became their sub-caste. Then on, the generations following, replaced ‘a’ with ‘i’ and Shekhra became Shekhri. In our time the community in Sialkot had been using its lighter version by omitting ‘h’ after the capital ‘S’ and the sub caste had become Sekhri.

Our community members as long as they stayed in Sialkot in their *mohalla* remembered Seva Mata alongwith *baba* Farid and *bibi* Fatima and her story on the occasion of the two important ceremonies in their families as mentioned before. At the division of the country, Sialkot which had continued to constitute the prime place of the Sekhri community, had been included into the Pakistan territory. That important ritual and the story of the origin was forgotten when the community got disintegrated after leaving Sialkot.

The story of the Sekhri clan's origin had always fascinated me. Though that ceremony which commemorated the clan's originator and her benefactors, ceased to be performed with the dissipation of the Sekhris after independence, the story remained in my memory as a special possession. As I grew up, a desire arose in me to explore into the roots of my family to see how far could it take me near the origin of our clan.

I contacted our clan's purohits in Haridwar and noted from their record book the names of all my ancestors who visited Haridwar from Sialkot. That list gave me the names of my ancestors back to more than 300 years. Har Bhagat Sekhri from Sialkot visited Haridwar in 1689 AD. Alongwith him was his old great grandmother, Sulakhni Devi. In 1689, India was ruled by Aurangzeb. Going three generations back from Aurangzeb, it was the reign of Akbar (1556–1605) which Sulakhni Devi may have seen.

I, then, tried to find the time of Seva Mata's story. The clue was found in *Sheikh Baba* Farid (II) who was a contemporary of Guru Nanak (1469 – 1539). The names I got from our purohit led me back to Akbar's rule. The gap of nearly a 100 years could not be filled.

From the names I noted I had been able to trace my lineage back to 11 generations, counting from my father. From my grandmother I had heard the stories of the grandparents of my grandfather, which may be of interest to my progeny.

The grandparents of my grandfather were Jwala Sahai and Bhagwan Dai. Jwala Sahai inherited from his father a part of the *haveli* in Sekhri *mohalla* for his residence and a group of eight shops in the wholesale market called Gunj situated outside the municipal limits of Sialkot city. The *haveli* and the *mohalla* where they lived and Gunj, where their business was carried on, had been built very long ago. My estimate is that those properties came into existence sometime in the end of the seventeenth century. Many of the houses in that *mohalla* had been reduced to ruins, the wreckage being only mud and small bricks as I saw in the years between 1932 and 1936. The Gunj had totally disappeared and there stood the main post office and a few buildings at its site.

Jwala Sahai, had carried on his father's business of a commission agency for commodities like dried fruits and general merchandise which he imported and warehoused in his shop on behalf of the wholesale dealers. But he used to import some quantities for his own direct sale.

Jwala Sahai died in 1880 leaving his widow Bhagwan Dai, a son and two daughters. He had married all his children before his death. I have not seen his son, my great grandfather, but I had the privilege of meeting both his daughters. Both were widows when I met them. The elder one was married in a well-to-do Sehgal family of Jammu. She was very old when I saw her smoking tobacco in a chillum in her room. Most of the members of her progeny continue to live in Jammu up to this day. The younger aunt of my grandfather named Hakim Kaur was married in a Chopra family of Gujrat (Punjab). As she was very close to our family and was a frequent visitor there, I knew her well and was also familiar with her family members.

She had two daughters and one son. The elder daughter was married to Ram Chand Tandon, who was a wholesale cloth merchant and the most influential aristocrat of Gujrat. He was a Congressman who hosted Gandhiji, during his tour of the Punjab in 1920's, when he visited Gujrat. The younger daughter of Hakim Kaur was a widow and her son was a bachelor. He, along with his widowed sister, lived in their ancestral house till partition of the country. After that, they migrated to Delhi where they had constructed a temporary structure for themselves near the house of Uncle Dwarka Das on the ridge side of Pusa Road. Both of them died there sometimes in 1960's.

Hakim Kaur had good influence on my grandparents and was the main consultant at the performance of marriages and other functions in the family. When I saw her first in our family, she commanded great respect there. She died in the year 1942, in Gujrat, on the day I happened to visit her. On the instructions of my father, I had carried a basket of fruits for her. Seeing her on her deathbed, I felt very embarrassed and silently came out of their house with the basket and reached back Sialkot to tell the story of what I had faced there.

After the death of Jwala Sahai, his wife Bhagwan Dai took care of the family, consisting of her son, daughter-in-law and their one daughter and two sons. Her son, Jevan Mal was a handsome carefree fellow, who had to take the responsibility of managing his father's property and business. Death again dealt a blow to the family as Jevan Mal's wife Mehtab Kaur died in the year 1883 at the birth of her third son. Jevan Mal, for reasons of his own, stopped staying at home after the death of his wife. Although he was quite young and well to do, he refused to remarry.

Bhagwan Dai, who had faced two deaths in three years, had to take on the responsibility to save her infant grandson. She faced the situation very ingeniously and courageously. She placed her infant grandson in the care of his *daayee* who voluntarily offered to take that responsibility. The *daayee* was a Muslim but a person sincerely dedicated to our family. She proved her sincerity by taking care of the infant boy like a real mother. She had her own small baby whom she brought to our home when she shifted there. She fed both the babies giving more attention to the one she helped to give birth to, even feeding it on her breasts. Bhagwan Dai too treated her like a family member.

The old lady, devoted herself to the care of the other three children. She also looked to the convenience of her only son and sent food to him regularly, two times a day to his shops. She also found time to visit him at his business place at regular intervals to see that he was not facing any inconvenience.

After a few visits, she discovered that her son, who had built a one room set on top of one of his shops, did not live alone in his market quarters. He had a mistress, a young and very beautiful Kashmiri Muslim woman. She handled that tricky situation very tactfully. She first talked to her son, then to his mistress, to find that both were serious about their relationship. She accepted that without any fuss and told the woman that she was welcome to visit her at home as and when she liked, assuring her of a nice treatment. She did exactly what she had promised and treated the woman well, whenever she visited the family. On all the family functions and on important festivals, she was invited to visit her home, and when sweets were distributed to the Sekhri community, those were also sent to the *Kashmiran's* house through a special messenger. The grand old lady managed not to let his son's affair become a scandal.

She ran the household with domestic help, and gave all her attention to bring up all the children as best as she could. Her son provided liberal financial help for the household needs and she took all care to see that he was not put to any inconvenience being away from home. To her further misfortune, her son died in 1892. It was too much for the old lady to bear. First she lost her husband, then her young daughter-in-law and then her only son in a span of 12 years. She survived to take care of her four grand children. She must have cried a lot which cost her the sight in both her eyes. She became blind but she never lost sight of her responsibility of her grand children, who were growing up fast. She must have possessed a rare inner strength.

After the death of her son, she had been left alone to manage the family and the Gunj shops and business. Considering the entire state of affairs, she thought out a way to handle the difficult situation sagely. Her eldest grandson, Gokal Chand was hardly 16 and not ripe enough to handle the business in the Gunj. She sought the help of one of her nearest relatives, Tara Chand Sekhri. She consulted him about the business and shops in the Gunj. He advised disposal of the Gunj business and the property there. Gokal Chand was asked to assist Tara Chand Sekhri in this. It could be done without much trouble. As Gokal Chand wanted to run a general merchant shop, those goods were retained and other stocks were sold along with the shops. Out of the money received by Bhagwan Dai, a small shop was purchased in the main bazaar of the city. The general merchandize was carried to it and Gokal Chand was asked to run that shop.

Bhagwan Dai found Tara Chand Sekhri a great help. She shared with him her thoughts about how she wanted to manage the family and the priorities she had set. Tara Chand Sekhri agreed fully with the views of the grand old lady and assured her that she could bank upon him for any future help. Her first priority was to arrange marriage of her granddaughter named Har Dai. In about a year after the death of her son she was able to marry her to a young stationmaster, Pran Nath Chopra.

Bhagwan Dai, after the marriage of her granddaughter, felt a big relief. She could then attend to other family affairs with a better frame of her mind. Her eldest grandson was attending to his general merchant shop with full responsibility. He had also shown maturity while assisting Tara Chand Sekhri in the disposal of his ancestral property and business. Bhagwan Dai, considering all her circumstances, arranged to marry him and this brought some pleasure to her stressful life. She also found big relief with the arrival of a young and beautiful bride in the family. Not long after the marriage, a son was born to the wife of Gokal Chand which provided another occasion of joyful celebration in the family. But the good time did not last long for her. A year or so after the birth of her great grandson, his mother died.

It was an extremely painful occurrence. The curse of death had not yet spared the blind old lady. She was the only person in the family on whom the responsibility of a small child and other family members had fallen. She knew very well that it was not possible for her to take proper care of the child at her advanced age and sightless eyes. But the Almighty God had bestowed her with legendary courage and foresight. She readily accepted the offer of a near relative living in the *haveli,* to adopt the child, named Ram Rakha. The relative was issueless and after the death of his first wife, had married a young girl in his old age.

After the customary period of bereavement Gokal Chand was remarried to a young girl, Malan Devi, who became my grandmother. Bhagwan Dai soon realized that the bride was a young, immature girl who needed proper training to manage the household by herself. Malan Devi on her part saw that the blind old lady was not an ordinary person. She was efficient, alert, courageous and could be a good guide and support for her.

Bhagwan Dai immediately created a good rapport with the bride and started performing her duty as a patron. She lead and trained her like a very experienced instructor. In her ingenious way, she imparted full training to the young bride to make her capable to run a large household; as also to have the correct attitude towards the other family members and towards different well-knit Sekhri community members.

My grandmother, who had come to the family as an innocent village girl, proved an intelligent and eager learner. In due course of time, she came to be known as a very capable householder. When she narrated to me the above story, she spoke about the blind old lady as her very respected ideal lady. Bhagwan Dai was respected not only in her own family but by the entire Sekhri community as "Bhani *dadi*".

My grandfather, Gokal Chand did not go to school. He knew only the Punjabi business language called Landay with its special script. But he could run well the general merchant shop. His younger brother, Brinda Ban did go to a school and having passed matriculation, did some job in Sialkot about which I could get no clue. The youngest, Labhu Ram, due to the circumstances of his birth, grew up to be a spoiled child. He did not go to school nor did he show any aptitude for any job. He, however, was coaxed to help his eldest brother when he started manufacturing steel trunks.

Bhagwan Dai performed marriages of all her grandchildren and lived to see her great grandsons and granddaughters even though she suffered many personal tragedies in her long life. She lived for 25 years after the death of her husband and 13 years after the death of her only son. A person of rare courage and capacity, she never gave up. The tasks which appeared grim and formidable were executed by her during her days of blindness. The grand old lady of the Sekhri clan passed away in 1905. She had the best relationship of mutual love, trust and confidence, with her eldest grandson Gokal Chand, who carried her ashes for immersion into the Ganga at Haridwar. Before her death Bhagwan Dai did see some happy days. All her grandsons were gainfully employed and married.

My grandfather, Gokal Chand, was only nine years when his mother died and his father refused remarriage and stopped staying at home. The death of his father dealt another cruel jolt to him. He was required to take the place of his father and earn for the family when he was hardly 16 years of age.

The general merchant shop, which he started, earned enough to support his entire family. He savoured his success in his very young age and that helped him to develop self-confidence. His grandmother's patronisation and sage advice made him a very responsible and socially acceptable. He continued meeting his father's Hindu and Muslim friends. He also had good foresight to make use of those good relations for business purposes. Soon he was favoured with an opportunity which he caught with both his hands and was able to change the fortunes of his family.

It happened one day when sitting at his shop, an English army officer, came there with a steel box carried by his sepoy. He enquired from him if he could get a similar box made. Thousands of those were required for the army *jawans*. My grandfather, showed enough guts and told the Army officer that he could try if the box was left with him for a few days. The officer agreed and left the box at his shop. He then used his contacts with skilled Muslim *lohars* and could produce an identical piece. That gutsy action resulted in making him the pioneer in the manufacture of steel trunks in India. In that business he earned a lot of money and fame. He sold his general merchant shop and went headlong into the new business. He expanded the new venture so much that he came to be known as Gokal Chand *trunkanwale*. All this happened at the start of the twentieth century.

My grandfather, Gokal Chand Sekhri, earned a good reputation as a gentleman and a pioneer in the steel trunk business. He had three sons and four daughters. I had lived with all his sons in a joint family in Sialkot. My father Durga Dass was his eldest son who with his family and those of his two younger brothers, Dwarka Dass and Brij Lal lived in one house in *mohalla* Ram Talai alongwith their parents. I had also known his four daughters and maintained very good relations with all of them when after partition they had all lived in Delhi. They were Vidya Devi, Shanti Devi, Leela Devi and Sumitra Devi. My grandfather had died in 1940 in Sialkot. My grandmother Malan Devi lived upto 1955 and died that year in my uncle Brij Lal's house in Patel Nagar, New Delhi.

Brinda Ban, younger brother of my grandfather lived with him in the joint family in their part of the old *haveli*. He and his wife Roop Kaur had two daughters and two sons. Both the daughters had been married and died issueless before my birth. It was too much for the parents. Roop Kaur who could not endure those tragedies herself succumbed to those in 1920. At that time both her sons were school going.

Brinda Ban, who was already aggrieved because of the loss of his married daughters, was so shocked and disheartened at the passing away of his wife that he left home entrusting the care of his two school going sons to my grandparents and went away to spend his life in the deepest interior of Kulu hills in the Lahul / Spiti valley.

I remember having seen granduncle Brinda Ban for the first time in 1933 when he had come to the *haveli*, where our family had shifted a year before after the burning of our new house. It was the occasion of the marriage of his elder son, uncle Baldev Raj. Both his sons uncle Baldev Raj and uncle Vas Dev, had been working and living in Lahore after completing their education in Sialkot, they came to Sialkot for the marriage.

After 1933 I had been seeing granduncle Brinda Ban every year in the winter months when he used to come back from the hills. I found him as the handsomest among the three brothers with a very proportional body. He was very different from all other elderly persons in the family. With immaculate white *khaadi* dress complete with a turban, and a convivial disposition, he talked eloquently about the simple and peaceful people of the hills, the herbal wealth of those areas, unknown to the people in the cities and the solace he got while he lived there. No one in our family knew about the other details of his life there. But he never made any mention of the tragedies he had suffered in his life. He looked a totally relaxed man, always cheerful and laughing and making others laugh with his witty and cynical references about situations and people in Sialkot. He was a *khaadi* wearing nationalist. His most frequent target was Hari Ram, the headmaster of K.C. Arya High School, whom he always called as "Haria Choondi Wadh" because of the headmaster's way of punishment to his students by pinching so hard at their hips as to make their skin red.

Granduncle Brinda Ban was specially close to my grandparents and my father. The education of both his sons had been completed in our family, their marriages were also arranged and performed in our family The marriages of both his sons were fixed with the younger sisters of the wife of uncle Dwarka Das. Both the brothers were living and working at Lahore whereas granduncle Brinda Ban continued to live in the hills, alone.

During mid forties, granduncle Brinda Ban had to face the greatest shock of his life when both his sons died within a gap of 6 months, leaving behind their widows with four small children each. The main person to whose care he had left his young sons before leaving his house, was my grandfather, who had already died in 1940. Those boys who were educated and married under the care of my grandparents, continued to consider themselves as our family members and used to consult my grandmother for any of their problems after the death of my grandfather. The next person in whom granduncle Brinda Ban and his two sons had faith was my father. On account of this relationship, uncle Vas Dev was taken as a partner in the running business of shovels. But destiny had intervened to change the whole situation. My grandfather's good deeds were pushed into oblivion and his sons failed to give justice to uncle Vas Dev as their cousin and business partner. Uncle Vas Dev, could not withstand that unexpected change of heart, left the partnership, fell ill and died in 1945. His elder brother, Baldev Raj, heard about the illness of his brother in Shimla where he had joined a service. He reached Sialkot with the intention of seeing his sick brother. But unfortunately, his brother had died a day before his arrival. The unexpected shock made him fall ill. He could not get over that shock and died within six months.

The loss of both his sons was too much for granduncle Brinda Ban to sustain. He lost all his geniality but somehow survived to give some comfort to his two young widowed daughters-in-law. He carried on till the partition of the country in 1947. After the death of his sons he stopped going to the hills and spent his days of suffering in the midst of his sons' families, living in the old *haveli*. After partition, while migrating with his families he was badly wounded near the Amritsar border by a fanatic Muslim mob. He was carried to Amritsar but died there. Thus ended his long suffering life. The worst of the whole story was that those poor widows had to pass their tearful lives unattended by the progeny of their original benefactor.

The third brother of my grandfather Labhu Ram was born in 1883. His mother died at his very birth and he was fed and reared up by the Muslim mid-wife who helped his mother at the time of his birth. He did not go to school, neither was he interested to work. He was married to the younger sister of Malan Devi, my grandmother.

When his eldest brother, Gokal Chand started the trunk manufacturing, he was coaxed to help in that business. Later, when a new trunk manufacturing was started for uncle Brij Lal, he shifted to Jammu. Shortly after the death of my grandfather, he suffered from cancer and died in our house in Sialkot. His family continued to live in Jammu till they shifted to Delhi after 1947.

Uncle Baldev Raj whom I remember for his congenial nature and small humorous anecdotes, was very fond of me from my infancy and used to narrate many episodes of my infant days.

Uncle Vas Dev came closer to me in 1941. I had a sort of comradeship with him. I respected him for his intelligence, knowledge of Urdu poetry and that of music. I used to treat him as a friend and a sort of teacher.

—10—

RECALLING SIALKOT

Even at my advanced age when I got settled in life to my satisfaction, I missed Sialkot very much. I continue to seek an opportunity to visit once my birth place, take in my hand the earth from its ground and put it on my forehead. I know that it had been physically snatched away from us, but no one can take it away from my system. The city of my forefathers for centuries. I was born there, rolled in its soil on my knees as an infant, played in its narrow grubby streets of our *mohalla*, educated in its schools and colleges. I know every inch of the city, its old and new *mohallas*, its schools and colleges, its playgrounds, its Mandirs and Gurdwaras, Its *Basakhi*, *Shivratri* and *Basant Melas*, its water tanks and *Baolis*, the fort of *Raja* Shalivan on whose slopes I used to run up, slip, fall and play, on whose wide stairs I ascended running in one go. There was the Puran Bhagat's well; Haqiqat Rai's *samadhi*, Babe-Di-Ber, Chuni Pehlwan Da Akhara, its very large sports goods and surgical goods factories, its railway station, *sarais*, restaurants and the big cantonment—all those had made me what I was. It was a city I always felt proud of for its being well-known in the whole world as supplier of sports goods, surgical instruments and hardware tools. For its thousands of small scale and domestic units spread throughout the city and also in the adjoining villages like Kotli Loharan, Godepur, Daska etc. And also for its being a city of skilled workers, capable of producing articles of an enormous range, for its being the city which was the first in the Northern India to take to the manufacture of steel trunks in which my grandfather had the distinction of being a pioneer. It was not possible for me to turn my eyes and mind from Sialkot.

Sialkot was the district headquarters and was one of the most fertile districts of the erstwhile Punjab. It is situated at the foothills of the Himalayas and is at the gate of Jammu and Kashmir. Nature has provided the district with three water streams called *Nalas*, named Aik, Dake and Basanter. The first mentioned passes through the city.

It is a very old city, probably one of the oldest in the country. Its first mention has been traced to the *Mahabharata* times when it was known as the headquarters of Madra Desh ruled by raja Shalya, the maternal uncle of Nakul and Sehdev, the sons of Pandu from his second wife Madri. It was called Sakel in those days. The old highway from Peshwar to Lahore passed through Sakel (Sialkot). It was this highway that was followed by most invaders from the Northwest. Madra Desh had become a part of the territory ruled by king Porus who fought Alexander heroically when the later invaded India in the fourth centuryBC. At that time Jammu was excluded from Madra Desh. Still later another Greek invader, Manindra invaded India between second and first centuries BC, captured the territory up to the river Ravi and ruled there, making Sialkot its headquarters. Even at that time it was known as Sakel.

The above mentioned facts of its being a very old city and that of its location on the old highway followed by most of the invading armies from the Northwest, lead us to believe that this city must have been the battle ground of many a skirmish in the past. Consequently it must have undergone several destructions and rebuildings.

When I lived there, the old city was in the shape of a dome, habitated densely from its top to every inch on all its slopping sides. The total construction was of small bricks and mortar.

From our childhood we were told the folk tales of that city of raja Shalivan, the father of Puran Bhagat. Its full story was told in the *Bhavishya Purana*. But we knew it as a legend of which two landmarks still existed. A fort of raja Shalivan and a well called the Puran Bhagat Da Khoo. The fort had an underground cell in which Puran, the young prince was held as a prisoner by his step mother named Loona, as per the story. The well was famous for its blessed water. It was said that the childless ladies who came to the well and drank its water would be blessed with a child thereafter. How the well got its blessedness is mentioned in the story of *Puran Bhagat* which had also been made into a movie by the New Theatres of Calcutta in the thirties.

THE STORY OF PURAN BHAGAT

Once upon a time Sialkot was ruled by one raja Shalivan. He had a queen, named Achhra Dai from whom he got a son who was named as Puran Mal. Puran grew up into a very handsome and talented young boy. The raja, seeing the exceptional qualities in his son, transferred most of his state responsibilities to him. Puran took up all the administrative work with full confidence and within a short time proved to his father that not only did he rule his state well but had also earned love of all his subjects.

In the absence of all worries of administration of his state the Raja naturally tended to spend all his time in seeking pleasure. Slowly, his indulgence increased and a time came when he wanted a younger companion to go with his luxurious lifestyle and soon he had married a beautiful young girl named Loona Dai. He started spending all his time with the newly wedded queen in her chamber. Loona was very young and Shalivan was too old to give her full physical satisfaction. The youthful Loona started feeling depressed which was notice by her maidservants as well as by the Raja.

He in order to provide some diversion to his young wife, gave her the commanding powers of state. On the advice of her most confident maidservant she started taking active interest in the affairs of the state. It was then that she came in direct contact with her stepson. She looked at him in amazement; he was so young and handsome with absolutely dignified gestures and expressions. Loona soon got captivated by the youthful prince. The peace which she had sought by diverting her attention to the state administration eluded her again. She could find neither rest in the court nor in her chamber. Her mind was totally enchanted by the youthful prince. Lying in her bed, she continued thinking of him and could not sleep even at night. During the days she could not put her mind to the administration work due to sleeplessness. She shared her problem with her chief maid who wisely suggested that she might take rest in her chamber and call prince Puran there for discussions over some of the important matters of the state. The maid's suggestion appealed to the queen and she told her to arrange for her bath and best dress so that she might be ready to meet the prince in her chamber.

Puran got the message that queen Loona was not well and wanted him to visit her chamber to discuss some important state matters. After he was free from his daily duties, he visited his stepmother's chamber. Queen Loona was lying in her bed feigning severe pains in her body. On Puran's enquiry she replied that she was miserable as her whole body was aching. The chambermaid's attendance and the nurse's medicine had not proven effective. Puran felt concerned and assured her that she might get well with rest and that she may not bother about the state matters for a few days. As he turned to go out of her room, she called him back and requested that he might sit on her bed for some time. As he did so, she took his hand in hers and placed it on her forehead asking him to feel if she was really feverish? She added that with the aching of her body her heart was also beating fast. With these words, she slipped his hand from her forehead to her breast and pressed it hard. Puran shuddered at the touch and Loona let his hand go free. She told him that she would be able to sleep well as she felt a little better by his affectionate words and soft touch, and that he could go to his own room and take rest. Saying that she turned her face to the other side. Puran stood up and as he was leaving, she asked him to come again the next day, at the same time.

Next day, when Puran arrived in queen Loona's chamber, she told him that something magical had happened from the time of his first visit. She was almost half cured and could sleep well the preceding night. Saying these words, she stood up from her bed and telling him to cure her fully, she took Puran in her arms. Puran turned pale with disbelief when she hugged him and started giving him non-stop kisses. He reacted strongly, extricated himself from her and pushed her back. He simultaneously implored why did she think about him like that when he had always treated her like a mother? But she hoarsely cried and told him that God meant them to be lovers and he should forget what he had been thinking about her before. His old father was impotent and he would not raise his voice if Puran agreed to her suggestion. She would give him all the jewellery and wealth she possessed. But Puran felt disgusted at her words and said "Mother, I have always given you the respect of a mother and can never think of you in any other way". Saying this he left her chamber hurriedly and went straight to his quarters in the palace.

He remained disturbed over the shameful behaviour of his stepmother and her disloyalty towards his father. On the other side, Loona was completely shattered because of the insult and rejection. Like a mad person, she started crying and called her most confidant maid in a frantic voice and told her that she had been ignored and discarded by the prince. She wanted to teach him a good lesson. Saying so she tore her clothes and scratched her face and body with her nails. She told the maid to go and call the *raja* to her chamber. When the *raja* arrived, he was stunned to see his favourite *rani* crying with her clothes torn, her breast and face bleeding all over with deep scratches. He went to her bed and asked her how did she come to that miserable condition? She did not say anything in reply but cried still more hoarsely. He then asked the maid to tell him what had happened, but she also remained mum, looking at the floor. When he shouted at her for an answer, she replied in a low voice that she only saw the young prince come to pay his regards to the ailing queen. He ordered her to leave the chamber and shut the door behind her. He sat on Loona's bed and in a painful voice he lovingly asked her to tell her who had done that devilish act. Loona replied sobbing that she felt ashamed to tell him but it was her own stepson, Puran. He came to sympathize with her but seeing her lying in her bed, he could not control his lust. After all he was also young like her. But she always treated him as her own son. He was all the more shocked to hear the unexpected words from her. She seeing his facial expression of disbelief, called in her confidant maid and ordered her to tell frankly to the *raja sahib* what she had seen happening in the chamber. The maid spoke hesitantly, that on hearing the loud cries of the rani, she opened the door of the chamber and saw that the young prince was naked and was struggling with the queen in her bed. The rani was shouting for help. The prince on seeing her, quickly wore his pants and went out of the room. She then ran to the queen and saw her torn clothes and her body and face badly scratched. It was then that the *rani sahiba* ordered her to call his majesty. That was what she had seen and she did not know anything other than that. The raja was dumb struck on hearing the maid and could not decide what to say or do. He left Loona's room and went to his chamber.

It was late in the night but he could not sleep. In the morning, he sent word to Puran to come and see him in his chamber. Puran at once went to his chamber and found him in a very disturbed mood. He anxiously went near him and asked sympathetically if he was all right? He looked towards his handsome young son and told him exactly what he had heard from rani Loona and her maid. Puran was also very much upset but he maintained his cool and told his father that his life and character were an open book. He could only say that he treated the younger rani with more respect than he did for his own mother. About what was alleged to have happened in younger mother's chamber, he could not utter a single word. He then asked him to clear the whole thing in his own version as it involved a very serious accusation. But Puran told his father that as his son whom he groomed himself and watched him everyday, he did not consider that he needed to say a word as he felt confident that *raja sahib* himself could judge his son better. Now the *raja* was more perplexed and decided to call Loona to his chamber and get the whole matter cleared in the presence of both.

Loona refused to budge from her chamber and conveyed her message that she preferred to die where she was rather than moving about in the palace in disgrace. The *raja* then sent Puran back to his chamber and went to his favourite rani alone. Finding Loona in the same wretched condition, he could not muster the courage to tell her Puran's version. Instead he consoled her with sweet and sympathetic words. But she reacted angrily and asked him to leave her where she was to end her life. The more he coaxed her the more vicious she became in her responses. At last she said that either she or Puran could live in the palace. Hearing this he got alarmed but in order to placate her, he said that he would transfer Puran to some other place in his kingdom. Sensing the raja's weakness for her, she said that Puran had sinned against her and therefore, she would decide the punishment. She insisted that Puran must be arrested immediately and put under her custody. He, overpowered by his craving for her, immediately yielded and ordered for Puran's arrest and putting him under the young *rani's* charge. In his lustful madness, he did not realize what he was doing.

Loona then embarked on her mission of gratifying the *raja* more zealously. She got Puran imprisoned in an underground cell of the Sialkot fort, and put two of her trusted guards on duty outside the cell. Puran, being a dutiful son, did not protest and surrendered to his fathers dictates. One dark night, Loona managed to move Puran from the cell to a remote place outside the city, got him killed and his body thrown into a well nearby. In the morning the guards on duty reported that Puran had fled from the underground cell when they had dozed-off.

He ordered the soldiers to be sent everywhere to find the absconding prince and bring him back to the jail. After several days' search, when Puran could not be found anywhere, the search was abandoned and the Raja, forgetting about his son, again lost himself under the carnal influence of the wily young queen.

Puran's own mother, *rani* Achhra cried and implored before her husband but the infatuated *raja* did not listen to her pathetic pleas. She was a God fearing woman and after sometime, she reconciled to her fate.

Time passed on till one day, a group of monks under their master Guru Gorakhnath, happened to arrive on the outskirts of Sialkot and encamped near the well in which Puran's body was thrown after he was beaten and considered dead. When these monks went to draw water from the well for their needs, their bucket was stuck inside. The monks tried to draw it with their united strength but did not succeed. Having failed they were afraid that some ghost or evil sprit might be residing in the well which could defy their united pull. Leaving the bucket inside the well, they ran to their Guru and narrated their experience to him. He accompanied them to the well and on confirming his disciples' experience, he shouted into the well, that he was Guru Gorakhnath and he had the power to rescue whosoever was in the well, from its fate. It might release the bucket and speak to him its problem. A reply came from the well that he was no spirit or ghost. He was a human being who wanted to be rescued from the well. The Guru at once told him to hold on to his rope and allow himself to be drawn out. He did so and when he was pulled out, the Guru was astonished to face a young and beautiful boy. He asked him how had he fallen into the well? Puran narrated the whole story to him. He heard the tragic story of the young prince and said that he would make the raja come to his senses and would teach him a proper lesson. But Puran requested him that he bore no ill will towards his father and his stepmother. He only wanted to become his disciple and if possible, to know about the fate of his real mother. The Guru was pleased with the young prince's reply and accepted him as a disciple promptly. Whatever wounds were found on Puran's body, were healed and he was given the saffron robes of a monk.

After some days, the Guru sent a party of monks to Sialkot city to beg alms. As the monks entered the city and started begging, some of the people in the city noticed that one of the monks looked just like their prince Puran. More and more people started whispering that one of the begging monks looked like their prince. When the news reached raja Shalivan, he invited Guru Gorakhnath for a meal at his palace along with all his disciples. The Guru accepted the invitation and on the fixed day, the full party reached the palace. Meals were served to all the disciples and the Guru was invited to have his meals in the raja's chamber. After serving the meal to the Guru, he enquired from him the antecedents of the monk who resembled his son. The Guru told him that he was his best disciple and was so noble and learned, that he might very soon be promoted as a *Nath Guru.* When the *raja* told the Guru that he resembled his lost son, and told him his story, the Guru admonished the *raja*. He told him that he had foolishly become a tool in the hands of his wily queen to throw away a gem of a son. The Guru then narrated what had been done to the prince. The raja, who had been blinded by lust, fell at the feet of the Guru and sought his forgiveness and the return of his son to the palace. The guru sent the prince to the raja's chamber. Seeing his son in the saffron robe of a *sanyasi*, Shalivan started crying and admitted that he had sinned against him by becoming a tool in the hands of Loona. He sought his son's forgiveness and promised to punish Loona suitably and throw her out of the palace. But Puran told his father that he was a *sanyasi* bearing no grouse against anyone and did not want the raja to punish his queen on his account. He had been lucky to find his Guru because of the behaviour of the queen and was rather thankful to her.

Shalivan then requested Guru Gorakhnath for his intervention but he refused and Puran Bhagat continued as a monk and in due course of time became Puran Nath, in the Nath line of gurus.

THE STORY OF *DHARAMVIR* HAQEEQAT RAI

The other historical place in Sialkot was the *samadhi* of *Dharamvir* Haqeeqat Rai in *mohalla* Dharowal. On the day of the *Basant Mela*, Hindus of the city used to go there and pay homage to the brave son of Sialkot who, as a boy of 13 years, preferred to die than to surrender to the unreasonable demand of the city *Qazi* for converting to Islam.

It happened during the last days of the Mughal Empire. Haqeeqat Rai was the son of Bhagmal Puri. At the age of 11, he was sent to a *madrassa* run in a Masjid near their house. A *Mulla* was the only teacher there and the curriculum was Urdu language and elementary arithmetic. Haqeeqat happened to be the only Hindu student in that *madrassa*. He studied there for two years and being intelligent, hardworking, and very well behaved, he was promoted to be the monitor of his class. One day the *Mulla* had to go out of the *Masjid* for some work and he instructed all students to continue studying in the class under the instructions of the monitor in his absence. As he left, Haqeeqat took up the duties of the *Mulla* and started giving lessons to the class. But the boys decided to enjoy their freedom. They started playing outside ignoring Haqeeqat's pleadings to stay in the class. He then threatened the boys that he would have to report it to the *Mulla sahib* when he came back. All the boys replied in chorus, saying that, he dared not do so. He then told them that they should not take his words lightly, he swore by Bhawani Devi that he would report to him. The two mischievous boys replied that they did not care who the devil was Bhawani Devi. Hearing such disrespectful remarks about his goddess, he was very upset. He told the boys that they may return to the classroom or not, but they must withdraw their unbecoming remarks about Bhawani Devi and express regrets. But the Muslim boys started using more abuses for the infidel's goddess. Haqeeqat felt angry and warned those boys that they should mind their bad mouthing otherwise they might hear the same derogatory words from him about *Bibi* Fatima. *Bibi* Fatima was the stepdaughter of Prophet Mohammad and as the Muslim boys heard Haqeeqat utter these words, they all pounced on him and started beating him with blows.

When the *Mulla* came back to the classroom he found it empty. He saw Haqeeqat sitting on his seat with a sullen face.

On enquiring Haqeeqat told him the whole story. The *Mulla* felt very angry. He at once called the boys inside the room and threatened that he would punish all the boys. The leader of the boys told him that Haqeeqat had abused *Bibi* Fatima and therefore they were not going to study in a place where their Prophet's daughter was abused by a Hindu boy. He told them sternly that it was their fault. The Muslim boys threatened him that they were going home to complain to their parents about Haqeeqat's remarks about *Bibi* Fatima.

He got scared lest the parents of the boys should take action against him. He went to the *Maulavi* of the Masjid and explained to him the whole problem. The *Maulavi* too agreed that Haqeeqat was not at fault but he also feared the parents of the boys. In order to make their position safe, they decided to detain Haqeeqat in the *Masjid* and get the issue decided by the city *Qazi* next day before the parents of the boys took any action against the *Mulla*.

Haqeeqat's parents waited for him and became anxious when he did not reach home. His father, after waiting for some time, went to the *Masjid*. The *Maulavi* told him the entire story and he was exasperated to hear that a small children's dispute was given such undue importance. He requested the *Maulavi* to allow his son to go home, and promised that he would bring Haqeeqat to the *Masjid* the following day for sorting out the matter. The *Maulavi* showed his helplessness, as he feared that the Muslim students must have reported to their parents their own version of an infidel abusing the Prophet's daughter. He, however, allowed him to bring food for Haqeeqat in the *Masjid*. Haqeeqat's father returned home crestfallen and told his wife about what had happened to their son. The poor mother started crying with her prayers to the Almighty for the safety of their son. Both the husband and wife carried food to the Masjid. They again saw the *Maulavi* and requested him with folded hands to be kind to their child but the *Maulavi*, though sympathetic, explained his own helplessness. Haqeeqat, however, was very calm and relaxed. He tried to console his parents and told them not to worry and have faith in God.

The next day they went to the *Qazi's* court. Parents of several Muslim boys were also there. The *Maulavi* and *Mulla* brought Haqeeqat before the *Qazi* and told him what had happened in the class. The *Qazi* asked Haqeeqat to tell his version of the incident. Haqeeqat stated the whole incident truthfully. The *Qazi* was impressed by the composure and faultless explanation of the episode by the young Haqeeqat. He felt that the Hindu boy was absolutely not guilty. The *Mulla* and the *Maulavi* felt the same way, but told the *Qazi* that it was not that they had any doubt about the innocence of Haqeeqat. They were afraid of the reaction of the parents of Muslim students who had taken the side of their sons. That was why parents of the Muslim students had gathered outside his court. The *Qazi* considered their argument and was confused. He took out his copy of the Red Book and went through the list of various types of crimes and the recommended punishment against each. In the chapter dealing with infidels, he found that doing or saying anything derogatory about Islam or Mohammad was a crime punishable with death, but what Haqeeqat had said was not about Islam or Mohammad. The *Qazi* was relieved for a moment but the *Maulavi* interpreted that insulting Mohammad's daughter by words, could be considered as insult to the Prophet. Those words made the *Qazi* doubtful and between the three of them they decided to send the case to the District *Hakim* for final verdict. It was announced that the case was complicated and the *Qazi* was not in a position to decide anything. The case would be sent to the District *Hakim* the same day.

Next day Bhagmal and his wife went to the court of the *Hakim*. Again the Muslim students' parents and other Muslim citizens reached outside the court, raising slogans against the arrogant infidels. The *Hakim* called for the case, went through it and felt exasperated to find the small children's dispute being brought before him. He was told that they were forced to do so under the pressure from the public gathered outside *Hakim sahib's* court. Moreover, the Red Book had a clause, which could be interpreted in two ways. They produced the Red Book marking the concerned clause for the *Hakim's* reference.

As per the *Hakim's* judicial knowledge, Haqeeqat was not at all guilty. He was only doing his duty as per his teacher's instructions. Hearing the threatening public gathered outside. the *Hakim*, felt weak in his sense of justice. He was sympathetic with young and innocent Haqeeqat. He discussed with the *Qazi* if there was any escape under any rule, which could be applied for saving that small precious life. The *Qazi* had already considered this point and had found an answer, which he immediately told the *Hakim*. The penalty of death in case of an infidel could be condoned in the event of his converting to Islam. The *Hakim* saw the clause in the Red Book and felt relieved. He then announced his verdict that Haqeeqat, though a school child, did commit a crime punishable with death.But he was happy to condone the penalty totally, if Haqeeqat agreed to convert to Islam.

After reading out his verdict, he asked Haqeeqat whether he agreed to his suggestion to enable him to declare him free. Haqeeqat calmly replied that he was a Hindu not of his own will. He was made to take birth to the Hindu parents by the Will of the Almighty and he considered he had no option to change this act of God. The *Hakim* was stunned by Haqeeqat's argument and more so by his composure. When the *Hakim* told him that his penalty was death, Haqeeqat replied that as a Hindu, he was taught that both birth and death are in the hands of God. Moreover, it was the body that was perishable and not the soul.

The *Hakim* was transfixed to hear the exposition of Hindu philosophy of birth and death from the young child, it kept him thinking for sometime. He was interrupted by the noise of slogans outside his court. He could not give the verdict as per the Red Book. He could also not free the boy for fear of public reaction. He then found an escape route and made note of the proceedings on the case file with full details, including the answers of the young boy Haqeeqat and ordered the case to be forwarded to the *Subedar* in Lahore for final adjudication. Hearing the judgement, Haqeeqat's parents gave out a loud cry of pain and helplessness.

Haqeeqat was taken to Lahore under police custody and a date was fixed for the hearing of the case by the *Subedar*. Haqeeqat was brought before him on the fixed day and his parents were also allowed to be present in the court. Besides them there were some parents of the Muslim students and Lakshmi—Haqeeqat's nine year old wife. The case had received good publicity in both Sialkot and Lahore. Many Hindus and Muslims of Lahore had also gathered outside the court.

The *Subedar*, looking at Haqeeqat, was impressed with his fully composed face. Going through the files, he got annoyed that such a huge mountain had been made of a small mole. He told the *Hakim* that the Red Book produced with the case did not proclaim anything, which could be safely applied to the step-relatives of the Prophet and that too in an innocent, unintentional child's remark. He was very sorry to see the miscarriage of justice in the handling of the case at all levels. The *Hakim* agreed to everything the *Subedar* said but pointed to the public agitation and reactionary slogans. The *Subedar* left his seat to have a look at the crowd and came back with fear in his eyes. The *Subedar* considered all aspects and addressed Haqeeqat in a fatherly tone. He said, "Young boy, your life is too precious to be wasted at this young age. The only course that can save you is your agreeing to embrace Islam". He assured Haqeeqat not only safe acquittal but also a bright future.

Haqeeqat replied that he had already given his answer in the court of the *Hakim sahib* and he would still stick to it in every detail. The *Subedar* addressed Haqeeqat's parents to intervene with him. They pleaded with their son to save his life by converting to Islam, but he refused. Finally, a verdict of death sentence in public on a particular day was announced.

On the day of Basant Panchmi, Haqeeqat Rai was taken to an open public place and beheaded by the government butcher in the presence of his parents and other Hindus of Sialkot and Lahore. At the fall of the sword of the butcher on the young boy's head, he had already uttered in a loud voice, "*Bhawani Devi Ki Jai! Hindu Dharma Ki Jai*!" The parents and the Hindu public cried uncontrollably so loud as to pierce the sky. His parents, his wife and her parents swooned at the sight of the cruel act. His beheaded body was claimed, wrapped in white cloth, and was decorated with flowers. In a huge funeral procession, in which the Hindu and Sikh public took part, the beheaded body found its way to the river Ravi. With full Hindu rites and *Vedic Mantras*, the body was consigned to the flames on the bank of the river. The Hindus of Lahore built his *samadhi*, which is a fit memorial to remember.

Every year on *Basant Panchmi*, the Hindus assembled there in a big congregation and paid their respects to the immortal memory of the great child. It went on till the partition of the country. His life had been regularly enacted in stage dramas all over the Punjab till the partition. In Sialkot, his parents' house was converted into a memorial and prayers used to be offered there on every *Basant Panchmi* day. The Hindus of Sialkot were proud of their immortal son, who at a tender age, had the courage to sacrifice his life for the honour of his religion.

Another memorable place in Sialkot was called "Babe-Di-Ber". Guru Nanak Dev, when he decided to visit Mecca, the sacred place for Muslims in Saudi Arabia, followed the old road that connected Lahore with Peshawar. That road passes through Sialkot and, he stayed there in the shade of a cluster of *Beri* trees for a day or two along with his disciples. The Hindus of Sialkot considered that place as sanctified by the great Saint. A big water tank and a large temple were built there called "*Babe-Di-Ber Da Talao aur Mandir*". Later, when some of the Hindus started calling themselves as Sikhs of the Gurus, that temple was converted into a *Gurdwara*. Every year, the *Baisakhi* fair was held in the open grounds of that *Gurdwara*.

RAM TALAI EPISODES

The other place of importance which remains engraved on my mind and memory is the Ram Talai. I may record the three special public meetings which I witnessed at Ram Talai. All of those were organised by the Indian National Congress of Sialkot.

The first was in May, 1932. All the prominent congress leaders of our city had been arrested when they offered their passive resistance in the form of picketing wine shops and those shops which sold English cloth. As a protest to those arrests, the Congress party held a meeting at Ram Talai and was addressed by a second rung leader, Mr. Kundra. Kundra spoke for a few minutes saying that all the Congress leaders in the country including Gandhiji and Pandit Jawaharlal, had been arrested. Our own city leaders of the Congress including women were also put in the jail. He exhorted the public to follow him in a procession to go to the Deputy Commissioner for lodging their protest for those unwarranted arrests of our great leaders. He added that all those who followed him would neither eat nor drink water till they had lodged their protest with the Commissioner.

In the same loaded environment, I joined the procession and walked alongside others. The distance from Ram Talai to the deputy commissioner's office was a little more than two miles. After going half way in the summer sunshine I sweated profusely from head to foot and started feeling thirsty. After covering some more distance, I saw that I was the only young child among all the grown up persons. I remembered the speaker's words "No eating and no drinking", on way to our destination and continued walking with that resolve although my lips were parched and I found it hard to walk. Suddenly what I saw bewildered me. Many of the people ahead of me were leaving the metalled road and going in groups to a handpump installed in an open piece of land. They were all drinking water from the handpump. I walked on my way ahead but that scene of men drinking water continued to trouble me. Those persons had broken the resolve set by the speaker. All the same, my thirst also became unbearable I stopped walking and in a second decided to go back home. On my way, I had my fill at the handpump. I reached home in a deeply depressed mood and felt so guilty that I did not talk about that episode to any one in the family.

The second occasion was the visit of Pandit Jawaharlal Nehru to Sialkot, to address a public meeting before the 1936 general elections. From early morning on the day of his arrival, people had been occupying seats in the Ram Talai, and soon all the steps were filled. Everybody in the city appeared eager to see their darling leader. The mass of men continued to flow into Ram Talai like many river streams flowing towards the sea. All the buildings surrounding Ram Talai were full with people crowding at their tops, terraces and windows. It appeared the entire city had reached there to see the *khadi* wearing prince of their hearts, their hero and the most beloved among all the leaders in the country. As a child I had heard many stories of how he had been brought up by his aristocratic father Pandit Moti Lal Nehru. He was nursed and taught by English nurses and teachers in their palatial house in Allahabad. As a young boy, he was sent to England for higher studies from where he came back as a barrister. I had heard many more stories, partly true and partly exaggerated, about his life before he joined the Congress at the behest of Mahatma Gandhi. One of the exaggerated stories was that his clothes used to be laundered in Paris. The other was that he was served his meals in the plates made of silver and the cutlery made of pure gold. But after he joined the Congress, he threw away all those items of luxury, wore *khadi* and started to live like a common man.

His photos could be found in shops everywhere in the city and in all those he wore a Gandhi cap, *khadi* shirt, *chooridar pajama* and a *jawahar jacket*.

I had also occupied a seat on one of the steps on the side from which he was scheduled to enter the Ram Talai. On that side was a small street connecting Ram Talai to the road on which our house was built. All other members of our household, including some near relatives, took their position at the first floor balcony of our house.

The central platform, fully decorated for the special occasion was abuzz with activity but no one could tell exactly when Panditji was arriving. On the platform, the best singers of Siaklot were singing patriotic songs. There were announcements from the stage every fifteen minutes about the movement of Panditji. At last the announcement was made that he was near Ram Talai. Every one of the mammoth crowd stood up on their feet and turned towards that side. Panditji had reached at the top of Ram Talai guarded by a squadron of volunteers who were trying hard to control the people wanting to have a good look at him and those who wanted to touch him. Panditji seemed to be very much disturbed because of pressure on him from the uncontrolled mass of people. Then I saw him stepping down the stairs, shouting to those around him to co-operate with the volunteers. When he saw the volunteers totally helpless to clear the room on the stairs for him to move, he lost his temper and started slapping all those who came in his way. His hands started flying right and left with his well known agility. Such was the leader's spell that once he was behind the mike on the stage, everyone sat still, prepared to hear him in dead silence. What he spoke could not be followed by me on account of my extremely high emotional state, but what I do remember was his style of speaking in a well modulated but halting voice. People appeared to go bananas in their devotion to him. Every sentence he uttered was received with appreciation by clapping furiously.

It was much later that I came to know that he stayed at the 'Pillars Palace', the best bungalow in the city, with *Chaudhri* Krishan Gopal Dutt, the aristocrat Congress leader of the city and one of the best speakers in the whole of Punjab. He was accompanied by his wife Kamla Nehru and his only child, Indira Priyadarshni.

The third episode was very grim and has remained in my mind ever since. After the Quit India Movement all the big leaders of India and the known leaders of our city had been arrested. Some of the common Congressmen and the socialists announced to hold a protest meeting against this in Ram Talai. They would hoist the Congress flag and then give vent to their resentment. The city authorities did not give permission for the meeting. Disregarding this, a spirited group of about 25 men got together at some place near Ram Talai and as per their plan, stormed into it tearing through the police guards. They swiftly took out the flag and started to hoist it. Following them immediately some of the policemen, commanded by the city inspector of police, pounced on Mr. Handa, a book-seller who was holding the flag. The policemen tried very hard to snatch the flag cloth from his hands but to no avail. The police inspector then ordered his men to use their sticks on his hands and body to remove him from the pole. Handa fainted because of the severe *lathi* blows. Within no time a very stout youngman, named Joginder Singh Baghi, a socialist, jumped in front of the charging policemen and took hold of the flag from Handa. The policemen attacked him with *lathis* but he courageously fought with them snatching a *lathi* from one policeman and challenged them to come near him. The police inspector became mad with rage and joined his men to attack him with full force. Joginder Singh fell on the ground badly wounded, his turban going off his head. The police inspector, with the help of his men, caught him by his long hair and dragged him around in a most savage and ruthless way till he became unconscious. Seeing such a macabre scene, all others who formed the group had surrendered to the policemen and offered their arrest.

It was the time when I had become a committed *swayamsewak* of the RSS. Inspite of this, or perhaps because of this I had a flow of tears in my eyes and a deep anguish inside my entire being.

In the Sikh history of the Punjab, the name of Sialkot is mentioned as the venue of various political agreements. After the defeat of the Sikhs in the Third Sikh War with the English, the Sikhs were required to pay to the English the reparations of seventy lacs rupees. The Sikhs had no money to pay. One of the independent Jagirdars of the time of *Maharaja* Ranjit Singh, named Raja Gulab Singh paid that money to the English on behalf of the Sikhs and in lieu was given that part of the Sikh empire which was known as the Jammu and Kashmir state. Sialkot was then included in that territory. Later, the English entered into an agreement with Raja Gulab Singh by which they got Sialkot in lieu of some areas in possession of the English on the western border of the state. The large population of Kashmiri Muslims in Sialkot explained this way the point of its being part of the Jammu and Kashmir.

Sir Mohamed Iqbal, the great Urdu poet, was born and brought up in Sialkot. He was a Kashmiri Muslim whose forefathers, were *Saprus—Kashmiri pandits*. The separate state of Pakistan was conceived by him during his stay in England in 1930 when he came under the influence of some fanatic Muslims. His concept was supported by some English politicians from the British government. In young days, he was liberal in his outlook and his poetry of those days bears the stamp of nationalism. The national anthem "*Sare Jahan Se Achha, Hindustan Hamara*" is his creation. When he came under the influence of bigoted Muslims, he had to change that song to make it Muslim exclusive. He was declared as the National poet of Pakistan.

PART - III

—11—

HUNT FOR WORK—START OF BUSINESS IN BOMBAY

On the fixed date, at sunset I boarded the G.T. Express for Madras with Shiv Kumar. It was a long journey and we had nothing to do but talk. Shiv Kumar who was closely associated with my family started enquiring about them. I told him how my elder sister Prakash was handling the household, and how worried my parents were about my sisters' marriage. As I was talking to Shiv Kumar, a South Indian sophisticated lady started a conversation with us. She asked me in good Hindi whether marriage of girls was a problem in the Punjab also. I was surprised to hear her words as she had understood the gist of our conversation in Punjabi. I told her that it was not a very serious problem in Punjab when the country was undivided. The problem stemmed from the uprooting of the families because of partition. The most serious problem was that of finding suitable boys for the marriageable girls because we had been torn away from the place and the society where our forefathers had been living for centuries. The hardships that we had been facing since the August 15, 1947 were totally unpredictable. What we were facing was enormous in magnitude and an absolutely bewildering phenomenon. My old parents with nine children had to bear all these travails.

The lady was very sympathetic and listened to me with obvious concern. She told us that marriage was also a very serious problem in the south, especially in the Brahmin community. In her family also they had to face this problem.

Her father, who was in Government service, had only two daughters. Both were given high education. She was lucky to get married without any problem. But misfortune befell the family when her father died suddenly. Her mother was left to look after the household. Her mother had been worrying all the time as she was unable to find a suitable boy for her younger daughter.

The lady continued that she had been married for four years and had a daughter. Her husband was a senior officer in the Madras State government. They had a very happy married life. Whenever she went to meet her mother, she found her grieving over the same problem of the marriage of her sister. On her own part she was also trying but they were unable to do anything in that regard. One day she was considering her own life and thought that God had been very kind to her in many ways. She received good education and got married without any difficulty. Her husband was an extraordianary person, highly educated, a very fine human being holding a very important post in a Government Department and they had a beautiful child. She considered that God had been very graceful to her and she felt totally satisfied with her life. The only thing which impinged upon her happiness was her own mother's grief. She being her only counsel or support, could not find any solution to her problem. Then she thought about her own all round satisfactory life. She then made up her mind to do something in the matter.

One evening when her husband came home from office and they sat over a cups of coffee, she told her husband that she had gone to see her mother. She was very much worried and was getting very weak, thinking all the time about being uable to marry her younger daughter. She requested her husband that he might kindly help in that matter, and with his extensive contacts, find a good boy for her sister. After all who else was there to help her except the two of them. Her husband gave her a sympathetic hearing and told her that all the time he was in office, he remained so busy that he could hardly think about any other matter. He was over-loaded with the official files. She then told him to give consideration to that problem when he was out of his office rut, and pressed on to ask him if he could think of any boy for her sister. He replied in the negative. She then said that she had a boy in mind, known to both of them, as also to her mother and sister. She found him suitable from all angles, the only question was if they could make him agree for the marriage.

Her husband became curious and asked her that if she knew such a person, whether she had ever tried to put the proposal to him. She said that she could not get a chance to do so as that person came to her mind only that day. He said, if that person was so well known to them, they could see him any time she suggested and they would fix next Sunday for a meeting. She took the responsibility to fix the meeting.

Next day she went to her mother and told her about her solution to her sister's marriage problem. Her mother was startled but she only asked if she had talked to her husband. She assured her that she would do it only when she had no objection. Then she talked to her sister in an indirect way inviting her to her place, on next Sunday with mom. Her husband would also be at home.

Next Sunday, her mother arrived at her place with her younger sister. They all sat together and the subject of the marriage of her younger sister was raised by her. Her husband remembered that they were scheduled to go for a meeting with the boy known to his wife and with whom she had fixed an appointment. She then told her husband that she wanted to have a word with him in the other room. There they took their seats opposite each other. She told her husband that they had been married for more than four years and she had enjoyed a perfectly homogenous and happy married life for more than four years. They also had a beautiful daughter. She was grateful to him for providing her with everything and in such abundance that she felt fully contented. She had only one request to make to him. Would he promise not to deny her that? Her husband found her conversation weird as he had never seen her speaking that way. He asked her did he ever refuse her anything. Why was she speaking in a queer way that day? She replied in a very sober and solemn tone that her request may be seen by him very uncommon and she wanted him to assure her that he would not refuse. Her husband became a little suspicious but said, yes he would not refuse.

She then took both his hands in hers and bringing her as close to him as she could, she told him that she proposed that he might marry her younger sister also. He felt aghast at her words and without knowing withdrew his hands from hers and stood up saying he could not understand what she was talking? She also stood up, her eyes full of tears, and in a voice at once sincere and beseeching, she said that she would consider it as a divine boon through him. She had already received from him so much that she had not been left with any human desire unfulfilled. She now wanted that favour from him for her soul. And she succeeded in making him agree. They both went to the room where the mother and younger sister were sitting. She told her mother that he had agreed to grant her the boon. Then she took her sister away, and as she explained to her the arrangement she had made for her marriage, the poor girl started crying putting her head in her sister's bosom. Both cried and when they became normal, she told her younger sister that she might consider that all had transpired as the Will of the Merciful God. Her husband, who was a virtual saint, would allow her to take from him as much as she could. He possessed an unlimited reservoir of love and humanity. That way she solved her mother's problem.

We both heard that lady and remained spellbound throughout her story. In the end, we had no words to utter except to show deep feelings on our faces. We felt that we had heard a story from a divine being.

As the train progressed from north to south, the difference of lifestyle was discernible in the environment at the railway platforms wherever the train stopped. Next morning as the train arrived at Madras station, Shiv Kumar's brother was there to receive us along with a military truck. We then drove to Shiv's brother's house.

Madras is a good city, and probably the first one developed by the English when they started conquering India. It had big cloth mills and big English business houses. I stayed there for two weeks, tried to get the canteen contract for which we went to Avdi to submit our application. Simultaneously we had been trying to find some other business possibility. We liked the city, its atmosphere and the *Punjabis'* brotherhood. There was a *Punjabi* club whose President was a gentleman named P.N. Dhawan. More then 75 per cent of good work done for the *Punjabis* and the creation of a sense of brotherhood among them was due to the selfless and helpful attitude of Mr. Dhawan. In Madras, we found another class-fellow and a *swayamsewak* friend, Keshav Duggal. He was also there in search of some business. We met at a *Punjabi* shop dealing in printing and stationery items. The owners of the shop were also from Sialkot and known to me. Keshev was probably staying with them.

We did not succeed in getting the canteen contract. Our efforts to find some other business also did not succeed. I felt that my visit to Madras was a failure. Therefore, I told Shiv Kumar that I was feeling embarrassed living with his brother for two weeks without seeing any ray of hope. Therefore I wanted to go back to Punjab. That evening we met Keshav who told us his story of failure in finding anything worth while to do in Madras. However, he suggested to us that he had a plan, which could be successfully executed in Bombay. The plan, he explained was to start printing and stationery supply business there. His friends, with whom he stayed in Madras, were doing the same business very successfully. Bombay was a bigger business city with bigger and larger number of business houses and mills. He was sure that he could find suitable living accommodation and business premises to start that business there.

I decided to give Keshav's scheme a try but Shiv Kumar was not convinced. He wanted to try his luck in Madras. As I lay on my bed that night, I thought about my departure the next day. At Sialkot railway station on August 13, 1947, I was not ready to board that train unless I saw Kapur Chand. Reaching Jammu Kapur Chand disappeared. I did not know his whereabouts for very long. I, however, could keep my contact with Balwant Singh and Shiv Kumar upto Delhi where we three stayed together for three months. Again when I made a programme with Shiv Kumar to go to Madras to find some work, Balwant could not join us. From Madras I planned to proceed to Bombay without Shiv Kumar. What my fate had in store for me I had no idea. I felt as if I was floating in muddy water without knowing which land the water jet would throw me on to offer me a shelter.

Keshav and I left for Bombay. On reaching the V.T. station, he took me in a taxi straight to a paying guest accommodation in Parel. Mrs. Pamento, a middle-aged Goan Christian landlady, arranged a clean airy room for us, with two fresh beds.

We refreshed ourselves by taking bath and had our breakfast in our room. Being tired from the night journey in train in the third class, we decided to take rest for the day in our fresh cosy beds.

Next day, we started to look for an office space for our business. Our preference was to have an office in the fort area. From *The Times of India* newspaper, we marked three addresses where the offices were available. We could visit all the three places but found them too expensive.

Next day, we followed the previous day's programme. Many addresses were marked and we started visiting them one-by-one. And that day we were lucky to find a place both suitable for our business and easy on our pocket.

It was the first floor of an old building but the space was cheap and other terms very reasonable. Out of the full first floor, half was offered to us with a telephone to share. Without wasting any time, we agreed to take the place on the terms offered and paid the landlord advance money in token of our acceptance. The landlord would take two days to get the rent agreement prepared for our approval and signatures and 3/4 days for arranging to fix the partition. We, on our part, wanted a few days to decide the name of the firm to start our business and to get some office stationery printed.

We agreed to name our firm as Grounds & Meadows, the same name with which I had started my exports business in Sialkot. We were lucky to find a printing shop, Ranjit Printery near our office from whom we got our letterheads printed. The printing shop was run by a refugee boy, Prakash Dewan, who was of our age from Multan (West Punjab). He also offered to do our printing work required in our business. In a few days, he became our first new friend in Bombay.

Within a few days of our arrival, the preliminary requirements for our project were in place one after the other. I was thinking about Keshav's charisma with adulation. He proved his worth by systematically planning and achieving his purpose efficiently.

For our office stationery requirements we went to Abdul Rehman Street where we contacted a big wholesale stationery shop, run by a Sindhi, and bought our requirements from them.

The day we set our business preliminaries in place we felt relaxed. We decided to have a walk on the Hornby Road towards V.T. station, looking around and reading the billboards on the buildings on our way to ascertain how many customers shall we be able to get for our new business from the firms situated on that most important business centre for our type of business.

The first signboard to attract our attention was 'The Imperial Surgical Co. Ltd.', a company from our hometown, Sialkot. It was a pleasant surprise as the firm had been floated by one of our class-fellow's family. We were urged to go up to meet the people there. Reaching the first floor, we found A.R. Wig, the big boss standing inside his office. We greeted him and introduced ourselves as class-fellows of Ramesh, his eldest son. He was kind to point to the seat where Ramesh was sitting. We approached Ramesh with broad smiles on our faces, also showing a degree of pride. He shook our hands, made us sit on the chairs opposite his seat and enquired what brought us to Bombay? I told him that we had started a small stationery business there and had our office nearby in a building on the Bank Street.

But he showed no interest either in us or in our business. We left his office crestfallen because of his cold response and continued our walk ahead keeping our eyes on the buildings and the signboards there. We again found a smaller signboard with a name, which was familiar to us. It was 'Punga Trading Syndicate'. This company too was from Sialkot. Though we were not known to the company's owner, but I remembered who they were and also that they lived in our *mohalla*, Ram Talai. I, being an over sensitive person, did not show any enthusiasm to find another firm from Sialkot but my companion, Keshav was not like me. He goaded me to visit them and pushed me upstairs, knocked at the door to find an elderly person, with spectacles and partly baldheaded, opening the door. We paid our respects and told him that we were from Sialkot and that I lived in Ram Talai with my parents. He invited us in and made us sit on the chairs on the side of a table at which his son sat. It was a small office.

The young son, Raj Kumar Punga, recognised me. I knew a lot about Raj as he happened to be the son-in-law of Anant Ram Nayyar, a friend of my father. I remembered very well, the accident in which Raj, leading the marriage procession as a bridegroom on his decorated white mare, fell down and was unconscious due to a very bad injury on his head. It happened near the bride's place and when the bride's father was informed about the accident, he rushed to the spot accompanied by some relatives and arranged to carry the bridegroom to his house in that condition. He called urgently the best doctor in the city and got the groom treated properly. As the groom regained consciousness, he was taken to the marriage *mandap* along with the bride. The marriage was performed at the *mahurt* time under the supervision of the same doctor.

Raj received us with a smile on his face. We told him that we had recently rented an office at 19, Bank Street, where we had started the business of printing and supplying office stationery. He listened with full attention and showed appreciation of our visit to their office. He was very sympathetic and asked us for our visiting cards. We told him, those were under print but we showed him our letterhead. Seeing our letterhead, Raj smiled and picking it from Keshav's hand, he folded it at its centre before us and showed us the corners of the form going haywire. Further, he pointed to the worn out types used in printing. He advised us that being in the printing business, our own stationery should be very impressive. But he was not criticizing us to discourage. He stood from his seat and offered to accompany us to our printer who had printed our letterforms. Arriving at Ranjit Printery and talking with Prakash Dewan for a few minutes, he judged that the young printer was as ignorant as we were. Raj talked to Dewan, explained to him in a few words that he might try to understand the basic requirements to run the business which he appeared to have no experience of. He also pointed to his very old printing machine and all worn out types. With his effort and attitude Raj won the appreciation of Dewan and became our spontaneous friend and a good guide for our business. Leaving the printery, he took us back to his office and placed a small order for some office stationery items. We left Raj's office expressing our gratitude for all the interest he had shown in us. We were deeply touched by his concern and the humane treatment.

As we walked out of the Punga Trading Syndicate, I was thinking about the good suggestions that Raj had given. How strange that all of what Raj had told us was very well known to me when stationery was printed at Sialkot for my export business. I remember my letterheads were very much appreciated by all. But the knocks of the partition had blunted my memory and judgement.

After meeting Raj Punga, I became alert and tried to retrieve some of my memory to enable me to improve my capabilities. Next day we visted Abdul Rahman Street and bought the items required by Punga Trading Syndicate plus some more for our own office. I remember the name of the firm from whom we purchased those things and continued to purchase as long as we stayed in that business. It was Zenith Typewriting Co., run by a handsome Sindhi aristocrat, a migrant from Karachi.

One of those first days in Bombay, as we were strolling at Marine Drive after having closed our office, we met Chaman Lal Agarwal, another friend from Sialkot. It was a totally unexpected encounter for all of us. Chaman told us that he had been there for a few weeks, staying with his elder sister, in a flat in one of those posh buildings in the Marine Drive. We told him that we had started a small business in Bombay, and had an office on rent in the fort area on the Bank Street. Chaman dragged us to his sister's flat, introduced us with her and served us tea with snacks. As we left the flat, Chaman noted our address and promised to visit our office the next day before lunch. He did come the next day, saw our office space, had the particulars of our business and while leaving, told me in private that he was also interested in joining us as a third partner. He indicated to me that he would invest funds according to his share, and even more in case required. I told him that I would talk about it to Keshav and let him know. He went away and I spoke to Keshav about Chaman's interest in our business and Keshav agreed to the proposal.

Chaman visited us again as promised and we both welcomed him to join us. We were then three partners in our business and a total of five friends in Bombay including Prakash Dewan and Raj Punga. We told Chaman about the first order which was placed on us by Punga Trading Syndicate. Next day, we took him along to see Raj Punga and deliver the files and other small things. Raj was happy to meet the three of us. In our talks, Raj told us more about his business and that he resided at Chambur with his parents, his wife and two children, in a rented house.

With the joining of Chaman, our business started moving fast. Chaman's brother-in-law with whom he stayed, was a director in his family's large company The Devidyals. They had been famous manufacturers of stainless steel utensils in India and Chaman could easily get a good order for stationery items from that company. We had also employed a Sindhi salesman with a good personality and good contacts. The salesman did not take long to secure orders from large Sindhi companies like Havels Ltd.

We had a reasonably fair start and all of us were quite enthusiastic about it. After about a month, Lala Dula Mal Soni with two of his employees met us at the Shere-e-Punjab Restaurant. Dula Mal Soni was one of the top businessmen of Sialkot and was related to me from my elder sister's side. He was in search of an office in fort area for his export company. In our introduction, he noted that we had secured an office in the fort area. He asked for our address and the very next day, he visited us. Seeing that we had enough office space, he told us that if we could spare half of our space with the telephone facility for him, he could pay us as much as we wanted. I asked Keshav and Chaman to talk to him. Keshav told him that we would talk to him the next day after speaking to our landlord. When we spoke to our landlord, he replied that, as per the agreement, we were his clients. As long as we fulfilled our obligations and there was no trouble, he would not object to any of our arrangements. Keshav and Chaman settled the terms with *Lalaji* the very next day for subletting half of our space. The new comers, arranged to erect partition at half space, brought their own furniture and started working there under the name of Northland (India) Ltd. The manager of their Bombay office was Vishwanath Behal, the younger son-in-law of Dula Mal Soni. He was of our age and we found yet another friend in him.

Chaman knew that Keshav and I were staying with a Christian family as paying guests. One day he told me that he had been staying with his sister for many months. His brother-in-law had three other brothers who all had flats in the same building. He was feeling embarrassed to have stayed with his sister for such a long time; he wanted to have his own independent arrangement. One Sunday he came to our room to see it. He found that the place was neat and clean and expressed his desire to shift there if acceptable to our landlady. Keshav called Mrs. Pemento to our room, introduced Chaman to her as our friend and an ex-class-fellow and added that our friend would like to stay with us as a third guest of hers. Mrs.

Pamento agreed readily. Keshav then requested her to arrange the third bed on the same terms and conditions. Thus Chaman shifted at Mrs. Pamento's adding to our pleasure of living and working together.

At the close of office, we three plus Behal would leave together. On our way, we collected Dewan from the Ranjit Printery and went straight to the Mongini Restaurant. There we spent half an hour over tea and pineapple pastry. After that Dewan went to Kalbadevi street, where he stayed in the working flat of his brother-in-law, and the other four of us to the Shere-e-Punjab restaurant for our dinner. After dinner Behal went to his hotel, and the rest of us to Mrs. Pamento's.

One day, Chaman suggested that we might hire a house where all of us could live together and everyone affirmed his suggestion. Keshav took the responsibility of finding a suitable place. Keshav was a God-gifted person in organizing things and in achieving targets in the shortest possible time. A few days later, he saw an advertisement for a five-room bungalow, newly constructed and electrically fitted, at the Juhu sea beach, at a reasonable rent. All of us reached the bungalow. It looked fine, and the only one in that area. From its verandah, one could view the sea. All around the bungalow there were palm trees. The accommodation was one longish hall and four rooms of different sizes with verandas on two sides. There was a tube-well with an electric motor for water. The rent was 250 rupees per month with no advance.

We booked the house there and then. The total travel time to the bungalow was about an hour. This was quite tolerable in view of the facilities that we would get. Both Chaman and Behal called their families to reach Bombay as soon as possible. At the fixed time we all shifted to the bungalow. Mrs. Pamento felt cheated of her income but when parting, extended us her standing invitation to visit her whenever we found ourselves in need.

At the Juhu bungalow, the mess arrangement was decided mutually. Behal would have his separate cooking. Chaman took the responsibility of common cooking for rest of us along with his family. After one month, he calculated the total expense, divided it propotionately and told us our individual share. All the three of us, bachelors, were obliged that Chaman voluntarily and generously took the burden for all of us. Chaman's family also included his mother-in-law and his youngest brother-in-law.

The five friends, living together at one place with its beautiful surrounding and near a charming sea beach, added to our pleasure. We used to play cards every evening; on Sundays and holidays, we took long walks on the sea beach before having a sea bath.

Due to his very close relations and childhood friendship with me, Chaman had told me privately that he would not accept the share money from me. Keshav knew this and also knew that Chaman was very close to me. Keshav unreasonably insisted that he would pay only when I paid Chaman in his presence. Though we tried to explain him but he did not budge from his point. I then felt annoyed and told him that either he paid his dues or he would be thrown out of the house and all his belongings would be held back. He then paid the amount, but took away his baggage from the bungalow. When he came to the office the next morning, I tried to soothe the ruffled tempers of the two partners by telling them to forgive and forget. But Keshav continued to be sulky. He would go out in the morning and come back in the evening saying that he was trying to secure orders and collect payments. But for almost fifteen days there were neither any orders nor any payments. Chaman smelt something fishy and sent our salesman to collect payments, which were overdue. The salesman came back with copies of receipts of payments made by some of the parties.

All the payments had been received by Keshav in cash but not deposited with the firm. This was something sinister for a partner to do and was totally unacceptable. When Keshav came to the office in the evening, we enquired about the payments. He replied that the parties had not paid as yet. At this, I showed him the copies of receipts. Seeing the receipts with his own signatures, he was staggered and could not speak. I made him sit on a chair and told him that I could hardly expect such dishonest behaviour from him knowing him and his family background. Why did he do it? I told him to deposit the money in the firm immediately, otherwise we would take action against him which might put him in great trouble. I do not remember how the matter ended, but Keshav did not come to the office after that.

Keshav's exit from our home and business did make a serious dent in our friendly circle. It did leave a very bad taste in everyone's mouth. The whole of our edifice, office and residence was mainly Keshav's enterprise. I just could not understand his behaviour, which caused the whole trouble. A few days later, I received a phone call from his uncle, G.S. Puri to whom Keshav had introduced me. He asked me about Keshav and why he had not visited them for many weeks. I told him that he had left our business and that I too had not seen him. When he further asked about the reason of his leaving. I told him that I would write to him. And I did that saying that he had started behaving strangely and also indulged in some unethical acts in our business. The result of this letter was that, after a week or two, I received a letter from my father, enclosing a letter written to him by Keshav from Delhi, in which he had abused me profusely.

The charm of living together at Juhu bungalow was over. Keshav was a trouble-shooter and the initiator of a lot of fun in which Prakash Dewan, though unwilling used to be the central figure. Almost every night before dinner, we played rummy or flash. Dewan, after a few days, refused to participate as he thought he was a consistent looser in those games. Keshav, in order to force him to play would sit on his bed and called everyone there, causing big annoyance to Dewan. But all this was in a good spirit. This thing stopped when Keshav went away from the scene.

Dewan's brother-in-law was in the business of stock trading in commodities such as cotton, silver etc. When Dewan, before he shifted to the Juhu bungalow, lived at the business flat of his brother-in-law at Kalbadevi, he also did some deals in that business of speculation. He continued with that business even after shifting to Juhu. When we were together at Juhu, he used to tell me about his deals daily. Though I listened to him as a friend, I never showed much interest in his speculation business.

After Keshav's exit, Dewan and I were left in the big hall. Dewan, after closing his printing press in the evening, went straight to his brother-in-law's office, and then came to the Juhu bungalow, somewhat late. One evening, Dewan came quite late and before going to sleep, he came to my bed and woke me. As I sat in my bed, he told me in my ear that he had got me also on the train with him that day. I did not understand and asked him to explain what he meant? He then told me that he had purchased some cotton bales and some silver caskets in my name. I was startled and asked him how could that be possible without any deposit from me against that deal. He said that he had done that against his personal deposit. Speaking this he went to sleep. I remained awake for a long time thinking what Dewan had done for me. A few days after that, Dewan stopped coming to the bungalow as he had arranged a room in Kalbadevi for himself. A month or so later, Behal left Bombay on his foreign trip.

Only Chaman, with his family, and I were left in that large bungalow. Now, it was not a safe place. When we were five young *Punjabis* living together, we had created a fear among the neighbouring *jhuggi* dwellers, who were well known as illicit liquor makers. After the going away of Behal's wife, Chaman's wife felt lonely and unsafe. As such, he had to immediately send his family back to Ludhiana and we vacated that bungalow. We found a room in a house in Andheri suburb.

The room we shifted to was found unfit for our living as the house being very old, sent forth whiffs of some suffocating odours.

We had hardly spent a few days there, when a fierce cyclone hit the whole of Greater Bombay one night. We were sleeping in our room with our mosquito nets and open windows when the storm, along with heavy rains, exploded. The strong rain-filled wind dashed against the open windows and sprayed its splashes inside our room to make it cooler. We had very good sleep that night after the clatter of the window doors had stopped. When we woke up late in the morning we spoke to each other lying in our beds about the nice sleep we had after several days. But as we sat up and moved our feet to the ground, we shuddered. There was ankle-deep water on the floor of our room. At that very moment, we heard a loud knock at our door; it opened with the appearance of our landlord, shouting at us angrily that we had not cared to shut the windows at night. This had caused tearing away of their doors from their hinges. Simultaneously his eyes fell on the floor covered with water, and the fellow started crying hoarsely that his room matting was also gone. Our satisfaction, after the pleasant sleep of the night, evaporated from our faces and we silently endured the genuine *hungama* created by the distressed landlord. But as our eyes fell on our suitcases lying on the watery ground, we immediately lifted them and placed them on our beds. The landlord left the room cursing us and his fate.

We stood on our beds, changed our clothes, and searched for our shoes drowned in the watery floor. We wanted to go out and find something to eat. But as we looked out, the road had become a jungle with fallen trees, uprooted electric and telephone poles with their snapped wires spread everywhere. The storm was still at its nastiest. We dared not step out. There was none to help. The landlord was busy going round his house, collecting the broken articles and throwing out water from rooms with buckets and bowls. We dared not look to him as he was still cursing us. We must have waited for hours looking out helplessly. Around midday, it seemed that the rains had stopped but not the strong wind. We decided to make an attempt to step out and reach the railway station with the hope to find something to reduce the pangs in our stomachs.

Arriving on the main road, we realized that the velocity of the wind storm was too strong. In that situation, we held each others' hand tightly and walked slowly towards the station sticking as close as possible. We had to find space to move amidst the fallen trees and poles and wires. We may have gone a hundred steps when a gust of wind hit our backs with a big thud and violently pushed us and knocked us down on the road, on our faces. We felt we were gone with that blast of the wind. But after a while we regained our senses. We found ourselves nervously clutching the road with both hands with as much strength as we could muster. I called out Chaman's name loudly and heard his reply in a feeble sound. I told him to hold on to the road as tight as he could. After some time, that seemed eternity to us, the wind appeared to come out of her rage. We carefully lifted our bodies to a sitting position and after waiting for a few minutes, stood up. On instinct, I shouted to Chaman to run as fast as he could to reach the shelter of the railway station, which was visible from our position.

The station was packed with men, women and children. No staff, no trains, no food. Everyone was looking at the cheerless and forlorn rails and praying for some providential mercy. Our minds were engrossed in finding some way to reach the centre of the city where we may find something to appease our hunger. It was a question of somehow reaching there. After some time, we saw some life on the rails at a long distance. There was smoke and a black engine. A mainline steam engine pulling a train, arrived and passed our platform without caring for the mob assembled there. Then there a man appeared in railway uniform at the station, opening his room. Many people rushed towards him but he swiftly entered the room and closed it from inside. He, however, opened a side window and shouted to inform the public that there was an unfathomable destruction of the local trains and nobody should expect any help from the railways and he then shut the window.

With the roads so heavily damaged and blocked, we could hardly expect any help from the bus service either. The drivers and conductors of the buses must also be suffering as we were. In that gloomy setting, we found a ray of hope when someone said that he saw a bus at the nearby bus-stand, going upto Bandra. We ran towards the bus-stop and reaching there came to know that a few buses had started service for short distance destinations. Late afternoon, we could get a bus to Bandra and from there to Dadar and then to V.T. The whole area around V.T. station was deserted. We decided to stride on a small street leading to Pheroze Shah Mehta road, carefully searching for any small open teashop but there was none. Crossing Pheroze Shah Mehta road, we walked towards our office on the Bank Street. On our way, we saw a man in one sidelane, opening his shop. It was a small teashop and clearly it was to help us that Providence had arranged it. The man offered us only two buns which we ate one each. Paid the man and reached our office building. It was dead dark at the entrance, but using our hands as our guides, we reached the stairs, and slowly went up to our office. Chaman carried keys in his pocket and he could open the door. Clearing our office tables of all papers and trays, we stretched ourselves on each and spent the night. The cyclone having passed, and with the normal daylight, people had started coming on roads. In the afternoon, small shopkeepers especially the teashops, bakeries and small restaurants started opening. Our office building was very old but luckily, it withstood the storm due to its being hedged between new buildings. After using the office toilet and bathroom facility, we went down and found a small teashop where we could get hot tea and biscuits. All government offices were closed but their employees in the essential services like electricity board, water works, railways, buses and fire stations were called to work on emergency basis. The city infrastructure had been damaged so much that in our estimation, it would take weeks to repair and put them back into service. But due to day and night rescue operations, it took just two to three days to get a working infrastucture. The government offices started opening. Newspapers containing the news of destruction and devastation started being published. We read that several small ships anchored in the harbour were drowned and thousands of boats and as many fishermen were missing. Hundreds of houses had their roofs blown away. The condition of the poor and the slums was very serious.

We spent one more night in our office using candles. I don't remember how we retrieved our baggage from Andheri but we did not live there another day. Chaman went to his sister and from there to Amritsar telling me that he would take a month or two to settle his accounts with his brothers; they had taken his name off the partnership of their ancestral firm. I shifted to Mrs. Pamento.

In office, I was alone on our side. When Behal was sent abroad, his company gave his responsibility to me till they made another arrangement at a salary of Rs. 300. With Chaman also gone, I tried to handle affairs of my office and those of the other company as best as I could. Only Dewan was left whom I met daily for my business and as a friend. The other friend, Raj Punga became much closer to me. He was most affectionate and in those days I used to go to his home in Chambur, on Saturday evenings to spend my Sundays with his family. Raj had a small three-room house in Chambur, not very far from the Tube station. He lived there with his parents, wife, two small sons and a grown-up sister. I came to know later that the sister was adopted and was the biological daughter of his mother's sister living in the Punjab. The family as a whole were very affectionate. His old mother, particularly, was very loving and friendly. She used to make me sit with her and we talked and talked for hours together joking and laughing. Visiting Raj's house and knowing his family closely, I observed a very strange thing. Raj was a teetotaler but his father was addicted to whisky. Every Monday, Raj used to buy a bottle of whisky of particular brand to be finished by his father during the week. In connivance with the rest of the family members, the bottle was kept out of the reach of his father and at a fixed time, two pegs were served to him. No more, no less and only on fixed times. But the bottle always remained with Raj or his mother.

Raj had maintained very close relations with his in-laws who had settled in Ludhiana. His father-in-law was a very well known head for foreign business but in Ludhiana he was trying to manufacture the measuring tapes with leather jacket and the printed metallic cotton tape. They used Raj's services for getting the feel of the Bombay hardware market for their products. During that period, a sample of a 50 feet long tape was received in Raj's office for showing it to the Bombay market so as to get a feedback on the quality and demand. Here, Raj availed of my assistance. I knew most of the dealers in the hardware market as I sold them shovels produced by my family in Delhi. When I went with the measuring tape sample to some of the major hardware dealers in Khokha bazaar and Nagdevi street, the big shop owners showed a lot of keen interest in the product. Some parties were ready to place their orders straightway. But Raj was not yet ready to book orders.

Dewan continued to maintain his close friendship with me. Besides our regular printing business, he had been taking me along in his speculation business. He also pressed me to shift with him in his room in Kalbadevi but I felt it was not proper for me to do so. However, once a week he used to take me along to spend the night with him. His room was in a very good flat owned by a Gujarati family with one small child. The landlady used to look after Dewan's room herself. Very fine, very humble and educated she used to knock at the door and then come to Dewan's room in the morning to see that everything was in order. I had seen her cleaning the painted walls with the *palloo* of her cotton *sari*. Sometimes she would send some special Gujarati dish for Dewan.

After Chaman had left for Amritsar, I had two dependable friends in Bombay, Dewan and Punga. In those days my elder sister had come to live near Poona. My brother-in-law, who was an ordinance officer, had been recently transferred to Poona. Their living quarter was in a military barrack in a Poona suburb, called Begarawari.

Once or twice a month, when I did not go with Raj Punga to his house, I used to go to Begarawari to my sister. This way I was keeping myself busy all the time and was spending my weekly holidays without getting bored at Mrs. Pamanto.

One fine day, while I was purchasing stationery in the Abdul Rahman Street I met Jagdish Mitra, another friend from Sialkot. We were together in school as well as in the RSS. Mitra was in surgical business and had been running a shop in Bhagirath Palace, Chandni Chowk, Delhi, in partnership with his two brothers, under the name of J. Mitra & Bros. He told me he had been staying in a hotel in Bombay for some weeks. He had to make purchases of surgical and medical articles from the wholesale market. He had also started importing a few items, which he sold in Bombay as well as in Delhi. I told Mitra about my activities in Bombay and my operations from my office in the fort area plus my residing there as a paying guest in Parel. Mitra showed interest in seeing my office, and accompanied me there. He liked the place and asked me if he could have a table space there. I welcomed him in the same friendly spirit with which he had asked me. I did not think that I should have consulted my partner, Chaman. Mitra brought his table and chairs in the next two or three days and I now had a companion in my office. After some days, he accompanied me to Mrs. Pamanto and decided to shift there with me the very next day.

Being together all the time I introduced Prakash Dewan to Jagdish Mitra. One day Mitra heard me talking to Dewan on phone about our speculation business. Dewan had continued making transactions in my name alongwith his own without even a reference to me. As a matter of fact, I knew nothing about that business. Only some information was shared with me by him and I considered it as a special favour done by him, due to his emotional attachment with me. I knew him as a very sincere and pure hearted friend. When Mitra came to know about it, he also showed interest to join us. I spoke to Dewan and he frankly told me that he was not in a position to do more in his own name. When Mitra insisted, Dewan suggested that he might do that independently placing Rs. 10,000 as the deposit money with the firm of his brother-in-law. Mitra was ready to deposit but wanted me to join him. When I informed Dewan, he told me that if I wanted to join Mitra, he had no objection. During the few months Dewan had been doing that business for me, he had kept that account separately. He told me that there was nearly six thousand rupees accumulated under my name and he transferred that amount in Mitra's name.

From that day, my speculation business was separated from Dewan and joined with that of Mitra's.

It was during Chaman's trip to Amritsar, and before my meeting with Mitra, that Shiv Kumar came to Bombay from Madras. As I left Madras and started our business in Bombay, I remained in touch with Shiv Kumar by correspondence. He stayed at his uncle, Pandit Sudarshan's residence in Mahim and phoned me in my office. Giving me the house address of his uncle, he invited me there to meet him. I went there and Shiv introduced me with his uncle and his family. Pandit Sudharshan was a well-known person in the film industry at that time. He had written some very popular stories first for the New Theatres in Calcutta and then for Sohrab Modi's Minerva Talkies in Bombay. At that time he was employed by Minerva. Shiv had some packets of imported nibs, which he wanted to sell in Bombay. He availed of my service to sell those for him. I helped him in doing so in Abdul Rahman Street. Shiv Kumar stayed in Bombay for more than a week and wanted me to be with him every evening. During those visits I developed friendship with two younger sons of Pandit Sudarshan, who were of my age. When Shiv left, his cousins Kul Bhushan and Shashi Bhushan continued to invite me occasionally to their place for spending my holiday with them.

A few days after Shiv left, I received a letter from my brother-in-law that he was coming to Bombay to admit his three years old son, in Tata Memorial hospital for Cancer. I received him at the station. Going straight to Tata Memorial in a taxi, my brother-in-law was able to get his child admitted in that hospital straightaway as he had the recommendation of his English commandant. I came back with my sister and her youngest son at Mrs. Pamanto's house; I had given her prior information about the arrival of my sister. Mrs. Pamanto and her daughter were very nice to my sister and took full care of her baby. My sister visited hospital two times daily and the baby was taken care of by Mrs. Pamanto.

After two days, when the child was examined fully by the concerned doctor, the hospital told my brother-in-law to take the child back home as he was found to be an incurable and a terminal case. Both my sister and her husband were very much depressed and went back to Begarawari with the sick child. They had wished that the child might get treatment in a hospital till the end. As I went to see them off, I saw their agonized and tearful faces at the station. I could not control my own tears. I was really sorry to be of no help to them.

Next Sunday, I had been invited at Pandit Sudarshan's place. I went there and while talking with Kul Bhushan he felt that I was not my usual self. I told him the episode of the sick child of my elder sister. Kul Bhushan happened to know one German doctor at Tata Memorial and thought he could help in the re-admission of the child. He immediately got ready and took me to meet the German doctor friend. Kul Bhushan introduced me as a good friend and explained the purpose of our visit to him. The doctor remembered the case and repeated his earlier view. But Kul Bhushan told the doctor that the child's parents had been greatly disappointed that their child could not be treated at the only Cancer Hospital and Institute in our country and given the best available treatment to his end. The doctor told Kul Bhushan frankly that there was not even a fraction of a chance to save the child but if it was only for the parents' satisfaction, he would readmit the child. The meeting ended with an encouraging note for me. We thanked the doctor and promised to bring the child back the next day. I thanked Kul Bhushan and took leave from him. At Mrs. Pamanto's, I informed her that I could get the permission for readmittance of the sick child and that I was leaving right away to bring him back. Mrs. Pamanto was very sympathetic and assured me that my sister was welcome to stay with her and that she would take care of her younger baby. I reached Begarawari at night and told my brother-in-law about permission for readmission. They made all preparations during night and we were able to catch the first train for Bombay early in the morning. We went straight to Mrs. Pamanto and after handing over the baby to her, we reached the Tata Memorial Hospital. I sought to see the German doctor who readmitted the child. The child died after three days, in the hospital.

All those days Kul Bhushan was also kind to come to the hospital. For many days, I had been thinking about these phenomena in human life. How could an innocent child of three years get a deadly disease? That child, especially, was the most beautiful one I had ever seen in my life. He could be compared to the best picture of child Krishna except that he had a very fair complexion. After this tragedy, my brother-in-law got himself immediately transferred to the North. My visits to my sister stopped.

With the coming of Jagdish Mitra, I got some good comradeship. Chaman's stay at Amritsar was prolonged due to his acute differences with his elder brothers. Mitra was doing well in his business. The speculation side was progressing in our favour in all our transactions. I was relieved of the responsibility of Northland Ltd. after three months. Chaman came back and stayed with his sister. He had been in contact with her from Amritsar and was trying to get her assistance in resolving his problems with his elder brothers.

He did not object to my taking in Jagdish Mitra in our office. What he did not approve was our speculation business. Jagdish's surgical business was doing well yet he had been taking keen interest in speculation business. This showed his craving for quick money. The extra gain in speculation made him hire a flat in Jogeshwari and call his wife there.

He pressed me to shift and live with him in the flat. But I was not inclined. However, he dragged me there with him causing another disappointment to Mrs. Pamanto. When we had shifted to Jogeshwari, Mrs. Mitra arrived in Bombay with her children and mother-in-law. We received them at the railway station and took them to the Jogeswari flat. All the things necessary to run the household had been arranged before the arrival of Mitra's family. One room was occupied by Jagdish, his wife and two kids, the other room by Jagdish's mother and me. I enjoyed living with Jagdish and it was lot of fun in the company of his mother. She had a jolly good spirit and was very witty. On Sundays, we used to go for picnics.

My stay at Jogeshwari was very peculiar in certain respects. First, that I was living with Mitra's family as their friend and guest, with no payment. Mitra never allowed me even to discuss this subject. The other peculiar thing was that Mrs. Mitra, from the day of her arrival in Bombay, did not utter a single word to me. Being shy in such matters, I also never tried to take any initiative. We might have lived together in that flat for many months, must have gone together dozens of times for picnics or shopping, but never did we come to speaking terms. The strangest aspect of this matter was that neither Mitra nor his mother ever tried to intervene. Both me and Mitra's mother were very comfortable as a company in our room. When the breakfast and dinner were sent for both in our room, we used to eat, talk and laugh heartily.

Time was passing smoothly. Mitra's coming in contact with me, our togetherness in office and at home, had cut short my meetings with Raj Punga. One day, as we reached our office and were attending to our respective jobs, the phone bell rang. I picked up the receiver to find Dewan's voice. Before I could greet him, he threw a bomb shell by telling me that there had been a ghastly crash in the market, the previous night, resulting in a steep fall in the price of both the commodities we dealt in. Further that all our money lying with the brokerage firm, had gone in loss. Mitra saw my face going pale and as I told him what had happened, he too felt shattered. Foolishly, we had never expected this eventuality though Chaman had warned me several times. The second phone call from Dewan was more devastating. The brokers said that adjusting the entire amount to our credit, there was a debit of four to five thousand rupees and that we were required to deposit another ten thousand with them forthwith. The third phone call from Dewan was picked up by Mitra to whom he said to arrange the money demanded immediately. Mitra felt aghast and was incoherent with Dewan on phone. The business transactions had been done in his name. Dewan, who was as much worried as we were, came to our office and told us that somehow or the other, the money must be arranged as the brokerage firm belonged to his brother-in-law. In fact, Dewan had introduced J. Mitra and therefore, he was morally responsible for the deals done in his name. I assured Dewan that we would stand by him and fulfil all our financial obligations. We only requested for a little time to arrange the money. Dewan himself had also lost heavily. The poor fellow was much more in trouble on account of his friendship with us.

Mitra became too nervous to talk about the subject. Chaman too felt concerned. After office, and while in the local train, we remained silent. But as we walked from Jogeshwari station towards our flat, Mitra suddenly broke down, started crying loudly and went down on his knees on the ground. As we followed the route by the rail side, there was nobody near us. I was stunned at his condition and as I tried to lift him up I found that he was ice cold all over. I helped him up with both hands and pushed him along with me up to the flat. I had been fervently telling him all the way that we should face the loss with courage but he could not control himself. I was feeling very much embarrassed. He kept on crying as he entered the flat, to the utmost distress of his wife and mother. They dragged him to his room and shut the door. I was alone in the other room feeling confused and ashamed. Mitra became calm after quite some time. When his mother entered our common room, I had already spread my bedding and had lied down there. In that environment, there was no question of eating.

Next morning, I packed up my bag and prepared to leave Mitra's flat. He requested me not to do so but I was adamant not to stay with him. I took my bag to my office. In the evening, I left for Mrs. Pamanto and started staying there thenceforth.

Next day, I explained to Dewan that he might co-operate and give us some days to watch the movement of the market. But he wanted more deposit money to do that. I had no money and I told Dewan frankly that I might be allowed to pay when I could. He told me that business was being done in Mitra's name and so, the money had to be deposited in his name.

Mitra appeared a total wreck. He did not want to discuss the subject with me or with Dewan. However, he started making preparations to leave Bombay as soon as he could. He had hardly lived there with his family for a few months. He wound up his business in Bombay and left within a few days, promising Dewan that he would arrange to pay the final loss once he was in Delhi. Dewan was helpless and so was I. We had to stay and face the situation jointly.

On the other side, the stationery business was not showing good results. Chaman talked to me about it. He told me that he had discussed it with his brother-in-law who, in turn, had offered our firm to market their stainless steel utensils in the whole of Bombay on commission basis. They provided us with the names of their dealers in Bombay and we had to visit those dealers regularly, collect their reports about their sales, book fresh orders and submit those to Devidayals once a week. They offered us commission on sales in that area. As Chaman wanted me to undertake that job, I agreed to do it without a second thought. I was then told to see the Director in-charge of sales of S.S. Utensils at Devidyals', Reay Road office. The Director Mr. Amir Chand Gupta interviewed me, was satisfied and gave me instructions about the way I had to go about that job.

I was to go and see each of their existing dealers, area-wise, in Bombay, note their sales figures for the preceding month, their suggestions about the sales improvement, then compile my report for each shop and submit those to the company every week personally. The reports would also include orders placed by some of the dealers. As the reports were submitted personally, the Director used to call me to his chamber and discussed with me about some of the important customers' suggestions and my personal impression of those customers.

I continued doing that job with all my sincerity and I could see that Mr. Amir Chand Gupta was happy with my work. I confined myself to the job and never discussed with Chaman about the remuneration for which, he himself was responsible.

A few months earlier, I had received a letter from my father that he was still in Panipat with the family. He had started manufacture of shovels and school children slates with his brothers in Delhi. He asked me if I could market those items in Bombay. He sent me samples of shovels and slates for the purpose. I had, therefore, also started marketing these two items. I fixed five days for stainless steel utensils and one day a week for shovels and slates. I could book orders for stainless steel utensils and took those to the Company alongwith my written reports every Monday. I had to work hard to attend to both the jobs but I felt happy to find that I could perform well on both sides and to the satisfaction of all concerned, including Chaman.

The orders booked for shovels were sent to Delhi for supply. The slates could not be sold but some shopkeepers were willing to buy from ready stock. I wrote to my father and he arranged to send at my address 25 cases of those slates, I stored those in our office. Some small shopkeepers in Abdul Rehman Street wanted one or two cases, and I started to deliver those. After Chaman told me that the stationery business was not doing well, we dispensed with the services of our salesman. I stopped demanding any money recompense for my expenses. I did not ask him and he did not pay me on his own. After some time I became penniless and impoverished. But I decided not to ask Chaman for any money. Every month, I had to pay Rs. 35 to Mrs. Pamanto. In addition, I needed some small amount for railway pass and some for my meals. With no money coming from the stationery business, I could not afford to buy some nourishing food for myself and as a result, started getting physically down.

The only source from which I could get some money to sustain my austere existence was to sell the slate cases. Each case was worth Rs. 72 and if I was able to sell even one in a month, I could manage things. But I started living like a pauper. For lunch, I used to go to a small shop making *poories* and *aaloo bhaji* at one *anna* each. Two *poories* for two *annas* and then a full glass of water. Another two for two *annas* and one or two glasses of water and I was satisfied for the day. A cup of tea was served in the office in the afternoon and for the night, I ate very little at some Maharastrian restaurant. In a month or so the meagre intake of food started telling on my health and I started feeling feverish.

Those days five or six young boys from U.P. had come to Bombay and lived in a room somewhere in Parel. Two of them reached some film studio in their hunt for jobs and there, they met Mrs. Pamanto's daughter. Knowing her home address, they started visiting their home and were introduced to me also. One of them was aspiring for the job of a lyric writer and the other for an actor. The poet could sing some of his poems in a good voice. They became friendly with me and told me that they were both socialists.

One day in the evening I was in my room at Mrs. Pamanto's when both those boys came to me. One of them started telling me about a socialist party procession, which they had also joined. They were all carrying their party's flags and shouting slogans. As the procession passed Dhobi Talao and was proceeding towards V.T. station, the police stopped them. The processionists resisted the police by using their flagsticks. Police had to resort to a mild *lathi* charge and tried to catch some of the violent processionists. The boy telling me the story ran inside the St. Xavier College building. He was followed by the police and was caught. He was *challaned* and asked to appear before a magistrate the next day. He said he was sure to be fined by the court which he must pay otherwise, he might be put behind bars. He had no money to pay the fine and he requested for some money from me. I was a little unwell and was lying in my bed. I told him that I had no money, as I was myself very hard up those days. He kept sitting there repeating his request for money again and again. He used to address me as *Nathji*. As the boy was persisting with his request, I felt more and more embarrassed. But he continued pressing me until I got up from my bed, took-off my trousers from the hook on the wall and emptied its pockets showing that all I had with me was less that Rs. 10. He then told me that only Rs. 50 would serve his purpose. He had been hardly known to me for a week or ten days. I told him that I had been honestly telling him that I was very hard up those days and that I had no money. Would he leave me alone. As I said these words, he sat on the floor and caught my feet, imploring for help. I was pushing his hands away from my feet when my eyes fell on the gold ring on one of my fingers. I pulled myself from him, took out the ring from my finger and told him, "Look, I have only this ring left with me. If that can serve your needs, you may take it". I was sure he could not be so mean as to accept the ring but to my utter disgust, he took the ring and thanked me. He told me "If I am fined, I will sell the ring otherwise tomorrow I will return it to you". When he was leaving, I asked him about the location of the court. He told me it was the Cruick Shank Road and if I wanted I could find him there around 1:00 P.M.

Next day, at 1:00 P.M. I reached the court and found that boy along with several others. They were all happy that they had not been fined. The boy came to me and very happily told me that he had been acquitted along with others. I saw he was wearing my ring on his finger. I waited for him to return the ring to me, but he did not do so and promised that he would see me that night. He did come to my room that night with his friend and after laughing, talking, and reciting some poems, both left my room without giving back my ring. I felt confounded but somehow checked myself from asking him for my ring. Next day, they did not come and were absent the second day too. I told Mrs. Pamanto the story of my gold ring. She was very upset with me and told me that I had acted like a big fool. Anyway, she asked her daughter the address of those boys. Her daughter gave me the building number and floor of the room. Mrs. Pamanto pushed me to go there immediately and get back my ring before it was gone. I went there, found the room, and saw the two boys sitting among the four others drinking beer. I called the particular boy out and asked him for my ring. He said, "Sorry *Nathji*, I had to sell it yesterday. I will try to pay you its price as soon as I get the money from the studio". I went back to my room in a sullen mood and told the story to Mrs. Pamanto. After that day, those boys disappeared without a trace just like my gold ring.

In those days I received a letter from Kapur Chand Jain that he would be visiting Bombay for some business and that he would call me at my office. He had also come a few months earlier, and from our office I had taken him to Shere-e-Punjab restaurant for lunch. He liked the dishes very much. He always remembered and used to tell me that never in whole life had he tasted such delicious food.

The day he arrived I had high fever and I could not attend office. I telephoned Chaman and told him that my friend Kapur Chand might come to the office to see me that day. When Kapur Chand arrived in my office and was told about my fever, he got my address from Chaman and reached my room in the evening. He sat on my bed for an hour or so. We talked on various subjects; he left having told me that he was leaving for Ludhiana the next day. I bade him farewell by leaving my sick bed and saying goodbye with an affectionate hug.

As usual, Mrs. Pamanto cleaned my room and redid my bed in the morning. The morning after Kapur Chand had come to see me, when I came back to my room after bath, I found Mrs. Pamanto standing near my bed after completing her job. She appeared to be waiting for me to talk, I was curious to know what the matter was. For the first time, she addressed me in an unusual mood. She showed me a Rs.100 currency note and warned me not to keep my money under my pillow. I became confused by what she said. I asked her, which money and where had she found it? She answered angrily that not only did I do such careless things but I was also very forgetful. She then handed over to me the currency note and left my room murmuring something I could not pick up.

As she left, I sat on my bed and wondered about the hundred rupee note she had handed over to me. Then it struck me. Kapur Chand could judge from my conversation with him that I was not in a good financial condition those days and might have slipped the note under my pillow when he was with me.

It was the beginning of November, 1949. Reverse winds were blowing all over my friendly circle. Jagdish Mitra left Bombay with his family for good. Prakash Dewan told me that he had put his printery on sale, as it was not worthwhile to continue any further. Chaman had already terminated the services of our salesman. Raj Punga was winding up his business as his exports had come down steeply and he had been advised by his in-laws to shift to Ludhiana. He would have their agency for their tapes for western India, which he could handle while living in Ludhiana.

In November end I received a telegram from my father that he was seriously ill and that I must reach Panipat immediately. Showing the telegram to Chaman, I left Bombay in a day or two and reaching Panipat found my father lying in bed and looking very weak. As I sat on his bed, he took me in his arms and started crying loudly. I was frightened as I could never imagine him to be in such a bad mental condition. Involuntarily, I also lost my control and broke down. After sometime we recovered and started talking. My father told me that he had waited for almost two years for my business to develop. His health was not good and he was going down day-by-day. He was not able to look after the large family alone. I told him that I had to wind whatever business I was doing and would be back with him as early as possible. After staying with my parents for two days, I found the condition of my father was getting better. I therefore, took leave and went back to Bombay.

—12—

RETURN TO DELHI—NEW BEGINNINGS

I explained the whole situation to Chaman and requested that he might try to wind up the stationery printing business to enable me to go back. Considering my position he suggested that I do Devidyals marketing job for two weeks and submit them my reports with my resignation, so that they did not face any inconvenience. I did exactly that; simultaneously I tried hard to sell all the unsold stock of school slates lying in our office. I could find a customer who offered to lift all at a very low price. I finalized the bargain, delivered the slates to him and received the money. Chaman was trying to wind-up stationery business as also to find some client for the office space. Anyway, he told me that after finalizing Devidyals' work, I was at liberty to leave. I took final leave of Mrs. Pamanto and thanked her for the very good time, I and several of my friends had, while staying with her. Finally, I left Bombay and reached Panipat in December, 1949.

Reaching Panipat, I found that my father had recovered fully. My mother was calm and quiet as usual. My sisters were working very hard in their studies and teaching in the nursery school, which had become very popular in the area. My three younger brothers were studying in different classes in school. The eldest of them, Satya Paul was also the captain of the school hockey team.

I sat with my father and tried to understand the whole position of the family including the small factory in Karol Bagh, Delhi, which was being jointly run in partnership with his brothers. It was on the government land, but the squatters who were registered refugees from Pakistan, were assured not to be disturbed as long as the government were not in need of that land for their own purposes. On one side of factory shed, uncle Dwarka Das had constructed two bedrooms and was living there with his large family. My father had also started constructing rooms for his family but he was unlucky. He could not complete the roof when the demolishing squad of the Land and Development Office raided and raised his incomplete structure to the ground, causing another loss to the limited money he had. My youngest uncle and aunty with their son and daughter, were living with my Shanti *Bhuaji* in a one room set on the top floor of their house. They were happily managing their household there.

I told my father to allow me to go to Delhi and help in improving the working of the factory. I assured him that with my plans, that business would definitely progress. When that happened, I might hire a house in Delhi and shift all of them there. My father agreed.

I went to Delhi and stayed with my younger uncle. Rai Sahib Tara Chand Chopra, Shanti *Bhuaji's* husband, was on the verge of retirement from his job in the Government of India. He was very well known to all the departmental heads as being a Deputy Secretary in the Union Public Service Commission, he was responsible for the examination of all ICS candidates. In that position, he knew most of the ICS officers. Because of his influence, our whole family received a lot of assistance in establishing themselves in Delhi. He had been a great support to us morally and otherwise. The factory place occupied by us was just opposite his house on the ridge side of Pusa Road.

The factory was actually a small temporary shed under which the partners had set up their tables and chairs. A large open space was being used for working. There were some trees under which the workers did their jobs. The slate-manufacturing unit, which was bought from some other party had been closed. Round-nosed shovels were being produced with old presses and dies purchased from a closed factory owner. I could judge that there was scope for progress in whatever little infrastructure we had. I expressed my views to both the uncles. First of all, I wanted to start the dies for square shovels for which there was much demand. Before my arrival, the three brothers were not ready to make any investment in tools and machinery. But when I made suggestions for expansion, nobody objected. Madan Lal, my cousin, was also working there, looking after accounts. There were four more employees, Mohinder Singh, a young Ramgarhia carpenter, Chhatoo Ram, an unskilled worker from Eastern U.P. and two more labourers. They were also introduced to me. I asked Mohinder Singh whether he could make a wooden pattern for another type of shovel. He replied that if he was explained or shown what was required, he could make an attempt.

After talking to Mohinder Singh, I told my uncles that we should start with making bending die for a square shovel. The pattern would be made by Mohinder Singh under my direction. I would not ask for money for the development of that die because I already had some money belonging to the firm. I gave them the statement of the accounts for the sale of slates in Bombay. They all were very happy and endorsed my plans whole-heartedly.

I bought one 'Tata' square shovel from the market as also the specification for Railway shovels from the Indian Standards Institution. With the help of these, Mohinder Singh could make the pattern. When we got the die cast and made our first square shovel from it, everybody felt very happy. And all this was managed within the funds I had brought from Bombay. The wooden handles for the shovel blades were received from

Batala, a border town of the Punjab. There, one of our old employees from Sialkot, a Sekhri from our old *mohalla*, was managing the production and supply of these handles.

When our square shovel was ready, I went on a tour, going straight to Bombay. All our customers were very pleased to see my samples and I could book orders for double the quantity than usual. Thus encouraged, we produced, one-by-one, other types of railway shovels to complete their full range as per I.S. Specification. In course of time, we had two sizes each of round, square and Loco shovels. My tours were extended to cover Gujarat and Madras.

When the range of shovels was fully extended, I devoted my attention towards some cycle accessories. Unfortunately, we had no facility in our factory for power nor any proper machinery. But Mohinder Singh, the young carpenter, proved a very good companion to work as per my instructions. As such, we could not only improve our existing presses and dies for shovels but could also manufacture some machines to be operated by hand. Thus we could produce, besides shovels, two types of cycle carriers and a cycle stand in that nondescript factory, which was only one small shed and an uneven hill side. I continued to undertake regular tours to sell our products and was able to earn for our firm a reasonably good name, along with improved profits, in a course of two years.

I worked in our family business for four years. Worked day and night virtually. My cousin, who had been doing accounts, fell ill after his marriage in 1950 and I took over accounts also from him. I did all correspondence, helped the processes of production in the factory, went on tour four times a year and purchased raw materials and accessories whenever the need arose. I could also secure foreign orders for our cycle carrier from Kenya. Before that I put in lot of work in the printing of our stationery and illustrated literature.

Throughout this period, I maintained the best personal relations with my uncles, aunts, their children, my four *Bhuajis* and their families who had all settled in Delhi. Similarly, all of them had a loving relationship with me. As long as my father and our family lived in Panipat, I lived and had my food with uncle Brij Lal, who had been very affectionate throughout. This is a matter of special mention that for more than a year that I lived with him, true to the best Hindu tradition, he did not eat unless he made me eat first.

During this period, there was only one occasion when I felt badly hurt. In the family firm, our elders were the owners and Madan Lal and I were employees, getting the same salary. The firm was getting a small quota of steel from the Directorate of Industries. For this, Madan Lal's brother-in-law, Panna Lal, was helping the firm as he had good connections in the Industries Department. One fine day, uncle Brij Lal told his brothers that Panna Lal could get the quota increased, provided Madan Lal was made a partner in the firm. As I was also standing there, I was stunned to hear this. I was so shocked that I could not hear the response of my father to that statement. When after a few seconds, I regained my equipoise, I told my uncle, "If this proposal is accepted, I will be the only employee left in our family firm. As this is not acceptable to me, I am sorry that I will stop working in it". After saying this, I left the scene deeply frustrated. That proposal did not receive any positive response from the other partners.

In this state of humiliation, a new idea flashed in my mind—could I not try to find out some person to help us in our quota increase. Next day I told uncle that let Panna Lal not help the firm; I would attend to the quota side also.

After a few days, through one of my friends, I could find a person who had direct approach to Mr. Seth, the Director of Industries. An appointment was fixed and I went to see him. I explained our case thoroughly and Mr. Seth appeared convinced of our bonafides. However, he said that, as per rules, our case for increase of quota could not be considered unless we got ourselves registered under the Factories Act. The Director told me that we must apply for increase in quota after getting ourselves registered with the Chief Inspector of Factories, Delhi.

I went back to the factory disappointed and told uncle Brij Lal, all about my meeting with the Director of Industries. Then I submitted our firm's application for registration with the office of the Chief Inspector of factories, Delhi.

As my mind was totally occupied to do something for the steel quota, I was losing all my vigour for the routine factory work. Finally, I decided to go to Calcutta to see the Chief Controller of Steel. It was a desperate act but I was in that mood those days. In my meeting with the Deputy Chief Controller, I submitted my letter with full details of our case. He read that letter and asked me to show him the recommendation of Director of Industries, Delhi. I told him frankly that the Directorate of Industries, Delhi was full of corrupt people; they helped those who bribed them even though they had only their letterheads and no factories. I showed him our pamphlets of shovels and cycle parts as also the export documents of our export of cycle carriers to Nairobi. He looked quite impressed and sympathetic. Wanting to help me, he told me that if he sent my original letter to the Director of Industries, Delhi and asked him to confirm the facts, would I be able to manage their reply. I told him that I would try.

He then called his steno and dictated a D.O. to the Director of Industries, Delhi, in my presence. I came back to Delhi and reported about the meeting I had with the Deputy Chief Controller of Steel. Also that he had sent a D.O. to the Director of Industries, along with my original representation to him.

Within a month of my visit, our firm received a permit for a full wagonload of steel sheet cuttings. I felt much relieved and happy to see the good result of my efforts. Our firm could make a handsome profit out of that deal.

Shanti *Bhuaji*, had also given us their garage for running our business office. Living and working in their house, I developed a special bond of love with her and her children.

All of us had formed a well-knit group, meeting on holidays and in leisure times, laughing, joking, telling humorous stories and titbits. *Bhuaji* was our elder "statesman" giving us love, help and protection. Being one of that group, I felt that I was getting special attention from almost all the members. I realized it only when I shifted to live with my parents. That living at a distance of two miles produced in me something akin to pain. I found myself not so strong as to face it and fell into deep depression that persisted for a year.

In the year 1951 uncle Brij Lal purchased a government-built house in Patel Nagar on cash payment of Rs. 7000. He had also arranged a similar house on rent for me just next to theirs. I then called my parents to Delhi.

The house we took on rent in Delhi was without electricity, and without municipal water connection. It had only a hand operated water pump. The front and back of the house had open compounds with mud floors. The handpump was used for cooking as well as for washing and bathing. Kerosene lamps were used in the night for working and studies. The accommodation was too small for our large family.

From August 1947, till beginning of 1950, our family had lived a nomadic life, going from one place to another. When I came back from Bombay, I found that they were still living there like refugees. I had returned from Bombay as a prodigal son, after having failed and having wasted almost two years of my life. But seeing the plight of the family, I was shaken to the realization of my duties to them as the eldest son of my parents. I made a fresh determination to start again with full vigour to perform well. In Delhi I started working in the family business day and night for nearly two years and succeeded to expand it to a respectable level. But I had exhausted myself and broke down both physically and mentally. In their best judgement, my parents proposed that I should agree to get married. Marriages of my sisters was my first priority. But I failed to achieve this even after so much of hard work. I had completed my twenty ninth year and felt the need of a companion. When my parents told me that there were some offers for my marriage, I agreed to marry. I got married on August 29, 1952.

My marriage was solemnized as a matter of necessity and with a shoestring budget. The family rituals were kept as simple as possible. On the day of my marriage, I had to collect my bridegroom's dress myself. Somehow I had to free myself from other duties, took my cycle and reached the tailor around 3:30 P.M. I collected my dress and carried it home on a hanger. As I reached home, I found everybody was waiting for me, including the *Panditji*. I hurriedly took a bath, put on those clothes, tied a white turban on my head and presented myself before the *Panditji*. All my close friends, Kapur Chand, Onkar, Charanjit, Sukhdev, Jagdish Mitra, Prakash Dewan and V.N. Behal were there. The marriage procession had to walk the distance from our house in Patel Nagar to the bride's house at New Rajender Nagar on that very hot evening. As a fully attired bridegroom with thick *sehra*, I perspired profusely. Seeing me in that state my cousin Balkrishan Puri walked alongside the decorated mare, fanning me with a hand fan all through up to the bride's house. It was a unique gesture and simply unforgettable.

Next day early morning I arrived home with my bride. My old grandmother specially came to me and remarked,

"Vishwanath, you must have donated real pearls in your previous life to get such a good looking wife." Her's were very heart warming words. My grandmother was well known for her knack for using such aphorisms on the right occasions.

Onkar and Charanjit came home and gave presents to my wife. Kapur Chand Jain, who was living in Delhi in those days, was the first to invite us to his house for dinner and we spent our night with them. Before my marriage *Bhabi* Pushpa Chopra had stressed on the point that I must manage to go for a few days to some hill station for a honeymoon.

When Kapur Chand invited us for dinner, he asked us our plans about honeymoon. I looked at him in disbelief as he was the one who knew my financial position better than any other person. But before I could say anything, he put Rs. 300 in my hand. I again looked to him with surprise but he explained that in our export business started at Sialkot, we had supplied a small consignment to Kenya in the month of July 1947. The bill for that was sent for collection through the Lahore Bank of Sialkot. That bank had shifted its head office to Ludhiana by end of July 1947 and wrote to all banks through whom they had negotiated their export bills, to send their payments to their head office shifted to Ludhiana. That small amount of Rs. 1500, the value of our export bill, had been received in Ludhiana. By virtue of my 50% partnership, half of the amount was mine. Out of this amount of Rs. 750 he was to take from me Rs. 450 being the price of the German revolver he gave to me for selling before my going to Madras. The amount of Rs. 300 given to me at that time represented the balance amount due to me.

That amount was a real manna from the heaven and we immediately started arrangements for our honeymoon trip. Deciding to go to Nanital, we reached there travelling first by train and then by bus. We checked in the Elphinston Hotel on the lakeside. It was an old English Man's hotel, very spacious and convenient. The charges were unbelievably low and we were allotted a big suite with a veranda overlooking the lake. We lived there for two weeks—mountaineering, horse riding, boating, photographing. We had a wonderful time there.

We returned to Delhi with a renewed body and mind. Coming back home, I went headlong into my work in the factory with renewed stamina. I found to my pleasant surprise that my wife was more hardworking and regular than I was. Further, she had no demands, no particular wants—she was very modest in spending and believed in conserving money.

Near our home, my cousin Pushpa was living with her husband. As she was very close to me, her husband Balraj Mago too became thick with me. After my marriage, Pushpa, became very friendly with my wife. We used to go for evening walks together. Balraj Mago's sister Raj also accompanied us.

Some time in the month of January 1953, my friend Jagdish Mitra, who lived in New Rajender Nagar, came to meet me at my factory. He enquired if it was possible for us to make some items of steel furniture used in hospitals? He told me that he had to supply three overbed tables to a local hospital and he had a problem in getting those manufactured. I told him that if he could show me one sample of the table, I could perhaps try to help him. In a few days, he came back carrying a sample.

I studied the item thoroughly and decided to call Mohinder Singh who had proved as an ace in my efforts to succeed in execution of all my plans during the last three years in Delhi. But when my eyes fell on Satya Paul, my younger brother who was working as a part time sheet-cutter, I changed my mind and called him. I handed over the sample to him and told him to study the same thoroughly as we had to copy it.

Satya Paul successfully made those tables, and once we got them constructed we got them spray painted and the wheels fixed. Two tables were thus ready as per the sample given to us.

All the three tables were carried to Mitras' shop. As I stood there a gentleman came to Mitras' shop and seeing the tables, enquired from them the source of those furniture items? Mitra introduced them to me and added that I was from Gokal Chand *Trunkanwale* family from Sialkot. The gentleman was Jagdish Singh who knew our family well. He asked me whether we had started manufacturing hospital furniture? I told him frankly that we had done those tables for the first time. We had no knowledge about the other items of hospital furniture. If other items were of a similar type, we might be able to make them also.

The very next day, one Mr. Puri, also from Sialkot, visited me at Pusa Road, and asked whether I could do for them some items of hospital furniture as I had done for Mitras. I told him I could if I was shown the items. He showed me a catalogue, which contained a lot of items like beds, bedside lockers, operation table, screens etc. and marked those he wanted. I told Puri that those illustration did not give any specifications of the materials used in the manufacture. I could understand in case samples were brought to me. He said that it was not possible for him to do that, but he could show me the actual items if I accompanied him to a hospital. I told Satya Paul to go with him with a copy and pencil to make notes of the details of the items shown to him. Puri gave us a list of four items which he wanted us to manufacture for him and showed these to my brother in a hospital.

We were able to produce all those items by working very hard in procuring all the right raw materials, making their gadgets, and painting those by brush but fine enough for acceptance. After the delivery of those items, a bigger order was placed by Puri with the condition that we might supply these after spray-painting them.

With the small supplies made and the next order in hand, we had developed certain confidence. But a serious thought arose in my mind when the entire open space of my father's unit was occupied with the finished goods of the last order. I was an employee of the joint family firm of my father and uncles. The manufacture of the hospital furniture items were done mainly by Satya Paul with tools belonging to that joint family firm at their premises. But in making those I considered that God had provided me with an opportunity to start something of my own separate from the family business. I, therefore, concluded that it would be proper to arrange our own space and tooling if we had to continue to do our separate business.

In compliance with my decision, I found two shops at a place at some distance from Pusa Road, on rent and started the manufacture against the new order there. I had also arranged some elementary working tools and bought a brand new portable spray machine from a disposal goods seller. My wife's savings and an advance from my client helped me to do all this. The new order was successfully supplied from the two hired shops.

It was the middle of 1953. Some more parties approached us with new orders of items like hospital beds which required larger space for working. The two small shops in a residential street proved unsuitable for many reasons. The first was that I had to attend to the new business as well as to my duties in my father's unit. It involved too much of hard work and lot of running about on my cycle. The other problem was that the residents of the street started complaining that their sleep was disturbed when we worked at night under gaslights. It was summer and those poor people had to sleep in the street outside their rooms. The third was that the two shops proved very inadequate. I therefore, started looking for some space on the ridge near our family's business premises. At the backside of my uncle's residence, there was a low area, forming a tiny valley, with accumulated rainwater at its bottom. I assessed that if we could clear the area around the water-pond of its small rocks and bushes, we might get some space to do our work.

I decided quickly and put two coolies with a pickaxe and a *phowrah* to clear the rocks and bushes. It took them two days to do their job of creating some workable space. I shifted all I had in those two shops, as swiftly as possible in two tempos.

One or two more small orders were also received from some new parties. To work in the open area without any cover whatsoever was very difficult. It was the month of June and the summer heat was too much to bear for any person who was expected to work eight to ten hours a day. Although we had only two coolies and one toolmaker, but still they were humans. Satya Paul managed by putting the table of the toolmaker and the drilling machine in the shade of the two trees. I arranged one or two tarpaulins and fixed those on top of bamboos to provide some more shade. Somehow, the work was started there without any problem from the side of the government. The whole area at the ridge was under the control of Land and Development office. The ridge was a reserved area, use of which was not allowed. Our elders' factory and the small residence of my uncle were put up there in 1948 with great difficulty. Whatever existed there was being tolerated because all our families were registered refugees in Delhi. In such a situation, our occupation of more space there was possible only as we were working without any new sheds and exactly at the back of my uncle's house. Further that area being much lower than the road, was not visible to those who passed by.

During this time, I had an awareness that the Merciful God's Hand was protecting me. I felt His Grace in the slow but steady improvement in the entire environment around me. Our first baby son was born on August 9, 1953. This brought a waft of fresh air and a source of joy in the family especially to my father.

Around the year 1899, when my father was born, my grandfather had to work very hard to avail of an opportunity, thrown in his way, to manufacture steel trunks in Sialkot. I followed his example in 1953, after birth of my first son, I worked day and night to take advantage of an opportunity to manufacture hospital steel furniture in Delhi. As the trunk manufacturing changed the fortune of his family, the same way, my venture into the manufacturing of hospital furniture changed my family's fortune.

—13—

FRUITLESS RANGOON VISIT

Around the time of my marriage, my friend Kapur Chand had started a new business of manufacturing tooth-brushes in Delhi. He was one of those friends who continued his close relations with me after the partition. He was also a great help in my new venture. One of those days, he talked to me about an international tender for the purchase of a huge quantity of tooth brushes by the Burmese Government for their Defence Canteens. He filled that tender in consultation with me. When the tenders were opened in the Burmese Embassy in New Delhi, the comparative statement showed best chances for his company.

I accompanied Kapur Chand to see the purchase officer of the Burmese Embassy. He told us that all the tenders and samples had been forwarded by them to the Defence Headquarters in Burma. He advised that we might follow-up our case in Rangoon. Kapur Chand asked me whether I could do that job for their company by going to Rangoon to follow-up the case. Besides the expenses of the Rangoon visit, I would be getting commission if they got the order. It appeared to me an attractive offer and I therefore accepted it. Then I talked to my father who concurred with me.

My newly started factory had not yet come out of the pangs of its birth. It was taken care by my brother Satya Paul, during my stay in Rangoon. Before leaving I acquainted him with all our customers and raw material suppliers at Loha Mandi. He assured me that he would do his best and I may go ahead. My wife with her new born baby shifted to her parents till the time of my return.

Kapur Chand's partner gave me an introductory letter to their family friends, Chopra brothers who were doing very well in Rangoon. I left Delhi and reached Rangoon safely. I stayed there in a moderate hotel. It was my first foreign trip and my first air journey.

The first thing I did in Rangoon was to visit the Chopras. I gave them the introductory letter and explained the purpose of my Rangoon visit. I was briefed very well by Achint Ram Chopra, the elder of the two brothers, about the Burmese people in general. I was told that they were happy-go-lucky type, easygoing and excessively self-indulgent. Those who could afford, had half a dozen regular wives plus numerous mistresses. During my stay I could see the difference in the style of living between Indians and the Burmese.

I went to the Defence Headquarters and met the captain incharge of the purchase department. I explained to him the purpose of my visit and also hinted in my talk that I was ready to co-operate with him if he helped me in securing that order. He confirmed that all the tenders and samples were received in their office but they had not yet been taken up for consideration. He assured me that he would manage to highlight my offer while putting up the case to his boss and advised me to address a letter to the Chief Purchase Officer. He told me to see him again the following week. When I did that, he showed me the file with his remarks in our favour. I invited him to my hotel and entertained him. When I asked him what I might have to pay him, he replied that after he handed over a copy of the order to me, I might pay him Rs. 2000. I told Chopra about my conversation with the Captain and the money that he expected me to pay him. At that Mr. Chopra handed over Rs. 2000 to me in cash.

The captain appeared to me a good man. I tried to remain in contact with him as best as I could. He once invited me to his house where there was some celebration. Many Buddhist monks, including one from Italy, were present there. They recited some Buddhist *Shlokas* followed by a big feast in which many non-vegetarian dishes were served. The monks were made to eat first. I was surprised to see the Buddhists and their monks eating non-vegetarian dishes with relish.

Anxious to know the result, I used to contact the captain on phone almost two times a week, to know the progress of the tender. I had been writing regularly to Kapur Chand apprising him of the position. It had been more than two weeks without any concrete information. Thus my stay was getting prolonged without any other job for me to attend to.

I confined myself to my hotel room reading books, writing reports for Kapur Chand of the day-to-day developments or writing weekly letters to my wife whose letters I used to receive every week. In the evening I used to go to the 'Jetty' which was like our Bombay Chowpati and Gateway of India combined. It had many stalls and hand driven shopping carts, selling mostly the eatable or some toys for the children. Inside the sea there were several small ships and ferries, some of them anchored. A small harbour building was also there. The 'Jetty' was a place full of people of several nations, enjoying their evening with friends or children.

It was then that I remembered home, my wife and the newly born son. My son was only 40 or 45 days old when I had to leave for Rangoon. I could not sleep for long hours. I used to take out my wife's letters and start reading them one by one. Then I noted that she writes beautiful letters full of loving words, as also many appropriate film songs. Reading and reading and reading I used to fall asleep.

One of the days at the 'Jetty', a boy confronted me with a broad smile on his face addressing me by my first name. It was a very pleasant surprise for me to see Dharam Vir, my friend from Ram Talai *Mohalla* of Sialkot. He introduced me to his cousin Ranvir who was with him. Exchanging information about the reasons of our being in Rangoon ended in Dharam Vir lovingly dragging me to their house. Their house was run by Ranvir and his parents. Ranvir's family was exceptionally affectionate. All the family members, from Ranvir's father and mother to their children were affectionate, warm and congenial, having a generous disposition. On the very first day of my visit and knowing that I belonged to Ram Talai *Mohalla* of Sialkot, they came closer to me as near relatives. They at once put me at ease, pressing me that I had to visit them daily in the evening. Having told them the purpose of my visit in Rangoon and my dealings with Chopra Brothers, I mentioned that I had received Rs. 2000/- from them. Chopras were well known to the proprietors of the toothbrush manufacturing company, which I represnted. Ranvir's father asked me whether I had been told by Chopras how much would have to be paid in Delhi against my loan of Rs. 2000? Surprised at the question, I replied that nothing of that subject was hinted to me. The elderly man advised me to talk it over to Chopras. I felt hesitant to do so as the money was paid to me on behalf of someone else. Ranvir's father told me that we might have to pay Rs. 1400 in Delhi because of the differnece in exchange rate. In case I felt hesitation in talking about it, then I might return that money to Chopras, and get the same from him and pay their man in Delhi Rs.1400. And the kind old man actually paid me Rs. 2000 from his safe.

It had then been more than a month of my stay in Rangoon. The decision on tender was nowhere in sight. I was told that the file was lying with the Army Chief. It was a big logjam for me. Diwali arrived and I had to pass my time in Rangoon. Though I missed my home, my wife and our child, I got good relaxation by the stimulating entertainment in the evening with

Ranvir's family. Diwali in Rangoon was a wonderful experience for me. It was celebrated with such gaiety, as I had never seen anywhere in India. All the streets of Indian shops were decorated with coloured lights. The whole area of the footpaths was usurped for laying tables with multifarious snacks. Majority of the dishes served were non-vegetarian. Every Indian, irrespective of any consideration of caste or creed, was welcomed and served with open handed hospitality. With the Diwali festivities over, Rangoon still remained a very gay town, very different from any Indian city. The people had different features, a different way of life. Quite a large part of those who moved about on the roads or were found at picnic spots, at restaurants and in the cinema houses were Buddhist monks with shaven heads and saffron robes. Those monks in Burma did all sorts of good and bad things like the average people.

In the city there were several hotels which were known for a special type of cooking. My friends took me to a hotel outside the city, run by a Chinese, where fresh roasted chickens were the speciality. The "fresh" there had a distinct meaning. We sat on the tables, layed in the outside lawn of the hotel, and gave our order for chickens. Soon after we heard the sound of "chi-chi-chi" from the hotel mess. I was told it was the sound of chickens for our order. Live chickens were thrown into a big pot of boiling water. They would be taken out only when they were boiled enough for further treatment and for service. It was a startling experience.

After more than seven weeks of incarceration in Rangoon, the captain phoned me to tell that the purchase against our tender had been dropped and that fresh tenders would be floated. Totally exhausted and depressed, I informed Kapur Chand by telegram, took leave from my Sialkot friends, met Chopras to return their money with thanks and took my flight to Calcutta, the very next day. From Calcutta I boarded the first available mail train to Delhi. Thus ended my first foreign adventure. I was depressed. Kapur Chand and his partners were also disappointed but it was as ordained by Providence. Nobody could do anything.

When I attended to my business, I found it in shambles. Satya Paul was totally devastated. He had been very shabbily treated by a big company whom he had supplied a lot of goods. Everyday they called him to their office in Darya Ganj with a promise to pay, made him wait and then told him that no payment had been received by them in their registered post. My coming back relieved him from the other jobs and he could revert to production work.

In course of time, and with a lot of efforts, we got released from the cruel clutches of that company. We had to put in lot of hard work to reorganize our infant manufacturing unit. I took up all the responsibilities of outside jobs and allowed Satya Paul to devote his full attention and energies to the production side. In the year 1954, we worked day and night. At the end of the financial year, I roughly estimated our gains and confidently told my mother and father that they might devote their attention towards arranging the marriages of my sisters. I had already resigned my job with my father's firm, sometime before I left for Rangoon. Before doing that, I had completed all the accounts and fulilled all my responsibilities in that firm.

In the year 1955, we put up a very small working shed with wooden *ballies* and old corrugated sheets. The height of the shed was kept low so that it was not visible from outside. On one side, exactly behind the residential quarters of my uncle, I got a small space created by levelling the ground and managed to put up a cement floor there. On that floor, I got a small office constructed with four walls of wooden planks, and the top of corrugated steel sheets. The office was good enough to accomodate two office tables and six chairs.

As our business was flourishing, one fine morning a young and handsome boy named Gupta, came to our factory. He introduced himself as a private agent to the Jammu and Kashmir Chief Minister, Bakshi Ghulam Mohammed, and said that he was on a mission for the purchase of huge quantities of hospital furniture for new hospitals being constructed in Jammu and Kashmir. He offered to introduce me to the Chief Minister if I accompanied him to Jammu. From our office telephone, he made a call to the State Secretariat and talked to Bakshi *sahib* on his secret phone. I considered it a good opportunity and accompanied the young man to Jammu by a mail train leaving in the night. On reaching Jammu we checked in a hotel at the Uttam Cinema Road. Early next morning, as we were sitting in the restaurant for our breakfast, a bearer came and told me that the owner of the hotel wanted to have a word with me. As I entered his cabin, a young, handsome boy stood up from his seat and respectfully asked me if my name was Vishwa Nath. At my affirmation he bowed before me with folded hands and told me that he was a *swayamsewak* and he knew me very well. He then told me that Gupta was a big cheat and asked me to get rid of him as soon as possible. After we had our breakfast. Gupta took me to the State Secretariat. Reaching there, he spoke to the gatekeeper asking to be permitted to go in to see Bakshi *sahib*. The gatekeeper replied that the Chief Minister *sahib* was in Srinagar. Gupta turned to me and said that we might have to proceed to Srinagar, but I told him that he had misled me and I would not go anywhere else with him. I went back to the hotel thanked the hotel owner profusely and left for Delhi. I told my brothers the story of the fraudulent person with whom I got entangled and how was I saved in time by the Almighty God through a *swayamsewak* from Jammu.

NEW ENTERPRISE WITH A FRIEND

Viswa Nath Behal, with whom I had worked in the same office

and developed close relations during my Bombay adventure had settled in Delhi and was doing very well in his export business of handicrafts. The cordial relations between us, were continued in Delhi. One day in the year 1956, he visited me in my factory and made an offer for expanding that business into a full surgical line under a separate constitution in association with him. He added that he knew about the surgical business through one of his closest pre-partition friends, P.S. Kant who had been working in the Imperial Surgical Company as their Bombay representative agent.

I also had been in contact with the surgical dealers of Delhi who had been doing very well in that business. I told Behal that I was ready and felt that if we could convince Kant, who was still working for Imperial Surgical Company, to join our firm as a partner, it would be a sure success. As per my information, Kant commanded the topmost position as an agent in the surgical trade. The proposal was to start a private limited firm with equal shares for me and Behal and me to take charge to run it. I had known Behal as a very astute business head with qualities of making quick decision and executing them with dedication and hard work. Within a few days of our decision, we could meet and persuade Kant for joining our new business as a shareholder. We put up a private limited company named, Dipak Agencies Private Ltd., and hired office space in the business locality at Asaf Ali Road. Kant, who had been living in Indore with his family for over a decade and had been serving Imperial Surgical Company for over two decades, managed to join us as a working director after about two months of our meeting. The company had three directors, V.N. Behal, V.N. Sekhri and P.S. Kant. Behal was the investor and the other two were working directors.

Thus Behal once again came close to me after our first association in Bombay in 1948. In the new company I had the overall responsibility to run the show. Behal, Kant and I were the three equal shareholders. I was known in whole of the surgical market as a manufacturer of hospital furniture. When the market people saw me and Kant joining hands to form a new surgical supply company, it created a sensation.

Kant booked his first order from Gwalior and arrived in Delhi to help make the purchases. I accompanied him to the surgical market where I found that Kant knew almost every dealer. The purchases against our order were made and Kant carried all the goods personally and delivered those to the Gwalior Hospital with our bill. He collected the payment of that bill and went back to Indore. On his way he stopped at a few other towns, booked orders from the hospitals there and posted those to me with detailed instructions. On the basis of those instructions I was able to make purchases and supply those goods to different hospitals. From the nature of the orders booked by Kant, till then, I understood that there were lots of imported instruments. Jagdish Mitra advised me that we could import against our own requirements and for securing import licenses we might seek the help of an import trade expert named K.K. Chhibber. I met Chhibber and he got us an import license in the name of our company. During my meetings with him, I found Chhibber a person of high IQ and sincere in his dealings. I spoke about him to Behal and proposed that such a person would be very useful if we could have his services exclusively for our company. I called him to our office to meet Behal. He impressed Behal also and we took him as our fourth shareholder. Kant concurred with our move.

At the time of making changes in the constitution to include K.K. Chhibber, Behal withdrew his own name from the Company and inducted his elder brother Mr. P.N. Behal. He first asked me whether I had any objection to that change. I understood that Dipak Agencies had not come upto V.N. Behal's expectations and gave my assent to his proposal.

That change brought two whole time workers in our Delhi office. Chhibber knew the surgical trade very well. P.N. Behal came as a raw hand, with no experience in the surgical line. But he was a sociable person, a hard worker with a desire to learn and succeed. So both K.K. Chhibber and P.N. Behal who wanted very much to settle in their lives, worked hard. In due course of time the company had three travelling directors which resulted in very impressive results. With their combined efforts the company could expand its business rapidly.

Started in 1956, our firm, in a few years, reached a position where it was counted among the top in our trade. All the four of us had very good rapport. With two directors managing the office, I could give more time to my factory. The bank operations remained with me upto 1962. V.N. Behal's initial investment, which never touched the figure of one lakh, remained in the company. With the improvement of turnover and profits, it became possible for V.N. Behal to withdraw all his investment without causing the least difference to the regular functioning of the company.

With prosperity, certain dormant weaknesses of my colleagues came to the fore. The basic principles of business and ethics were compromised, and that resulted in creating differences between the two Delhi directors, on a personal level. Their frictions and conflicts increased and in 1964, K.K. Chhibber and P.N. Behal felt that they could not work together and decided to part. My personal intervention could not mend their rift although they both held me in good regard. Kant was called from Indore. A decision was made for separation. Accounts were immediately prepared and meetings held at my residence. All of us decided for mediation and Kant, Behal and Chhibber chose me as a mediator. I placed the details of the accounts and the amount of total assets before all. Each of them signed the statements in token of their approval. Behal and Kant expressed their desire to run the firm. K.K. Chhibber looked to me for support. Being the arbitrator, I could not do that, although in my opinion, Chhibber's contribution in the progress of the company was the foremost. But he needed me to join him so that we could bid to take over the company. In my heart I knew that Chhibber's regard for me surpassed that of the others. He used to say that although he was elder to me but he considered me as the duplicate of his real father who had died long ago.

When he needed my support the most and could not get it from me, he felt very frustrated and while opting out, he started crying. After some time, he calmed down and the meeting was resumed. I told both Kant and Behal that as Chhibber had opted to go out, his dues must be paid within two days. Behal had come prepared with his cheque book; he wrote a cheque in Chhibber's name for the full amount due to him and handed it over to me to pass it to Chhibber. When everything was settled and Chhibber also became normal, I asked them all whether they were convinced of the correctness of the accounts and the personal statements of share holders before them? Both Behal and Kant said yes and thanked me for my mediation. I then told them that I had to make a request. On the figures agreed to by all of them, I also begged to withdraw my name from the company. Both Behal and Kant disagreed but I insisted and told them that my decision was irrevocable as I had some private reasons of my own which did not allow me to continue. I requested them to settle my account as per figures arrived on that day. If needed they could take their own time in paying me my dues.

My association with Dipak Agencies lasted eight long years. I must add here that during my tenure in Dipak, I enjoyed the maximum respect and regard from all my partners. All of them were older than me by 2 to 3 years, yet each one of them treated me as their elder. I never had any difference or dispute with anybody and had been very close to all of them.

Today, as I write this, all the three have passed away. Kant was the first to go. He was hardly 50 or 51 when he died of heart attack in the year 1970. Then P.N. Behal passed away sometime in early 90s. Third was Chhibber to go. But all were very kind to me and I have the best and sweetest memories of them all.

—14—

THE FAMILY BUSINESS PROSPERS – MY FIRST VISIT TO LONDON

A few months before the birth of my first son, Sudhir, in August 1953, I was able to start my own business, Paul Engineers. A few months after the birth of my first daughter, Geeta, in February 1956, I started Dipak Agencies (P) Ltd. as a promoter share holder. Both these enterprises were progressing well, when my second son Pradeep was born in October 1957 and my second daughter, Reshmi, was born in October 1959.

Paul Engineers was started by me and Satya Paul, who had stopped studying. Raj Paul, my third brother after passing his matriculation joined us in Paul Engineers. He was also asked to look after another small firm started by me for manufacturing of steel chairs, tables etc. in the name of Sunshine Steel Industries. When my fourth brother Govinder Paul quit studies, he too joined our business. Govinder Paul filled an important gap in our growing business, that of liaison job. Whereas I was able to control all other aspects of business, I failed in the liaison work with government offices for steel quotas and import licenses. Govinder Paul took from me that job with full confidence.

He proved a hit in the liaison job. So much so that in the office of the Directorate of Industries, Delhi, where the inspectors used to harass us no end, he was, in a short time, considered a formidable personality. He did not care for the inspectors in that office. The assistant and deputy directors were also ignored and he would go direct to the Director and got his work done. Watching him and the force by which he conducted himself, all the inspectors, assistant and deputy directors started looking at him with awe and sought his help in getting their problems with their administration, sorted out. In the same manner, he created an impact in the import-export office. He had tremendous guts and a presence of mind to enter the room of the top man in any government office and get his job done. With his coming into our business, this weak side of our firm had been taken care of and we made rapid progress.

Before the start of Dipak Agencies, Paul Engineers had become known in the entire surgical market for supply of any hospital furniture item. After my joining Dipak Agencies, the prestige of Paul Engineers had gone up. Both these firms were asked to become members of the Surgical Manufactures and Traders Association. Soon after joining the association I was elected as the General Secretary of the Association and held that position for many terms. I was also the promoter of Surgical Manufacturers Cooperative Society which was able to get allotment of Industrial plots for many of its members at a very prestigious site. I maintained very cordial relations with all the surgical dealers.

In 1955, my youngest sister who had done her M.A.Ed, was proposed by a young boy, who had been introduced to our family very recently. He had been a co-student of my sister Prakash, in the Gandhi Ashram, Wardah. The boy belonged to a very respectable, well-to-do family and was working as a Director of Education Nai Talem, Faridabad. They had their own houses in Faridabad and Delhi. The proposal also included that the marriage would be solemnised at an early date. It was a proposition, which needed serious consideration in the family as the early marriage of the youngest meant jumping over the two elder sisters. It was likely to affect the morale of the elder girls and could give them a feeling of rejection. Daman was also not agreeable for marriage before her elder sisters were married. It appeared that my sister, Prakash, had assured the boy in private that their proposal would be accepted. Finally, with the concurrence of the two elder sisters we prevailed upon Daman to agree. The marriage was fixed, and was performed with the pleasure and happiness of all concerned. It was again the Almighty's blessings that everything was done with elegance and style which earned appreciation from everyone.

Later in that year, my sister Prakash was also married. Hers was a very queer type of marriage.

The boy lived in Jalandhar with his widowed mother and a younger sister. They were refugees from West Pakistan where the boy's father was a very respected landlord. Unfortunately, during the family's migration to India, they were attacked by an armed Muslim mob, who murdered their father and the boy's younger brother. The boy reached India carrying his badly wounded mother and sister, who could be saved with proper medical treatment. The boy had done his LLB and was doing some sports business there. I went to meet the boy with my mother and wife and we liked him. He was a *khadi* wearing young man with spiritual views. My sister too wore *khadi* and held very unconventional and socialist views. A meeting was arranged between the two and both agreed to marry. My sister then told my father that she would carry nothing by way of dowry. We argued with her that such conditions from the bride's side were not practical but she stuck to her principle and told us that she could handle the matter with her in-laws herself if we found it embarrassing to talk about it. So she talked to the boy and they both agreed. My sister's insistence was on "no dowry" but the boy added to it "no *baraat*" also. The boy's stipulation of "no *baraat*" was not acceptable to his widowed mother. She, like all Hindu mothers, had some genuine aspirations to see her only son with *Sehra* and riding a white mare. The controversy was not being resolved and my parents had to go to Jalandhar to help in arriving at some decision. I was waiting for the news from my father about the outcome but instead I received an express telegram from him, reading "marriage fixed for tomorrow. Come with Prakash". I was shocked to read the impracticable and brief message. There were no details and there was no time for thinking and no one to consult. In my totally confused state I sent the same message home to Prakash asking her to be ready to leave for her marriage. I could only think of purchasing two kilograms of mixed sweets and left with Prakash by the afternoon train. We reached Jalandhar at night and went to our maternal uncle's house. As we reached there, we found two or three gentlemen from the groom's side discussing about the marriage formalities with my parents. The discussion was all the more astonishing. We understood that they had come there to tell *pitaji* that he might prevail upon the groom to accept his mother's wish and agree for putting on a *sehra* and riding the mare at the head of the procession of *baraatis*. My father told the visitors that he could not intervene in their family matter. They left with a promise to inform us the next morning by 8:00 whether there would be a *baraat* or not. I was dumbfounded to hear that. Next day was the marriage. Till around 10:00 P.M. there was a doubt whether there would be a *barat* or not. If it was decided in favour of *baraat*, how would the arrangements for its reception be made? Nobody could suggest a way out of the tricky situation. My father suggested that we might eat our dinner and sleep. Prakash said boldly that we should not bother at all. If it was something which we could not do, we would tell them frankly that it was not possible.

We got up very early next morning and again started talking on the same issue. Till 9:00 A.M., there was no message. My maternal uncle suggested that we should go to the boy's house to find out. As we left our quarter, a man from the groom's side met us on the way to tell us that there would be a *baraat* of 20 people and they would arrive at our place in a procession between 7:00 to 8:00 P.M. Both of us stood where we were, and without losing our balance, we started counting the jobs to be attended. *Halvai*, the provisions, tents and crockery, some decoration items. It was a Sunday and the tent shops were closed. I asked uncle whether he knew some *Halvai*. He mentioned Phool, a very good one and from Sialkot. We both reached his shop. But he was not there. We were informed that he was working for the marriage of a daughter of Seva Singh of Sialkot. The son of Seva Singh was my class fellow in college. We went to their house, met my class fellow, found out from him that his sister was to be married three days later. When I explained to him about the immediate marriage of my sister, he called Phool and graciously told him to leave their work to some of his assistants and go with us for the evening party. Phool knew me very well and asked us the details of the party and the dishes we might want to serve. When we told him that the marriage party would be only 20 persons and maximum twenty from our side, he assured us that our work would be done in time. He then called one of his assistants, gave him our house address and told him to reach there with the required number of cooking pots and a chullah (an open top coal oven). Phool then made us write the provisions, spices and vegetables needed for the party.

We first went to the provisions shop in the main bazaar and gave the list of provisions and spices, telling the shopkeeper to keep those ready for us to be collected after an hour or so. We then rushed to the place where we could buy fresh vegetables, loaded those in a rickshaw who promised to carry these to our address. From there we went to the tent shops, and found all the market was closed but outside one shop, there was a labourer sitting. When we told the man our immediate requirement of tents, crockery and furniture for the same day marriage, he told us that he knew the house of the owner and accompanied us there. The owner, hearing about our immediate need, took our list of articles, promised to send everything immedietly to our place and arrange to fix everything in time. He also arranged a *Pandit* for us.

I had given uncle Rs.2000 and he managed everything required. Coming home, we called two local scavengers and told them to do their best to clean and cover the open drainage in front of our house. Uncle had to go to the bazaar again to buy readymade Choorha (Ivory bangles, the maternal uncle had to give to his niece at the time of her marriage) for the size of Prakash's wrists. Inside the four walls there was enough vacant space in the compound to accommodate 40 chairs and tables that were ordered. Tents, shamianas, *Vedi* provisions and *Halvai* all arrived and before 7.00 p.m. everything was under control. The *baraat* came with more than thirty persons and were served well. The marriage ceremony was performed between 3 to 4.00 a.m. The bride was ceremoniously sent off in the morning. Everyone, big or small, in the family heaved a sigh of relief. I sat down, tired to my bones in an intensely reflective mood. The Almighty God, my Great Benefactor and Protector, was always there to do for me such impossible things. What had been accomplished was no less than a miracle.

By the grace of God, all the arrangements were made and the wedding took place without any inconvenience or problem.

A year after this, my third sister Kamla, also M.A.Ed was married to an Excise Inspector who had his own house in Gurgaon near the house of my eldest sister, Shakuntla.

We continued to live in the same rented quarter. My three sisters left after their marriages and the space created by their departure was filled by my growing brothers. The house remained as crowded as before. But we had made some improvements like getting electricity, the municipal water connection, improvement of toilet facilities, paving of both the compounds with bricks and raising the outer walls.

With the regular growth of our business, we could extend the area of our working by clearing some hillside and were also getting bold to put up some temporary sheds. But all our production work was in the open with no secret. That position encouraged some of our customers to copy our manufacturing processes and start their own units to manufacture hospital furniture for their own requirement. One of my cousins who happened to live in the two room residence at that place had secretly started his factory for the same items. He not only copied us but also did some unethical deeds. Those developments were a serious cause for my anxiety. Some of our customers took advantage of that development and started delaying payment of goods supplied by us to them. I, therefore, started thinking seriously to find some solution to the problem.

In the year 1960, I happened to see a tender advertised in the newspaper for supply of shovels to the Government of India, Defence Department. I got the tender and also purchased the specifications and drawings of the shovel. Shovel was the main business of the firm run by my father and uncles. I took the tender to my father and uncles and asked them whether they were interested to quote. They saw the papers and told me that they were not interested in doing government business. Moreover, the type of shovel advertised had never been produced by them. They allowed me to fill the tender if I liked. Considering that it might be an opportunity given by God to come out of the difficulties we were facing in doing business with dealers, I filled that tender. I was sure in my mind that our family was growing larger and my Maker in the heavens was creating additional avenues of income for its sustenance. Our firm succeeded in getting the first government contract for the supply of 33400 pieces of defence shovels in the year 1961.

In the month of May, my younger brother, Satya Paul got married. I solved the accommodation problem by vacating my room for the newly married couple; I shifted with my family to a rented place near our house. After living in the neighbourhood of my parents for two or three months, I shifted to the vacant first floor flat of my *bhuaji* at Pusa Lane. Exactly after 10 months Raj Paul's marriage took place. Again the new couple's problem was solved when Satya Paul and his wife shifted with me in the Pusa Lane flat.

Raj Paul got married in March 1962. A few months after his marriage, we received a much bigger order of the same type of shovels, required on top priority basis due to the Indo-China war. Wagon loads of steel were supplied to us direct from the producers like Tatas, on defence priority. Inspectors were posted in our factory for quicker clearances of the goods. Working at the same jungle land, without proper sheds and without power, we were able to fulfil the defence needs at a speed at which even companies like Tata Agrico could not match. We were placed in the Hand Tools Advisory Committee of the Government of India. Our name was included in the approved list of the Directorate General of Supplies and Disposals (DGS & D) contractors. I was selected a member of the Minimum Wages Committee of the Delhi Government. I continued to be The General Secretary of Federation of Delhi Small Scale Industries for many years. We purchased our first car in 1962. The same year I purchased two industrial plots in the Modern Industrial Estate, Bahadurgarh, one in the name of Raj Paul and the other in Inder Mohan Chopra's name. In 1964, before I opted out from the directorship of Dipak Agencies, I purchased a residential plot of 2533 sq. yards in West Punjabi Bagh.

How was it happening without our planning and almost automatically? The doer was none other than my all time Benefactor. I felt it and silently bowed my head to Him.

Sometime after Raj Paul was married, I sensed that there had developed some reservation between Raj Paul and some other members living in the Patel Nagar house. I did not like any unpleasantness to happen in our family and started looking for some solution. One day, I read in a paper that the Punjab government was constructing industrial estates in some towns near the Pakistan border, and were offering liberal incentives to encourage people to settle in those areas. I applied in the name of Sekhri Brothers. in the industrial estates at Batala in Gurdaspur district. We were allotted a unit on instalment basis for the manufacture of stainless steel Hospital equipment. Raj Paul was sent there to manage it.

He rented a house there and took Gulshan Rani, his wife there. He was able to create there a circle of good friends and started living happily there. His first baby girl was born there.

Everything was going smooth there till Pakistan attacked India in 1965 and Batala had the misfortune to be one of the places where bombs had fallen. The war did not last long and after cessation of hostilities, we decided to shift our Batala factory to some other industrial estate in Punjab. It was not permitted and after a lot of effort we got permission to shift our machinery from our factory in Batala to Bahadurgarh subject to the surrendering of our unit and foregoing whatever had been paid by us towards the price of that unit.The Sekhri Brothers factory was shifted from Batala to Bahadurgarh.

For the past year or two I was considering to go into exports. An opportunity came our way when the Government of India participated in an industrial exhibition in Tripoli in Libya. Paul Engineers was allotted space there. Govinder Paul was sent to attend the fair. He got no response in the exhibition. However, after the exhibition, he managed to reach London, on his own and wrote to me from there.

Govinder Paul came back to Delhi after spending more than a month in London and brought with him big orders for Garden tools set, garden chairs and vice-grip wrenches, alongwith samples of all those items. By booking such big orders for many new items, he virtually brought to us a big challenge. All those items of his orders were sophisticated and required proper machinery and premises to produce them. The production of all items was started after approval of samples by our foreign buyers; who also opened their Letters of Credit. But very little could be produced within the time stipulated in the orders. For an unorganized unit like ours, to produce so many new items of export quality and deliver those in time was not possible. Garden tools sets and garden chairs were for the summer season and as we were late, the parties refused to accept the goods and did not extend their letters of credit. Our firm was left in a hot soup, with huge stocks of finished and unfinished goods.

The tin shed that was erected for manufacturing, was converted for storing those stocks. During the time we had been busy in production of export items, we could not attend to the DGS & D tenders and therefore we had no other work to do. But as a result of the Indo-Pak war of 1965, we succeeded in obtaining shovel contracts expeditiously from DGS & D. We switched our production towards those orders immediately. More contracts of camp furniture were also placed on us. We were again overloaded with work and began working day and night forgetting about our misadventure in exports.

In 1967, Punjab was divided into three states viz; Punjab, Himachal Pradesh and Haryana. Sekhri Brothers factory at Bahadurgarh fell in the Haryana State. This unit had to undergo another shake-up. Raj Paul had been running it alone. I felt he needed some help and asked Govinder Paul to give some of his time to work for that unit in the liaison job.

Govinder succeeded in doing a marvellous job for Sekhri Brothers. He secured a very big import license for stainless steel sheets for that unit which had also started manufacturing steel utensils. With his help the unit became well off and was able to secure a big showroom on the main Darya Ganj road.

In the year 1967, Paul Engineers had received good DGS & D contracts. The business was good in this firm but all other smaller units were not running properly. Inder Mohan Chopra, our brother-in-law, was partner in every other firm except Paul Engineers. At that time it occurred to me that we were living comfortably but Inder Mohan could not live that way. His children appeared to be leading a somewhat different standard of life. This thought would just not leave me. I spoke to my parents and suggested that Inder Mohan be taken as a partner in Paul Engineers. Both disagreed with me and asked me to help him more to develop the other units which were under his control. But when I insisted they did not oppose. At that time I did not consider it necessary to consult my brothers. I directly spoke to Mr Relan, our C.A. He showed surprise at my suggestion for the reconstitution of Paul Engineers, but did what I said, only asking me whether I had given the matter my full consideration.

Sometime after the reconstitution, the business of Paul Engineers improved further. I decided to fulfil a long cherished wish of our parents and planned to construct our residence on the plot purchased in 1964. Considering winter *Navratras* of 1968 as an auspicious time, I managed to start the construction. I had discussed about the requirements of our four families with my architect thoroughly. The plot had been bought in the name of four brothers represented by me alone, in compliance with the Punjabi Bagh Housing Society's rule.

I started devoting most of my time on the construction attending to each and every minor detail. Since I took very keen and impassioned interest in the construction from day one, the house turned out to be an elegant building.

Govinder Paul's marriage was performed at the new house in the winter of 1970 when families of all four brothers also shifted there alongwith our parents.

A marriage in the family and the construction of a big house created a serious financial crunch, but somehow we could manage to pull out.

Some new contracts were thrown our way, and specially favourable relationship came to be developed without our directly soliciting them and without our fully understanding their import. Near the end of the year 1971, a very large DGS & D contract, almost beyond our dreams, was placed on us for defence hospital beds.

Our family had been granted ample affluence by our merciful Master during the war years. A building of a large two storeyed house and a highly dignified marriage of Govinder Paul were the one sign of our comfortable life. The other sign of His grace was the fulfilment of the wish of our parents to enjoy witnessing the marriage of their last child and then live with all the families of their sons at one place.

But that quick opulence appeared to have produced some imbalance in the thought channels of one of my brothers, and I instinctively caught the hint. But I was so full of the gratitude for God's mercy and His steady guidance that I remained steadfast on my duty and worked as devotedly for the family as before. Making mention of that change of heart in an important family member was considered necessary because all through the foregoing years, we were regarded as an ideal family with impeccable unity, devotion and genuine respect for elders. I had a feeling that some evil force was trying to intrude and inject the selfish motives in a particular member.

As we were overburdened with many more orders, I could not get time to think about those inklings. I kept myself busy with making arrangements for the house-warming ceremony which was performed on a grand scale.

The government had allotted us an Industrial plot of half an acre in Mayapuri a few years earlier. We started construction on that plot again in the winter *Navratras* of 1971. The big factory was completed in 18 months, with full basement. In those days our factory was considered as one of the finest buildings in that area. Its inauguration was done on the *Basakhi* day, 1974. All relatives, business friends and other well wishers were invited for lunch.

As the surge in our business subsided in the year seventy three, our large new factory building equipped with new machinery had nothing sufficient to do. We felt the need for expansion and diversification of our existing business to be commensurate with our advanced infrastructure. Considering that need, we decided to work again towards exports. Govinder Paul had booked large orders from London in 1965, which could not be executed in time because of constraints of proper factory premises and other infrastructure. In 1973 we had both the spacious modern factory and good machinery. Considering it the right time to go into export business, I made my programme to go to London and try our luck there once again.

It was on November 2, 1973 that I had to leave for London. My family joined by a few members of my in-law's families, assembled at our house, to say good bye to me. The ritual started in our traditional way by applying of vermillion mark on my forehead and rotating of a tray full of flowers and a lighted *diya* before me by my wife. Other members placed garlands around my neck. Many of them accompanied me to the airport where they were joined by several relatives who had reached there directly. It was a very heart warming send-off by nearly 30 to 35 relations.

Inside the airport I went through the check-in to hand over my suitcase and receive my boarding pass. Thereafter, I passed through Passport check, the immigration check and finally the security check, to proceed to the airplane. I ascended the stairs to reach into the belly of the plane and was guided to my seat by an airhostess. My hand bag was placed in the box above my seat.

After the call for tightening of our belts, the plane moved slowly and then suddenly took a flight into the air. Higher and higher it flew until it attained its required height. After that it was as smooth as if it were resting in the sky. I took a glass of orange juice from the serving hostess, and went to sleep till I was woken to prepare myself for the descent of the plane at its destination after half an hour.

Finally it landed at the Heathrow Airport. Everything that came in my view and every movement I made through that large complex, presented to my hungry eyes a novel freshness. Its elegantly huge structure, its carpeted floors, the escalators, the movements of the well-dressed and agile airport personnel, the long disciplined queues of passengers of every nationality of the world for passport, customs and security checks, the slowly rotating conveyors for delivery of the baggages, the trolleys for the passengers for carrying their bags out of the airport, the brilliant arrival lounge, with its counters for tourist information, banks, hotel booking, ticketing counters and the restaurants and waiting lounges, all enchanted me.

I moved ahead thoughtfully rolling my baggage trolley before me and stopped at the Hotel Booking where I booked my room in a moderate hotel in the center of the city and was issued a reservation slip by the lady at the counter. For reaching my hotel, she placed before me options to choose between a bus, the underground train or a taxi.

Out on the pavement, I stopped to look for the taxi stand. An up-to-date gentleman, wearing an overcoat and a felt hat approached me and asked me whether I was looking for a taxi? I could hardly say yes, and that man swooped on my trolley to pick up my bag, telling me to follow him. Totally confounded I went after him carrying my briefcase to a taxi. When he placed my bag on the front seat, made me sit in the back, himself occupied the driver's seat and asked me where I wanted to go, did I realize that the gentleman was himself the taxi driver. I gave him my hotel reservation slip and he drove his vehicle on.

The taxi speeded ahead and I fixed my eyes at its meter which appeared to me moving faster than the taxi. As the meter reached at the figure of GBP 3.00, I put my hand on the driver's shoulder and asked him how far was my hotel? He replied, not very far. "But I have only GBP 3.00 cash with me", I told him with anxiety in my voice. Without showing any concern, he snapped back that I must be having the traveller's cheques. As I replied in affirmative, he nonchalantly speeded on and at last stopped in front of my hotel. The taxi meter showed the figure of GBP 4.30. The driver came out, took out my bag and opened my door to tell me again to follow him. He entered the hotel lobby and placing my bag near the receptionist's counter, he gave my hotel reservation slip to the lady sitting there. She confirmed my booking, handed me the key of my room and helped me in the encashment of my traveller's cheques. I gave the taxi man GBP 5. He gave me back the balance of GBP 4.40 meter fare and stood looking at me. Seeing that I could not decipher his look, he said, "sir, tip". Hearing that, I returned all what he had given me back from my GBP 5 currency note.

Going back to the reception I found standing near my suitcase a handsome young boy, telling me "Your room key Sir". And as I gave him my key, he picked up my bag, directed me to take the lift and himself proceeded towards the staircase with my bag.

Using the small lift I reached the second floor and to my room, where the elegant boy (called porter) stood outside. He handed the key back to me, showed me in my room where he placed my suitcase and left. The room was very small but trim with facilities like a shower, a washbasin, a small reading table with chair, a telephone, a small cupboard and a single bed. The room rent was GBP 6.50 without breakfast. The toilet was outside in the corridor, to be used by three or four persons.

The first thing I did after entering my room was to phone my childhood friend, Balwant Singh Ghura, to tell him of my arrival in London that morning and the name and address of my hotel. He came to my hotel and accompanied me to the bus stop to take me to his warehouse.

Since the time I landed at London airport and reached my hotel, whatever I saw, appeared to me something wonderful. Waiting for the bus in a queue the first thing that caught my eyes gave me a severe shock. A young boy and a young girl stood in front of us cuddled tight and kissing endlessly. Agitated in my mind I pointed the couple to my friend and asked him, what was it? He told me that I may look towards the road for the bus and should not bother about those scenes as it was the way of life there. The bus arrived and we reached the warehouse in a few minutes.

Balwant had started the business of importing fresh vegetables and fruits from India and Pakistan and selling those to various shopkeepers of London from his warehouse, situated on the Commercial Street in East London.

I spent my first day in London with Balwant at his warehouse. In the evening he helped me to travel to my hotel by the "Underground" rail. The "Underground" rail system was another wonder for me. It was an unbelievably extensive and intricate network of rail lines to cater to the people living in all areas of the great city of London. The underground map I got from the Liverpool station showed twenty different rail lines operating in London.

I could easily pick up the Central Line, from the "Underground" map, that catered to both the locations of my hotel and Balwant's warehouse which would be my most frequent place of visit. However, I found the map a complete guide to reach any destination I liked.

My first business appointment was fixed with Mr D.K. Bakshi, the foreign officer of the Engineering Export Promotion Council of India. He saw my products and advised me to have an agent to take me round the interested parties for my items. He also recommended an agent named Mr. N.N. Rao, who had been the first foreign officer of the E.E.P.C.London. He gave me his phone number and told me that I might mention his name to him when I met him.

I first fixed my meeting with Mr. Dabber, the Export Officer of the British Steel Ltd., and went to see him for my requirement of high carbon steel sheets. He told me that they had been manufacturing high carbon strips mainly to supply to the West Indies for their requirement of chaff cutters blades. Their supply to India was limited to one single party in Jalandher. But currently they had almost stopped production of that item. However he noted my yearly requirement and told me that he would discuss the issue with his production department and let me know about the outcome after one week. Mr Dabber, was very cordial with me and I asked him to have dinner with me one evening convenient to him. Dabber had never visited India nor had he ever tasted Indian food. He told me that he would talk to his wife about my invitation and confirm his date and time the next day.

Mr. Dabber came to my hotel with his wife one evening in response to my invitation for dinner. They had their drinks in the hotel bar. During the time we had our drinks Mrs. Dabber showed her keen interest in knowing about India. I replied to her queries about India in the best way I could do. To her last question about my liking of her country I said that I had reached

London only a few days back, but whatever little I had seen impressed me very much.

We went to an Indian restaurant and Mr. Dabber ordered dishes and drinks for himself and his wife. After we finished our dinner, I presented to Mrs. Dabber a silk blouse piece, as a gift which she accepted with hearty thanks and after taking it out from a plastic bag, she felt its surface by her hand and offered me her plentiful appreciation and gratitude. After dinner Mr Dabber was kind to drop me at my hotel in his car and we parted company.

As I went to my room, and took to my bed I kept thinking about the first English couple I had come in contact with. Mr. Dabber was reserved and brief in his talk. His wife was open humble, sweet, gentle and sociable.

On the following Sunday, I went to Balwant who accompanied me to his eldest married daughter, Mary's home. I had seen Mary when she was a child. She had grown into a very tall and beautiful girl. She was very nice to me when Balwant introduced me as his childhood friend. We then went to Balwant's own house. I was expecting a cordial reception from Balwant's wife as I had stayed in Balwant's bungalow in Sialkot for one week in August 1947. Also, I had arranged my *Bhuaji's* New Delhi Quarter for her, when she had arrived in Delhi after migration from Sialkot. But I was surprised and embarassed when she refused to recognize me even after I reminded her of living together in Delhi for a month where she cooked and served the meals to both her husband and me. My first week in London passed this way.

On Monday, I phoned Mr. Rao and he came to see me in my hotel room. He represented a few Indian firms including Gedore India Ltd., He saw my literature and samples and agreed to work for me and took me to his office in his car to make and sign the agreement for representation as our agent in the UK.

From the next day, he started driving me around London to meet various importers of hand tools for whom he had been booking orders for Gedore. One by one we visited Hardware and Tool dealers all over London during all the week days. We could book one small order from one firm but received a lot of inquiries for better quality lock wrenches, garden tools sets and various other items of hand tools and hardware that we might be asked to develop.

The next Sunday I went to Oxford Street with Balwant. I was dazzled by the magnificence of the showrooms of Marks and Spencer, Mother Care, Selfridges etc. and was amazed at the disciplined behaviour of all the people in the stores and on the footpaths. The slow and orderly movement of cars and buses through the much crowded street without the sound of a single horn and without any of those vehicles showing a single scratch on their bodies appeared something beyond my imagination. I bought my overcoat at Mark and Spencer. It had started drizzling when we came out of that store.

The following week, Rao had made plans to try other towns and he drove me to Birmingham, its suburbs and then Manchester. We could secure one order from a company called Redmore Ltd. The order was for an item called Rose Pruners, which we would have to develop and supply. Again many parties contacted by us wanted large garden tools or some other garden tool and hand tool items. I collected a lot of samples for development.

On that weekend, I went round in a conducted tour for which the bus collected me from my hotel. It was a luxury bus furnished with superb facilities. It moved with a running commentary, giving names of the roads it passed through. It stopped at the London Bridge Museum.

Almost thirty years have passed since I saw that Museum and I may have forgotten many things I saw in that large building. But I would try to recollect some of those.

The museum exhibited the entire history of that country. The collections were arranged in such a manner as to bring out for the viewers the full picture of the life of the people from its beginning. At its start I felt that I was transported among the ancient islanders. It showed how the old society of that island comprising smiths, farmers, traders lived in the small hamlets and towns along with their women and children and domestic animals. The things which I clearly remember were the changes in life brought about by the invaders from outside on their land particularly the difference in the matter of warfare after the coming of more advanced people in that secluded island. The most conspicuous among those articles were the paraphernalia of warfare such as the arms and the armours, protective as well as attacking both for men and their vehicles, animate and inanimate, development of new towns and improved living standard of the people, the small ships and new sailing gadgets. All that was very absorbing. The display was the progression from darkness to the dawning light slowly moving to bright sunshine. The primitive society started its advance towards the modern time which lead to the rule of the kings and queens. The development primarily worked towards the shipping as the island was surrounded by seas. The growth of its Navy coupled with the new found inquisitiveness and the spirit of adventure brought many laurels to their land and thereby opened new vistas for its people.

I moved on to the section displaying the heavy bejeweled dresses and crowns of the kings and queens, the *kohinoor* studded crown which Queen Victoria had worn. Another section contained a large variety of jewels, gems, precious stones and pearls of many sizes and shapes. There was a section displaying the arms and defensive equipment of the present age both used on land, sea and in the air. There were statues of the great Kings, generals and other persons. It was the total history unfolded in that multistoreyed building.

Coming [illegible] of the Museum I retraced in my mind, the coming of the Eng[illegible] men in our country, after having covered thousands o[illegible]les on the sea to start trading in the beginning of the seven[illegible]th century and then, by the middle of the eighteenth cen[illegible], they had conquered the whole of India.

From there w[illegible]re driven through to the Trafalgar Square, 10, Downing Stre[illegible]e parliament house, the imposing Queen's palace, the Big Be[illegible]d the Westminster Abbey Church. There the bus stopped ag[illegible]nd the passengers were allowed to see the church. I looked [illegible]amazement at its seating arrangement, the pulpit, the multico[illegible]d glasses fitted to its windows going high up on all sides to [illegible] the very ceilings. From there we were taken to Lady Tus[illegible]. It was a novel museum of wax statues of mostly the Briti[illegible]eats and also those of the Europe and other countries of the [illegible]. Mahatma Gandhi, Jawaharlal Nehru, Indira Gandhi and M[illegible]med Ali Jinnah were from the Indian sub-continent. Attach[illegible]his Museum was the big hall with light and sound display [illegible]o horrible for the children, ladies and timid hearted menf[illegible]- the moment it went into complete darkness and the stran[illegible]adows moved wickedly on all sides of the hall with frightf[illegible]unds.

I had already been very much imp[illegible]d by many more things that I saw in London. The river T[illegible]s, so vast, deep and calm and the steamers and ships plying [illegible] surface unimpaired by several bridges on it. The uninterrup[illegible]iling of large ships with heights much more than that all[illegible] by some of the bridges, was another wonder for me to [illegible]hen the bridges parted at their center to open up to all[illegible]se ships pass through. One day I had gone to see Shak[illegible]re's house in Stafford on Avon. We were allowed to see [illegible]00 years old building from outside only as probably it was [illegible] renovated.

After going through all the above I slipp[illegible] a reverie thinking about the achievements of the people [illegible] island.

Men from that small island had reached all the four corners of the world with their ships and soldiers and went on conquering country after country, with land mass, people and riches much more than what they possessed in their own country. I was unaware of it till I reached my high school and was told that the sun never set on the empire of the people who ruled our country. Throughout the years of my education, I carried a feeling of intense hatred for the despotic and cruel rulers who ruled our country for nearly a thousand years; the British were the last who ruled over us for more than 200 years. After my college, I had gathered much more information about all those rulers most of which related to their misdeeds, ill treatments, and barbarous and ruthless acts. But my first visit to London changed those ill feelings for our last rulers, from intense hatred to deep appreciation.

What I actually saw were people who were very well-behaved, co-operative, honest and clean in conducting themselves in all spheres of their life. Their railways, roads, buses, trucks, cars; also the way all their transport system was managed even in the crowdest of the areas — all this was simply marvellous. I used to stand in one corner of the footpath of the Oxford street for long time seeing large numbers of people, including men, women and children walking around me in big crowds without pushing or pulling. Then I looked towards the road which was full of slow moving cars and buses. Out of about 100 cars or buses, I hardly found any vehicle with a scratch on its body.

During that time I saw the young educated boys sweeping the footpath of the dried fallen tree leaves, during their spare hours. I also saw workers hurrying to their work places very early in the morning in extreme cold or rains; the nurses working with extreme devotion in their hospitals; teachers, very loyal and devoted in their duties. The punctuality and discipline were visible everywhere in the system, whether it was the shops or the railways or the offices. I realized the importance of dignity of labour by actually seeing it in life.

Domestic animals like cats and dogs belonged to special breeds. The care and love which was shown to them and with which those pets responded to their masters, was something I could not dream of. Stray animals were an unknown entity in that land.

Everything that came in my view in that country appeared very different and superior. Sometimes when I travelled by the Underground in rush hours, I realized that some passengers were not able to buy their tickets from the starting stations. Those ticket-less passengers had the cash ready in their hands equal to the price of their ticket. They handed over that cash to the ticket collector at destination station, who had a small wooden plank on top of one side of the exit gate, where he placed the coins. I had seen those planks with hundreds of such coins collected from the ticket-less passengers. Neither those passengers tried to dodge the collector nor the collector took that money home. At the end of his duty, he counted and put all the coins in a bag to deposit them in the cash department.

I realized that the cows had achieved a vital position in the life and economy not only of this country but those of the most European countries. Cow's milk, milk products and its meat formed an essential part of the diet of the people. The nation had taken full responsibility to breed and keep cows and provide its people of their benefits. Cows were divided in two categories — those required to provide meat were fed with a special diet which created more of flesh on their bodies and the others which provided milk, got a different dict which went to form more milk. Both were very well looked after. Their habitats were kept very neat and clean with all those facilities of heating in winter and fans / air conditioners in summer. As their diets had been well researched, so were the medical facilities available to them. All the benefits of scientific developments were passed on to them.

Similarly, strict rules were applied for the development and care of children who, though were the responsibility of their parents, were considered as a national property. Parents had to follow strict government rules about their upkeep. Abusing and beating a child was a criminal offence. To convince me about children's rights, a family friend settled in London told me of an interesting episode. His old father was once called there to enjoy the benefits of good life his son was having there. The old man was happy to see the prosperity of his son and his family but being illiterate, he could not move out independently. He spent a few days going with his son to his shop but sitting idle the whole day, without understanding anything, he felt tired and bored. He then decided to stay back at home where he could take rest, listen to *bhajans* on the radio or see some Indian programmes on T.V.

His son and daughter-in-law worked at the shop. The children went to school early. He remained alone in the house till the children came back from school. The children, after coming home and eating what they wanted from the refrigerators, started enjoying themselves by playing, jumping and laughing. The old man rested in his own room. One day he found the children so noisy as to get disturbed in his room. He came out of his room and told the children in Punjabi not to be noisy as they were disturbing his sleep. The children did not understand what their grandfather told them repeatedly, nor did they care for him. They continued in their games and making noise. The grandfather got irritated and strongly warned the children to behave. But still the children neither understood what he was saying nor bothered about him. When the old man could stand it no more, he came out of his room, went to the most noisy boy and thumped at his back. All the children stopped their play and could not understand the way the old man behaved. The grandfather having succeeded in quelling the noise, went to his room and rested peacefully in his bed.

The boy who was hit, silently went to his room, picked up the phone and dialled the police number to tell that he had been hit by an old man living in their house and gave them his address. In a few minutes two policemen arrived at the house and enquired from the children if one of them had phoned. They confirmed and guided the policemen to their grandfather's room. He was resting peacefully when he was jolted to come to his feet and was utterly confused to see the policemen standing there. One of the policemen addressed him if he had hit the boy. He could not understand what the policeman said. The boy who phoned the police, confirmed that he was the culprit. The policemen took away the old man to the police station in their van. The children happily started playing again.

Late in the evening when the children's parents arrived home from their warehouse, the old man's son went to his father's room as usual. Not finding his father there, he enquired from the children about their grandpa. The boys told them that the police had taken him away. He was stunned to hear that and asked the children, why? The boy who had phoned the police, volunteered to tell him that he had phoned the police as the old man had hit him. Hearing it both the man and his wife rushed to the police station near their house. Their father sat there on a bench with tears in his eyes, and an expression of helpless humiliation on his face. With a lot of explanations, pleadings and requests, they could get their father freed from the police and brought him home. The old man sat in the car silently shedding tears not hearing the apologies of his son. Reaching home, he went straight to his room, packed his bag and told his son that he may be immediately taken to the airport and sent to India. His son and daughter in-law begged that they might be pardoned for the children's folly and requested him to take his food. They succeeded in consoling the old man with a clear promise to send him back the next day by the first available flight.

For me that story came very handy to tell my people when I went back home with a lot of humour and fun.

In nutshell, my first visit to London convinced me that the people in that country follow faithfully the tenets of our religious scriptures and we, who consider those books sacred and swear by them, fail to follow them. That is the reason why Britain could rule over the world and we, having ignored our seers' dictates, remained in bondage for centuries. I felt that those of the people in our country who could afford, England was the best place for pilgrimage.

During the last week, I had a call from D.K. Bakshi of E.E.P.C. who wanted me to see him in his office for an inquiry from a firm wanting a manufacturer who could economically produce a machine that they had designed. A pamphlet of the machine with address of the firm named Spray Master & Co. was given to me. The firm was run by an Indian, named Mr. K.R. Menon. The address was not far from my hotel. I fixed an appointment with Mr. Menon and went to see him at his address. It was his home.

Mr Menon was a fine man who had been settled in London since 1934 and had married an English lady. He showed me the machine, which he had himself developed by working in his garage with a small tool room. During our discussion, I discovered that Mr. Menon was the younger brother of Mr. V.P. Menon who was the home secretary of Sardar Vallabh Bhai Patel. He had worked as his right hand man in obtaining accession to India of 365 small or big princely states at the time of the division of the country.

I found Mr. Menon very affectionate. After our first meeting in the afternoon, he did not let me go away from his home until his wife came from her office and cooked rice and *daal* which both of us ate together in his drawing room with Indian pickles. Thus our first meeting was like 'love at first sight' as we became very close friends. After my visit in 1973, I again went to

London in 1975 and I had a standing invitation from him to be with him in his house every weekend. I specially remember one occasion when Mr Menon phoned me at my hotel to reach his house at 6.00 p.m. sharp as there was a TV Programme on Indian Railways that day. I reached there before time and joined Mr Menon to see the TV programme. Dinner was also served and we both ate and witnessed the TV programme. It started from the time the Railways were brought to India. The steam engine-driven trains traversing the Indian countryside and also the small gauge trains working their way through the lush hills was so beautiful and nostalgic as to bring tears in the eyes of both of us in remembering our beloved motherland sitting in a foreign country. But unfortunately, Mr Menon died of heart attack during my next visit, a day before I was invited at his home.

I spent most of my last week in the purchase of clothes, dresses and saris for each member, young or old, of my joint family. All the purchases were made from the three large showrooms in Oxford Street – Marks & Spencer, Selfridges and Mother care.

On one of my last Sundays in London, I went to Paris by the morning flight and took a conducted tour from the airport. The tour showed us the Versailles Palace and Museum. That museum was very different and altogether a wonderful place. The museum was actually a palace constructed and reconstructed or renovated by successive kings. It was started by King Louis XIV and went on to be used by Napolean. There were different Chambers for all the Kings and their Queens after Louis XIV, insides of which, was all gold and golden, from their doors and beds to the upholstery and furnishings. The palace had more than 1000 rooms and a huge collection of unique articles of antiques, which were mind boggling. It was a museum which needed a full month to see it thoroughly. I pushed through the chambers of King Louise XIV and XVI and those of Napolean Bonapart and his wife Josephene. I remember a long corridor in the palace called the Hall of Mirrors, all studded with beautiful mirrors on all its sides and the ceiling. The palace had also collected many world famous paintings and sculptures done by famous artists of Europe. To go through some of the Kings rooms and through the hall of mirrors, I was not left with enough energy to enjoy the marvellous paintings and pieces of art and sculptures.

There were large open spaces in the precincts of the huge palace and on one side there were two parks beautifully laid with lawns and large beds of flowers of numerous shapes, quality, colours and sizes. The two were little different but near each other.

I was awestruck even when I came out after seeing the chambers, paintings and statues and felt that I totally lacked the capability to assess their great artistic value or even to be able to appreciate those and put them in writing. Coming out I had something to eat from the outside shops and boarded the bus for the airport. I got down at the Airport and came back to London by an evening flight.

I did not succeed in getting the business I expected. A day before I was to fly back, Mr. Rao, our agent, came to my hotel and placed before me four samples of some tools and asked to quote my prices for those immediately as the enquiry was genuine and urgent. I examined the samples and found those items simple. Calculating the cost exactly to make offers was not possible without going into details of consumption of each raw material in those items for which there was no facility in my hotel room. I told Rao that if the enquiry was genuine, I might make my open offer to book the order at 10% less prices, than those which the party was paying already.

From my hotel room Rao phoned the interested party and after discussing with them my offer, he wrote on a paper, prices for each of the items. I considered those prices suitable and gave my acceptance. I was told to take those samples with me and send my counter samples with written confirmation of my prices. If the samples were acceptable order for one hundred thousand of each items will be placed on me. That way my first tour of a Western country was ended.

I reached back Delhi exactly after one month on the 2nd December, 1973. My reception at the Palam Airport was just like my send-off. Many of my family members and other relatives were waiting for me to come out of the airport. Again I stood overwhelmed by the number of persons and the different way each offered their regards to me. The car that carried me home was full with those who wanted to be with me whether there was enough space inside or not. I reached home and met those who could not go to the airport.

When I was taken to my room, the first thing I did was to open my bulging suitcase and emptied it on the surface of my bed, whatever I had purchased for each member of my family. It was a scene to watch. The children were transported to another world on seeing the brilliant colour combinations and brightness of their dresses. I felt an extreme sense of satisfaction when I found every one overflowing with joy to meet me and then to receive their gift.

— 15—

SIGNS OF DISUNITY AMONG BROTHERS

Resuming my duties in our business, we produced the best samples that we could and sent those to our agent with confirmation of our prices. Our samples were approved and we received, from the concerned party, an order for 2,50,000 pieces of each of the three items with Letter of Credit for 25,000 pieces of each item as part supply. Thus started once again production of export items in our unit. I was giving more attention towards the development and the timely execution of those orders. Satya Paul attended mostly to the production. Govinder Paul looked after the government office jobs at all levels. Raj Paul attended exclusively to the affairs of Sekhri Brothers and Inder Mohan Chopra worked as a 'minister without portfolio', helping wherever his services were needed in all the units.

1975 onwards, I undertook my foreign trips more frequently and the export business started growing. It expanded from the UK to the other European countries, and hence demanded much more attention from me. When I was not on tour abroad, I was on a procurement mission in north India. That left me with little time to pay full attention by my large joint family. But somehow, I could feel that the family was drifting apart. It hurt me but I did not show. I felt ashamed in telling anyone about the failure of my lifelong mission to create a homogeneous and an ideal joint family. All the same, the persistent inner turmoil made me sick with deep depression.

All my brothers had developed under the umbrella of my protection. Each one of them could stand shoulder-to-shoulder alongside me in any society. My parents were contented with my humane attitude in the family and in the society. Then why all the hints of disaffection? I had no answer to my inner query and I continued to be wracked inside.

The continuous mental pressure and my unceasing mulling over the deteriorated position led to my disregard of personal comforts and a sense of detachment. After some time I started feeling like a spider caught in its own web. I slipped into a state of deep depression. One early morning, when no one was up, in a muddled frame of my mind, I caught hold of a shoulder bag, stuffed it with some articles and left home. I took a morning bus to Rishikesh where I rested for the night in a tourist bungalow. Early next morning with the same state of my mind, I left the tourist bungalow and took the first bus I found on the road, heading towards the mountains.

It was early February. I had no idea where I was going to and for what? I told the bus conductor to issue me a ticket for Badri Nath. He replied that Badri Nath was closed for winter and that the bus was going only upto Joshi Math. I then told him to give me the ticket upto that destination. The bus went its way crossing many bridges on rivers joining other rivers called *Prayags*, When the bus was about to reach Joshi Math, it suddenly stopped and the conductor announced that it could not go further as the road ahead was blocked with a massive hillslide. The bus would go back to the place it had started from.

I saw two young boys getting out of the bus at that deserted place, I followed them involuntarily. On enquiring they told me that they were hill-people and hillslides did not bother them much and they planned to walk to their village which was quite close to Joshi Math. On knowing this I requested them to take me along. They were surprised at my request and were apprehensive that I, a city dweller, could walk through the hill slide. I told them I would follow them closely through the mud and was confident to ford it out with them. They advised me to be careful and to manage my steps so that they fall on their foot prints. Luckily the mud we had to cross was only ankle deep and I had no problem. The blockade was spread wider than I could guess.

When we reached Joshi Math, those boys walked swiftly away. The city was dark and deserted. No shops were open and there was nobody in the *bazaar* whom I could ask for help. It was freezing cold and misty dark. I had no alternative but to stand where I was and wait till somebody appeared there. After some minutes, I saw a figure of a human being coming out of the mist on a hill track. I went to him and requested him to guide me to a tourist bungalow. He looked to me with incredulity appearing on his face, and said that the tourist bungalow was closed in the winter and he was not sure if there was any watchman on duty. Nevertheless, he guided me to the bungalow. The building was all dark and locked. There was a small room outside the main building and I knocked its door. There was no reply. As the door was not locked from outside, I continued knocking harder. At last there came a very feeble sound from the room asking who was there? I replied that I was a pilgrim and the door might kindly be opened. A little after, the door opened and a small man, looking at me in surprise, addressed me "It is no time for pilgrimage, sir, in this harsh weather?" I told him only that I had to pass the night there and would feel obliged if he could arrange for me a bed inside the building. The poor man was perplexed seeing me with no baggage. However, he not only cleaned the room for me but also surprised me by cooking *daal* and *chapaties* for me.

Although the watchman had arranged for me three blankets to be used as mattress and the other three to cover myself, it could not provide me with sufficient warmth. The night was too long and too cold to give me any restful sleep. At the first light of the day, I left the tourist bungalow after handing over the six blankets and some money to the very kind watchman and went down the hill. In the *bazaar*, I found one *halvai* shop where the servant was heating a coal *choolah*. I stood there till the *choolah* was fully fired. I ordered a glass of tea and drank it along with some rustic snacks. I then thought over my next step. The experience of the last night dissuaded me to go towards Badri Nath and I decided to turn back. It involved crossing back the blocked road and walking all the distance up to the town where the bus went back last night.

It was daytime and the sun was rising above the hill tops. I found it easy to pass over the hillslide following the last night's experience, and continued walking. I had to walk about 12 miles and by the time I reached that place I was dead tired. After eating at a *dhaba*, I boarded the afternoon bus going towards Rishikesh and got down midway at Vishnu Prayag late in the evening. There, I ate my dinner and got a room in a tourist bungalow. With a proper bed and bedding I had a restful sleep during the night. In the morning I had a hot bath which somewhat eased my fatigued body. I left that place after lunch. Picked up a bus and alighted at Rudra Prayag to spend one night there. Next morning, it was raining and I had to buy an umbrella. Boarding again a bus, I arrived back in Rishikesh.

All my aimless wandering did not do any good to me. My mind was as restless as before and my head was totally blocked. Next morning I crossed the Ganga from the Sivanand bridge and after selecting a lonely place on her bank, I seated myself on the stony steps. Looking towards the crystal water of the Ganga, I felt as if I was seeing her for the first time. Being her dedicated devotee for decades it appeared to me that she had been lost to me for long and that, I had only that day rediscovered her. Putting off my clothes hurriedly, I jumped into the sparkling cold water. Touching the bed of the river, when I came up, I felt that a miracle was happening and I was seeing everything afresh. I swam to the bank and again sat on its stairs. I felt that peace was dawning on me and my head was getting cleared. I asked a person sitting on the stairs near me about the day and the date. I realized then that I had been away from home for five days. After that miraculous experience I decided to go back home.

It was late in the afternoon when I reached the gate of our house and peeped inside. The children were playing joyfully. My entry through the gate of the house created such an excitement among the children that it virtually brought the whole household down. Being Sunday, everybody was at home. I did not know how I was carried to my room on the first floor. One after another, Raj and Govinder sat down before me and cried aloud, clutching my feet. Touched by their respect and love, I also started crying. It was only Satya Paul who was calm and composed. He was conspicuous for lack of any sentiments. He lifted Raj Paul and then Govinder Paul from my feet and told them to control their emotions. My mother, father and every single person embraced me with overflowing love. Santosh stood crying at one side waiting for everyone to calm down. At her turn, she hugged me long and fast and then touched my feet crying in repentance for no fault of hers.

I realized that my act had caused much pain to all members of my family. I felt ashamed when my mother came to me with folded hands and expressed her regrets for something, which I could not understand. I was dazed by the overwhelming affection showered on me.

After some time, everyone departed leaving me alone in my room. My wife brought my dinner in my room. Immediately after dinner I went to bed. I had a very restful night after almost a week of my wandering.

Sudhir, my elder son, had joined St. Joseph School, Nainital, where he studied for two years. But I found that he was unable to adjust to the environment of that school although his results were good. My father was so upset by the embarrassed face of Sudhir when we went to see him off at the Delhi Railway station after his second year winter vacation, that he started scolding me when the train left. Next year I did not send him there and got him admitted in St. Xaviers School, Delhi from where he did his higher secondary. He got admission at Kurukshetra University for Engineering and he completed his B.E. honours in mechanical engineering in 1976. He then went to Poona for his six months probationary work in New Standard Engineering Co. Ltd. In that year Satya Paul had a slipped disk for which he was confined to bed for many months. I was feeling the slowing down of production due to his long absence. In order to fill the gap, I called back Sudhir, leaving his training midway. He came and followed my directions to look after the production at Paul Engineers. After sometime, Sudhir suggested that I may assign him some work in which he could hold independent charge without any guidance. I considered the relevance of his proposal and told him to take up Sun Shine Steel Industries at Naraina. He worked there for a month and reorganized the unit. I went to see it and found a visible improvement in the production set-up of the unit.

After that he came back to Mayapuri. I then thought of using his talent at the right spot. We had several different production lines at that time. For the government, we manufactured various types of tools, camp and hospital steel furniture. For exports, we did some items of welding accessories and some of garden tools. Satya Paul was the production man for the entire factory. I decided to guide Sudhir to look after the production of export items and made him sit in my large room by my side. When Satya Paul started working, Sudhir again told me to assign him the task of production of the welding items for exports which he could handle independently.

His suggestion came handy to me and I managed to hire a small factory in 'C' block of Mayapuri. Sudhir was told to set up the unit there and start the manufacture of export items independently under the name of Industrial Products of India. As expected that unit proved its worth and our export production improved. Sudhir continued to work there for a few years.

With the steady growth of exports, its work load had started increasing. The responsibility of procurement and financial arrangement for the entire show also rested on me. I did not mind the hard work in India but the exertions that I had to undergo during my regular and frequent foreign tours were of a very different nature. In those tours, I had to carry the bag of my personal things as well as that for the samples and walk long distances. That had to be done that way to be economical. And I had been doing it as my solemn duty.

Govinder tried to help me in those tours but his habit of indulging in excessive drinking forced me not to use him for that purpose. Satya Paul went to Europe once but he took his wife along to make it a pleasure trip. This also did not help.

I never considered that load of work as a drudgery. Providence had arranged some relaxation during my duties in India. My procurement tours towards the Punjab ended at Jalandhar. There I found an old college friend, Sansar Vadehra who had settled there after partition. He ran a sports goods factory in an Industrial Area in Jalandhar and was living in the cantonment, with his wife, father and a younger brother's family. In the beginning of our meeting I used to stay in a hotel and spent my evening at Vadehras. As we became closer, I started staying with them.

Vadehras were a wonderful family, living a life of happiness, enjoyment and pleasure. Hence the time spent in Jalandhar, used to rejuvenate me.

The more our business expanded to new countries in Europe, the more wider fields appeared before my eyes and my ambitious mind guided my steps towards that direction. In the year 1978, I decided to explore the markets of the USA.

I therefore visited America for the first time in that year. One of my good young friends, P.C. Sethi was settled there and I stayed with him in New York. I stayed in the country for about three weeks, but could book only one small order from a welding accessories dealer in that city. However, the dealer was kind enough to advise me to see Mr. Jerry Robinson, who was considered as the King of welding accessories business in the USA. He also gave me Robinson's telephone number and full address in New Jersey. When I phoned that number, I was told that Mr. Robinson was out of the country. I had to postpone seeing him to my next tour and made plans to see my wife's elder brother, Professor O.P. Madhok who had been settled in Minot, North Dakota. My air travel to Minot proved a big adventure.

I booked my seat with North West Airlines from New York to Minot. As I reached the airport with my friend and went for check in, I was told that my ticket had been wrongly issued. There was no flight of the airlines to Minot. My friend argued with them that if they had no flight, how was the ticket issued? The airline was in a bind and requested us to wait. After sometime, their officer called us and offered to get us a new ticket for the next day. But it was not acceptable to us. Then they told me that they could arrange to fly me that day but I shall have to change three flights to reach Minot. And those three flights had to be caught within 20–30 minutes gap between landing and departure. I would have to run direct from one plane to another. He assured me that their staff would be helping and guiding me at every change. I agreed to do that and they issued a new ticket to me.

My first flight landed at Mineoples and from there I hurriedly boarded a plane that took me to Milwalkee and from there I was taken to Rizmak. When I landed at Rizmak, it was cloudy and dark.

The flight to Minot was ready. As I entered the plane, I felt as if I had been pushed into an antique model of a first tiny plane. There were 12 or 13 seats. Three other passengers were occupying their seats. The seats were like those we had in our old buses, crudely made of pipes and cushions. I was simply looking around and feeling astonished. Soon, there was a fierce storm with lightening and loud thunder. It was followed by heavy rains. The captain of the aircraft announced that the plane could not take off because of the bad weather. The weather was getting so nasty that our small plane quivered while standing. We waited with baited breath, without a murmur. Then suddenly I heard the voice of the Captain, saying that he had decided to fly and the plane jerked to move forward and shortly after, took to the air. I caught the front seat's top of naked pipe with my two hands. The lightening continued its flashes with its faithful thunder, as I tightened my grip on the pipe with belt in place round my body. Without my knowing, I had closed my eyes and my lips moved in prayers. The bird like aircraft was swerving and dropping then ascending, sometime violently. It looked like a never ending journey when suddenly the announcement was heard that our craft was landing and we actually did land. I opened my eyes, let go the front seat pipe from my hands. Coming out of the plane I entered the small enclosure of Minot airport, and saw standing there, with pale faces, Om, Urmil *bhabi* and their daughter, Reena. They had been anxiously waiting there for several hours hearing regular announcements about the flight being caught in the stormy weather and they felt a tremendous relief seeing me.

It was a very happy occasion for all. They had received in Minot their first-ever relative. After a couple of days, Om noted that I was a little hard of hearing. The very next day, I was taken to a hospital where they got my ears tested. I learnt there for the first time that my hearing in both ears had been reduced and it was beyond repair. On the weekend, We went for a picnic about 25 miles away and stopped at a small hutment in a secluded place. We ate our home-made food, and spent some good time there gossiping and laughing. From that place we went further ahead to reach some bushy strip of land where an insect stung me. The next day I had fever; I was again taken to the hospital where my illness was diagnosed as malaria. The hospital authorities recommended not only hospitalisation for me but also that I be quarantined till I was cured. Om had to use his influence with some of his student doctors and got me released from the hospital assuring them that he would be keeping me in a separate room and administering me their medicine regularly. I remained confined to bed for seven days and it was only after I had recovered that I left for India.

In our foreign business trips I came in contact with a party in the UK. who showed a very keen interest in our product. In a short time they increased their turnover of our product and became our topmost client. They further developed their personal relations with us through one of their Anglo-Indian employees. All that was consummated in our decision to give 'Our Best Customers Award' of a Gold medal to that company in the year 1979. They were invited to New Delhi to receive the medal. Three persons arrived in Delhi, including their Managing Director Mr Vic Adams, who received the gold medal in the presence of a very select gentry of nearly 100 guests in a big hall in the Claridges Hotel. The award giving function was a great success and it enhanced our prestige a good deal.

The same year, I could find a suitable match for my daughter Geeta, who had completed her graduation from a Delhi college. The boy was an engineer employed with an electronic goods manufacturing company in Washington DC. His parents had settled there with their whole family after their father had retired from the Indian Foreign Service. An early marriage was fixed as desired by the boy's parents.

When Geeta's marriage was announced in my family, Satya Paul proposed a meeting of all brothers to consider the manner in which we had to go about it. I felt proud that my brother had thought of sharing the responsibilities for the performance of the first marriage of the next generation. Being closest to me among my brothers, he had watched me working day and night in fulfilling all the responsibilities of the marriages of my sisters as well as of my brothers. My thoughts continued having their soothing effect on me till the meeting was actually held.

We sat in our drawing room. Satya Paul opened the subject by saying that the first marriage among our children had been fixed. It would be the marriage which shall be considered by all brothers as an example to follow. We might, therefore, consider, how much money should be spent on the entire marriage. I replied that I had been attending to the expenditure side of all the marriages celebrated in our family after coming from Pakistan and I had the experience and knowledge of every aspect of a marriage. From my own marriage in 1952 to Govinder's in 1970, I had acted with full responsibility according to the time and the financial situation of our family. This time too everything would be done in the same spirit.

But Satya Paul was not satisfied. He proposed that we might fix an amount within which the marriage would have to be performed. His words caught me by total surprise and while I was thinking on the import of his sentence, he continued to say that an amount of rupees one lac should be fixed.

I was startled at his rude boldness. Simultaneously, he asked Raj Paul and Govinder Paul, their opinion and they both quietly concurred. Till that time the two had been sitting silently. Again Satya Paul carried on like a very sagacious person and addressing me, said, "*Bhai Sahib* when you would fix one lac for the whole expenditure, the ladies would stretch it to 1.25 lacs".

Inside my room I pondered over the proceedings in the meeting. To me it was becoming clear that the meeting was an expression of loss of faith in me and my honest conduct. But I started wondering, how Satya Paul, my most dedicated and obedient brother had all of a sudden changed so drastically? He had never performed any of the marriages in our family; how could he advise me about all such details. It took me no time to understand that he had been influenced and tutored.

Geeta's marriage was performed and I kept the account of everything spent there. With my experience and good connections, every function was performed with respectable elegance, at the minimum expense. About 1500 guests attended the marriage and nearly 1200 of them stayed for dinner. The dinner was so good and so well served that, our caterer told me, that nearly 100 guests had taken his address. But none of my arrangements could be called "extravagant" or "ostentatious". The total expense could not be limited to 1.25 lakh. It was 1.70 lakh, and I told my brothers that it could not be reduced. None of my brothers offered help to me in the marriage arrangements. Even the stainless steel utensils which we manufactured in Sekhri Brothers had to be purchased from Punjab Steel, Chandni Chowk.

In the Hindu society, marriages of girls are considered as responsibility of the entire small community like our Sekhri community. In a joint family, it is a virtual family marriage where all put in their best efforts and resources together. I myself had worked in all the marriages of my cousin sisters in Sialkot so hard that all the family members used to compliment me. Coming from Pakistan, it was the Almighty's grace that I was able to perform all my family duties in the same spirit and had continued to remain steadfast upto this time as a true example of a joint family.

I took the hurt caused by my brothers' attitude stoically, thinking that all what had happened was God-ordained and it might be for my benefit. The business and home affairs continued to be attended to by me as before. No one from outside could have the slightest hint of the inner position of our family.

After Geeta's marriage, the environment in the family started changing fast. It appeared that the entire household had been infected. The edifice which I had erected with the blessings of my parent's and full support of my brothers, appeared to be crumbling.

That drift in the family continued and one day, in the factory, Satya Paul came to me and sitting before me told me very seriously that he found it impossible to live in the house with *bhabhi* i.e, my wife. I asked him what prompted him to say such a thing. He said it was not one thing that he could tell. *Bhabhi* was very petty-minded and small-hearted. I was stunned to hear such words against the person who came to our family as my wife thirty year ago and had carried on most of the burden of the family, especially during the hardest years, without any hassle. I also remembered that when Satya Paul brought his family to live with her at Pusa Lane flat, she bore all their burden. His two elder children were born while living there and my wife had taken full care of those two for many years like a real mother.

I controlled my feelings and told him that I knew my wife was simple and not clever like his wife. She was honest and good-hearted. She was married to me, was mother of our four children and had been totally dedicated to me and our whole family. If he and his wife could not pull on with her, I would arrange some separate accommodation and would shift there, leaving him and his wife to live there in peace. The subject was closed and I left my seat. The next day he again came to me and told me that he did not mean to live separately. All what he had tried to express was that *bhabhiji* should also be as broad-minded as his brother. I told him that he must understand that no one in the world was perfect. Every person born as a human, possessed some good qualities and some shortcomings. In a family, the correct attitude of those who lived together was to look at the good points in others and ignore their weaknesses. I pointed out to him that he must know that I had brought all of them up with that attitude.

When Govinder Paul, who had come back from Kathmandu, came to me and talked the same way and with the same reasoning about Santosh, I realized that somone was working determinedly against me in the family. These two episodes occurred in July 1980. Santosh, the simplest and the sincerest of all ladies in our Sekhri *parivar,* was being made a scapegoat. The real target was her husband. I continued to be tormented all the time with thoughts of the uncharitable attitude of my brothers. I was now convinced that the distrust had made its entry in our family and it was spreading very fast. But I was not mentally prepared for what I was witnessing.

In addition to what was happening in the family, a new problem had cropped up. After Sudhir, the children of other partners, having completed their education, had also joined the firm when there was hardly sufficient work for all of them. I decided to consider the situation in a meeting where we four brothers, our father and Inder Mohan Chopra discussed this subject. No practical solution could be found inspite of several meetings.

But we continued to discuss the problem in our regular meetings. Finally, Inder Mohan proposed that he might be separated, with the Naraina factory and the Sun Shine Steel Industries, as his share. All agreed on his offer and we went to our CA's office. When the separation deed was prepared, our C.A Mr Relan phoned me and I got both the Separation and Dissolution Deeds collected from him.

Those were placed in a meeting in which all partners including *pitaji* participated. Everyone signed those Deeds except Inder Mohan who wanted to take them home and sign them only after proper scrutiny and legal consultations. Thus this meeting also ended in unpleasantness.

Up to the time of my writing this book, those deeds remain as they were left on that day. The premises have been in the possession of Inder Mohan since then and has been conducting his business there with the help of his sons.

Sudhir too, after sometime resigned from Paul Engineers and started his own garment export business. With Sudhir's exit and Neeraj and Pankaj having left earlier, only Vikram remained in our business. The problem of Inder Mohan's refusal to sign the papers of his separation remained unresolved. For this problem we held a meeting and decided to wait for Inder Mohan's next move.

Inder Mohan's attitude and my failure to convince him of my sincerity had given me a very rude shock. It shattered my self-confidence and created some apprehensions in my mind about the future of our family relationships. To set my concern at rest, I held a meeting with my brothers and asked them to suggest any future plan for the reorganization of the various sections of our business. Satya Paul promptly suggested that every one of the brothers might control one section of our business. He added that he would control Paul Engineers independently. As I was prepared to hear something of similar nature from him, I promptly agreed to what he said and told him to control that firm from the next day. Raj Paul who had been controlling Sekhri Brothers independently for a long time, wanted Govinder to help him but he did not specify in what capacity he wanted Govinder Paul to help him.

To my mind, Govinder was indispensable for the liaison jobs of both Paul Engineers and Sekhri Brothers, but independently he might not be able to manage any business successfully. Satya Paul only made exception about the export business but thought that he would handle liaison work of Paul Engineers himself. Govinder Paul said that he wanted to run the rolling mill together with the manufacture of the portable welding machines, which he would market in the domestic territories. To start with, he wanted the machine from Paul Engineers and welding accessories and garden tools for domestic sales from Industrial Products of India which had fallen to my lot. The meeting came to end and I felt that I had a complete picture of the mind of each of my brothers.

From that meeting, everyone seemed to go in a happy mood. On my part I stopped taking interest in Paul Engineers and Sekhri Brothers from that day onwards. I did go with Satya Paul to introduce him to the DGS & D officials in New Delhi and to CIGS people in Kanpur but did never touch even the fringe of his finances. A rough demarcation in the factory was also made.

Govinder Paul, who wanted to run the rolling mill installed in the premises of Sekhri Brothers, will start working in the space next to that unit. The export section would be shifted to the backside set-back of Paul Engineers. I told my brothers that what was done that day was only provisional and experimental. The whole business would remain as family business and the outcome of the new arrangement would be discussed after a year or so.

For the first time in several decades, I had to be on my own to conduct the business and I was no more young. I had to go on foreign tours almost every quarter of the year to secure sufficient export business to make my firm a profitable unit. I did all the purchases, attended to the manufacturing, arranged dispatches and to be able to do all those, I had to arrange the finances. At the same time, almost unknowingly, I had to take on myself the total responsibility of the firm newly started for Air Commodore Jaiswal who had just retired. He had come close to me when I worked for Paul Engineers as he was an officer in the Inspection Directorate of General Stores.

I had been putting in my best efforts all the time to recreate and maintain good atmosphere in the family and in business, but failed. I realized that my time as the family head was up and that I must find a way for an amicable parting. It was the most challenging situation in my life as I had to extricate myself unscathed from the web I had created in pursuit of my life's mission of family unity.

The provisional allotment of different sections of business, after sometime, metamorphosed practically into the final division. Everyone had started doing business in their own way and had reconstituted the old joint firms into their individual firms. With that development, the household was automatically segregated into four separate segments. It was a virtual division except that the house and the factory buildings were not yet formally divided.

Raj had decided to change his product line from utensils and surgical dressing drums to kitchen sinks. He received blessings from his Guruji for that change and was working hard to make the new product successful. Govinder had started to produce portable welding transformers in his unit and was managing domestic marketing through agents and by taking tours himself. Besides the portable welding machines, he was getting welding accessories and garden tools from Industrial products of India. Satya Paul had successfully executed the government contracts which were already placed on Paul Engineers or for which the spadework on our tenders was completed in our favour. He was very happy of his initial performance. In one of our meetings he had stated that in the year after separation and under his independent control, his performance had surpassed the best year's performance of Paul Engineers when there were six persons contributing their might in that firm. That boastful statement shocked me as well as others. I felt that so much of conceit would not be good for him. But no one had said anything in response.

I continued to be stressed due to the bad vibes from those who had been closest to me in the family. Tragically, the onus of dividing the house and the factory buildings was put on me.

I took-up first the factory where the business had virtually been divided. I could find a solution in my mind and worked on it to give it a practical shape. In a meeting I told my brothers that the infrastructure of the factory was set up for one family business. It could not be divided like a commodity on a weighing scale. I had thought the best way it could be done. The built-up factory was divided in four equal sections from the basement to the top. On one side Raj Paul was working with his machinery set up on concrete foundations. He could not be disturbed. He was told to have that section of the built-up area with all the adjoining open areas. Next to him, I told Govinder to take the adjacent portion with its open areas. Govinder's portion cut into the administrative block, but since it could not be avoided, I had to stick to it. Half the factory was thus divided. The other half that remained, constituted the corner part of the building with two side roads. In that portion my son Sudhir had rented a part of the mezzanine for his export business. That space happened to be towards the main front. I therefore, divided that part north-south wise so that one part attained the corner position, including Sudhir's rented space, and the remaining part was left at the back. The corner portion had the advantage of large front and opening onto two roads. The other portion, which had a very small front, included a bigger open area on the back of the factory. While making those divisions, I told Satya Paul to choose any one he preferred. I simultaneously told him that if he could leave for me, the part where Sudhir was working, I would feel grateful. But he chose the corner portion. I put my seal on the division without any show of feelings. The important subject of division of machinery was not touched as I considered that since the division was being made in the spirit of basic oneness of the family, it would automatically go to the side where it was needed.

Everyone appeared satisfied and the meeting dispersed. Sudhir's space being on Satya Paul's side, did not make any difference as the rent paid by Sudhir had been already collected by Satya Paul.

I called our architect and got the division plan prepared with marking of different portions in different colours bearing name of each one on his portion. When Satya Paul saw that his set-back part was lesser than that of mine, he did make a protest. But I told him that he had himself chosen that part in spite of my request to leave it for me. Further, if he liked he could still exchange. But he was not prepared for that. With the division of the factory and business, one hurdle was overcome.

—16—

FAMILY DIVIDED AFTER THE DEATH OF PARENTS

The exit of my mother from the family, its escalating disunity, the increasing vanity of my younger brother, had all contributed to vitiate further the environment at home and at work.

When business was separated and the four families of brothers were tearing apart the person who started the process of the disintegration was the one who had to face its consequences first. The business about which he claimed to have achieved excellent results when alone, started giving him headache and he had to go to his brothers for help.

The trouble first confronted Satya Paul in the running of Paul Engineers as Inder Mohan Chopra, one of the erstwhile partners had refused to sign the dissolution papers of the old constitution. In order to reconstitute the firm, he had to dissolve the old constitution which needed the signatures of all former partners on the dissolution deed. Everyone had signed but Inder Mohan refused, telling him that he may first arrange the allotment of Naraina factory in his name. I had to accompany him to Inder Mohans's house and request for his signatures but Inder Mohan did not budge. When I told Satya Paul to visit him again alone, and request him for an alternative, he gave him the alternative to pay him Rs 2.62 lacs which the DDA had demanded for executing the lease in his name. He had made a concession of Rs 50,000 to Satya Paul and wanted 2.12 lacs by cheque. Satya Paul who had done excellent business in the last year did not want to pay from his sources and wanted me to pay that money. This was the irony of the situation. A little earlier Satya Paul had refused to pay the personal loan taken by Paul Engineers from A.C. Jaiswal and another government officer, because I had arranged those when I was heading Paul Engineers. In Inder Mohan's case too I was forced to pay which I had to arrange partly from Sekhri Brothers and the major amount from Welspring Universal, my new export firm. Inder Mohan signed the papers after receiving payment by cheques, and Satya Paul could reconstitute Paul Engineers as per his plan.

After that episode all of us could concentrate on our separate firms. I was finding it very hard to handle my business. From 1953 to 1982, in every business activity, I had worked in a team though I shared the major responsibility. I had been working with the psychological strength of my being one of a group of my own people.

Soon, my Saviour had arranged good working hands in my firm and though I had to work much harder, I had the consolation of the smooth progress. At home, it was getting worst and very painful. Alongwith other pin pricks the circumstances of *mataji's* departure and *pitaji's* condition exerted tremendous pressure on my mind.

Then all of a sudden, a new problem cropped up in our household which shook the very foundation of our joint family. Raj Paul and Satya Paul started marrying their school-going daughters in extreme hurry. In doing so, they disregarded all the joint family ethics and traditions that the elder daughter in the family should be married first. Raj Paul arranged the marriage of his eldest daughter to the son of one of his Gurubhais in Bombay. He went to Bombay with his family and married the girl in two days without informing anyone in the family. Similarly, he performed the marriage of his second daughter in Delhi without any consultation with anyone. On my own I went to him and offered my contribution. Though I felt aghast on his behavior but when I sat alone to think about it, I could understand Raj Paul's position. He had four daughters and no son. His wife was incurably sick. His business in spite of his best efforts and hard work was not showing good results. I knew his mental pressure. It was through his *Guruji* that he found some solace. He performed both the marriages in a sober manner not putting pressure on others. I felt bad because of his ignoring of my existence as his eldest brother.

Satya Paul too started the same way. Moreover, he also did it in a most undignified manner. He settled the marriage of his daughter with one of our neighbour's family and performed her *thaaka* ceremony with such pomp and show that it could be an envy for the millionaires of that time. Arranged in our front lawn, both Satya Paul and Usha Rani acted as masters of the ceremony, distributing gold and moneybags to their new relations with immense pride on their faces. It was a function so ostentatious as to flout every stricture on expenditure so gallantly set by Satya Paul at the time of the marriage of my daughter, Geeta. But the worst part for me was the position of my daughter, Reshmi who was much elder to all the three girls and was still unmarried. She was seeing all and feeling totally helpless and demoralized.

Three months after that grand *thaaka* function, Satya Paul fixed the marriage. At that time, he unexpectedly knocked at my door, wanting money for the marriage from me. As his eldest brother, I was never consulted about the marriage. Both Satya Paul and Usha Rani started forcing me to arrange the money as I had done for them in the case of payment to Inder Mohan. But how was I responsible for giving the money after separation. Moreover, Satya Paul had got the main business which was the only profit giving firm. Not only this, he had claimed in the presence of all the brothers that he had been running the business much better without his partners. Where was the money going which he had been earning due to his excellent performance? But at that time they did not listen to any of my arguments and questions. They both continued their pressure on me for money. Ultimately, they forced me to arrange it before I could attend to my own business. I had also to come back for the marriage leaving my foreign tour half way and was made to perform the duty as father figure at that time.

It was the beginning of 1984 when Satya Paul married his daughter. That year turned to be full of problems from its very beginning. *Pitaji* with his penance after *mataji's* death, fell badly sick. He had to be hospitalised in his bad condition but he could be saved and brought back home. At home he needed regular nursing. At the same time I also arranged for weekly visit of a doctor. But whatever we could do, when he did not want to live, how could he be saved? He started languishing both physically and mentally. The later development was creating problems for which I had to give more time to him and also sleep in his room at night. With all our efforts we could prolong his life for a year more. In December 1985, he had to be again taken to Ganga Ram Hospital where his severe voluntary ordeal ended with his last breath in 1986.

After my father's death, I attended to the division of our house between the four brothers. That time I found a way to do it in a manner which suited the changed conditions. What I did in the case of the factory did not do the proper justice to all. The person who received the lion's share just in a brotherly division, did not play his part as a brother. He shared a little with Govinder Paul but openly worked against my export unit. My purpose of a brotherly division was , therefore, defeated.

It was almost 3 years after factory division and during that time I had to go through severe mental agony. I therefore, decided to complete the separation by dividing the house as well. An architect was engaged to get the house and the land valued at market rates. The house was divided in two parts in a way that it might require the minimum possible alterations. The open land at the back was divided into two plots. The value of every divided part was calculated for us by our architect and in a meeting I explained to everyone how the residential property had been divided and the manner in which every part had been valued. Govinder, the youngest, was told to have the first option to choose any of the four parts. He chose the open land at the end. As per the calculated estimate of the price of each part, Govinder would get Rs. 3 lacs for construction from one of his brothers who might get the part of the built-up portion on the driveway side. Second to have his choice was Raj Paul. He opted for the second open plot. He was to get 3.50 lacs, for construction from the other brother getting the other built-up section. Third was Satya Paul's turn and he surprised me by graciously telling me, *bhai sahib* this time you choose first". This was the way, like which he had been acting before 1970. I was touched and told him, "OK, let us not disturb the way, we are living already". This time the division was in a proper and just manner.

All of us would continue to live as before till Raj and Govinder constructed their units as and when they found it convenient.

My father's death resulted in the separation of his four sons. He had been the overlord of his family and alongwith his wife, was the cementer of the unity of the family.

—17—

MY PARENTS—AN ENIGMATIC UNION IN MARRIAGE, IN LIFE AND DEATH

In the year 1917–8, the *barat* of my father, left *mohalla* Wadehrian, and reached the brides village called Dugri, on *tongas*. They were received and accommodated in a hall as honorable guests. The marriage was solemnised and the *barat* was ready to leave with the bride after their having been entertained for customary two days and nights, when it started raining. It had to wait for the rain to stop.

But the Rain God had a different plan—the rains became heavier. The *barat* could not move out of their resting-place and hence had to stay on for another night. The whole night, the rains did not stop and in the morning the marriage party found themselves in an unenviable position. The compound outside the hall where they slept was full of water and still the rain had not relented. The helplessness of the *barat* and the delicate position of the bride's parents started turning more and more embarrassing because of the non-stop of rains for another two days. The roof of the hall started leaking and the compound water started entering the hall. The *barat* had to survive wearing their underwear, sitting on their steel trunks The bride's parents could not arrange to give proper food to the bridegroom's party after two days and two nights. Then on they served simple *dal roti*. On the fifth day of their arrival, when no improvement in the weather was foreseen both the bride's and groom's parents had mutually decided that the *barat* should depart in that unforgiving weather in whatever way they considered fit. The best *tonga* was earmarked for the newly married couple. The rest of the *barat* members were told to adjust themselves and their bags in the other *tongas* in the best way they could. Some young folks volunteered to walk by the side of the *tongas*. Half the way to Sialkot from that village, which was not brick laid, was the most difficult to traverse even by the horses; the other half which was brick laid was easier. By the nightfall, all the members reached their houses safely, to the great relief of their family members.

This was the story of that eventful marriage of my parents Shrimati Daya Wanti and Shri Durga Dass Sekhri. My father was then a student of ninth class and my mother was an illiterate village belle.

THE LIFE

My father, after his matriculation, started working with his father in his steel trunk business, and my mother started living as the first bride in a joint family consisting of the families of my grandfather and his two younger brothers. Individually, the couple was very different. My father was educated, my mother illiterate. My father was autocratic, angry, short tempered, outgoing and vocal and my mother was obedient, calm, silent and soft. Their lives went on smoothly even though the family had to face some tragedies and hardships. My mother gave birth to 10 children out of which one died soon after birth. They had five daughters and four sons.

Sometime after marriage they had to get separated from the joint family and during that period they had many ups and downs. But the smooth life of the couple was mainly due to the qualities of tolerance, patience and forbearance of my mother. The most testing moments for my mother were when I and other children were treated mercilessly by our angry father. Still she continued to be proud of her educated, hardworking, sacrificing and spiritual husband.

THE END

My mother died in July 1982. She suffered for almost a year from asthma and was confined to her bed. She was looked after by her sons, daughters-in-law, her daughters and by her only brother's wife. My father who had a separate room did not contribute in any way during her illness. Even before that since both lived in their own rooms since 1970, my father sometimes would tell me in good humour that he had seen my mother after four days. Such was the position of their relations at that period. But when my father was informed in his room that our mother was dead, he silently stood up from his bed, brought his *havan kund* and started giving *ahuties* with *vedic mantras*. At the cremation ground when her pyre was lit, he fainted. He was brought home somehow and given the required medical aid.

But it was not the end of the problem. My father became totally silent, stopped eating his regular diet. Unfortunately, I was not present at the time of my mother's death. I reached home about 10 days after her death. When I came to know about her demise, I cried aloud for quite sometime in her room placing my head on her bed. The whole family assembled around me to offer their solace. As I came out of her room, I went to my father who did not move from his room. I was surprised to find him sitting tight. I expected him to speak something and allow me to give vent to my aggrieved feelings but he remained sitting like a statue. The other family members told me about his reaction on my mother's death.

Next day I went to my father's room in the morning to pay my respects and found him in the same position as the day before.

I continued meeting him every morning and evening for paying my respects but he did not change his stance. He had totally abandoned all his spiritual programme which he had been following for half-a-century. After one week on a Sunday morning I went to his room and sat beside him. I started the talk by addressing him, "*Pitaji*, ever since I have come back from my foreign visit, I have not seen you performing your daily *havan*". He did not speak and continued in his posture of silence. I again started and told him that he had been so much overpowered with grief after *mataji's* death that he had forsaken those very things which constituted his lifeline. With such predilection towards religion and so much of vedic study and knowledge, how could he drown himself totally in grief and forget all those noble acts which he had been performing daily for the last fifty years? Did he think that our *mataji* was immortal or did he expect that both he and *mataji* would leave this world together? Ever since this universe came into existence, had there been any two partners who were born or died together? He stopped me there by raising his right hand and then spoke, "My son, you are telling me those things which had been taught to you by me. I have not forgotten those. But now that the vital spark has been snuffed out of me, I am no more alive to do those things". I was stumped to hear those words from him. He carried on, "Vishwa Nath, your mother and I had been married for 64 years. All those years we remained steadfastly united, loyal and sincere. All you are telling me to do is not in my control anymore. You leave me as I am." I silently got up from his bed and left his room.

Going back to my room, I wondered whether the simple and unassuming mother was the real sustainer of our family? And was she the Holy Spirit behind all that was good and noble there in our house? The more I thought about it, the more I was convinced that with her exit, our family was orphaned.

I also could see that my father had made up his mind to commit a slow suicide. He exactly did that and was reduced to a bundle of bones. Finally, he breathed his last on January 4, 1986, at Ganga Ram Hospital.

— 18 —

LIFE AFTER THE FAMILY SEPARATION

When my father left his physical body, and our separation was completed with the division of our house and the factory buildings, the position started easing for me both at home and at work place.

At that time I got the feeling that my father who could not put an end to the rift in the family while he was in his physical body, could do it soon when he turned into a spirit. I came out of the cobweb of the responsibilities I had voluntarily woven around me. After our final separation, I felt as if I had come out of my long incarceration to see the light of the day. I could give attention to my family.

Both my sons having become engineers were working independently, Sudhir in Delhi and Pradeep at Richmond, Va. USA. My elder daughter, Geeta was married in 1979 and living happily in Washington DC with her husband. She also had a daughter and a son. My son Sudhir was also married in 1981 and had twin sons. A year after my father's death, my son Pradeep was also married to a girl of a Punjabi family living in the UK.

My business was improving and after working in Europe I extended it to USA. There, Pradeep was giving me a helping hand. The only problem I could not handle successfully was that of getting my younger daughter, Rashmi, married. She was getting older. All my efforts for fixing her marriage were unsuccessful. When Pradeep was married and took his wife to Richmond, Rashmi and her mother also went with them.

We, then started finding some suitable match for her in America, among the Hindus settled there, but failed. Finally Rashmi, who had started working there, told us one day that an American who visited the place of her work, asked her if she would marry him. It was an utterly unexpected and queer proposition, and we did not give it much attention. But after a few days that person again came to her store and repeated his proposal. I was in America those days and I told Rashmi to call that person to our home to meet us. When the gentleman met her again, she could fix the time and date with him for his visit to us. We called our daughter Geeta and son-in-law, Ravi from Washington DC for that day's meeting. The gentleman arrived with two of his relations and after they left, my son-in-law having satisfied himself of the credential of the boy, recommended that we might go ahead if Rashmi was agreeable. It took a few months for the family to decide and finally Rashmi got married to an American.

She is now settled in Richmond, Va with a son and her own large house. Nearly five years after her marriage, she obtained a divorce from her husband and from that time, she has led her independent life there with her son.

A new chapter of reconciliation had also begun with my brothers. It was after many years of family separation, that Govinder's daughter, Sonu, was to be married. He used his God gifted talent of a liaison quality with his approach to his three elder brothers. He called a meeting and told us that they had each married one of their daughters at the time of the joint business. He being the youngest, his daughter's marriage had been fixed when there was no joint business. He pleaded for justice from his elder brothers. The three of us agreed to jointly spend Rs. 5.00 lacs for Sonu's marriage. Each one of the three brothers had volunteered to contribute Rs. 1.70 lacs towards that amount. I was made incharge to manage the event. The marriage was performed satisfactorily in every way respecting the wishes of both Asha and Govinder. A little more than Rs.5 lacs was spent. Raj gave his share money to me. Satya Paul could not do it.

All the brothers were living separately but in the same house as before. It's the Grace of the Almighty and the good deeds of our parents that we were considered as one family even after separation. Sekhri family of Punjabi Bagh was known as a family with a special flavour of respectability. After some small irritants and pains of separation, we continued with respect and love as in one good family.

After Sonu's marriage Santosh, my wife, went back to USA. Raj Paul's wife Gulshan, though very weak with her incurable disease, had participated in the marriage in good spirit joining fully in the ladies *sangeet*.

Being an early riser, I attended to the important matters of my business at that time. One morning, after I was free from my work, I came down to collect the day's newspapers. Seeing Raj Paul standing in the lounge, I went to him and casually asked him about Gulshan's health. He told me that she was still sleeping and added that those days she appeared to be very cheerful. Talking about her, I moved with Raj Paul to the room where we found her sleeping with Charu, his youngest daughter. Both of them were in sound sleep. The cover sheet which both were sharing had slipped fully to the Charu's side and Gulshan was uncovered with her legs exposed. In order to cover Gulshan's legs, I pulled the cover sheet from Charu's side and in the process, my hands touched Gulshan's leg. Finding it abnormally cold I was alarmed. I put my hands against her mouth and nose. There was no breathing. I looked at Raj standing close to me and told him that she appeared lifeless. He hurriedly came forward touched her and confirmed that she was no more.

We were stunned at this unexpected scene. Raj pushed Charu to get up from the bed. Pulling the cover sheet from the bed, we spread it on the floor, lifted the dead body from the bed, placed it on the ground on the sheet. I then hurriedly went upstairs and informed Satya Paul, Govinder Paul and Sudhir of Gulshan's demise. All the family members came down. Raj phoned his Guruji in Gurgaon. Satya Paul and Sudhir phoned our relatives. My sisters and some of Raj Paul's *Gurubhais* started arriving. Raj Paul, after the initial shock, had regained his balance. No crying except for the children who could not control themselves. Gulshan's was the third death in our family after that of our *mataji* and *pitaji*. Gulshan's mother and her only brother were already dead. She was the third to go from her parent's side too.

Gulshan, ever since her marriage, remained unwell. Slowly and slowly her health problem developed to make her hysterical and she started passing into fits of a strange type. In that condition, she forgot herself and showed disregard for every one in the family. Mysteriously she only spared me and sometimes only I could control her in that condition. It was something which I could not understand but I could feel some strange inner connection and that connection may have led me to be the first in the large family to discover that she was no more with us.

Santosh, my wife, continued to spend more time with Pradeep's family in America. The couple who had been married for four years, had one son, and could easily manage without her help. I stayed in Delhi with my elder son and attended to the responsibilities of my business all alone. I had to undertake regular foreign tours and when in India, I had to travel for procurement of different types of raw materials from places outside Delhi. I was almost seventy years old and the magnitude of work I had to do, did not allow me to do justice to all sections of the business. In addition to my own business, I had involuntarily involved myself in the business of my friend Jaiswal. Although, his son had joined that business but the boy's association, instead of reducing my workload, increased it because of his mistakes. All that accounted for much more than I could normally take.

I talked about that to Sudhir to know if he could share some responsibility of the engineering business. He expressed his inability to do so as he was exceedingly busy and fully involved in his own fast developing business.

At the third death anniversary *havan* of our father, I had undertaken to construct a hall at a new Arya Samaj in East Punjabi Bagh, in memory of our parents. That hall could be completed and its inauguration was done in 1991. After I got free from that responsibility I visited America in 1992. I discussed with Pradeep about my growing business and social obligations to request him to come back and help me. Pradeep was very sympathetic. He put before me the major factor which came in the way of his shifting to Delhi. It was his wife Renu's apprehension that as she had been born and brought up in the west (UK), she might not be able to adjust to the Indian environment. She was then in her mid-twenties and had never lived in India. I realized the genuineness of her fear. After listening to Pradeep, I continued deliberating with him to find the solution to the problem. He thought that I might find a way out, and requested me to do so. Giving the problem a deep thought and in view of Pradeep's explanation, I tried to find a solution. One of those days, I decided to speak to Renu myself.

One of those days I took her for an evening walk. Giving her the resume of my discussions with Pradeep, I told her that I appreciated her apprehension about life in India, where she had never lived except for a couple of weeks before her marriage. I suggested to her to go to India for a month or two as a trial. I assured her that she will have a living accommodation as good as she had in USA. In addition to the accommodation, she would get a new car with a chauffeur for her exclusive use, a modern kitchen with a cooking range, refrigerator, washing machine and other household gadgets along with a cook, a maid servant for her children and spacious lawns in that house. She would find good schools for her children. With those facilities if she found the life in India good for herself and her family, she might continue, otherwise she would be free to go back. Renu did not raise any objections and agreed to my suggestion. Pradeep managed the rest and all of them shifted to Delhi as early as they could. I thanked the Almighty for His gracious help.

I was confident when I spoke to Renu because I could judge that our living quarters and other resources in India were in no way inferior to those available to her in America. After Pradeep's marriage, my elder son Sudhir had renovated our house to create two self-contained and modern flats each on the ground and the first floor. When Pradeep's family arrived, they were heartily welcomed to occupy the ground floor. I had been already using one room on that floor. Renu found everything to her liking and never thought of going back. At the time of her arrival in Delhi, she was in the family way and had registered herself for delivery again in Leister. At the appropriate time, she flew there and gave birth to her second son on December 1, 1992. After staying there for about two months, she came back to Delhi with the newborn son, whom we named Rahul.

Pradeep's shifting to India had reduced my burden and it helped in introducing several good measures for the expansion and improvement of our business. I had suffered some betrayals in the export business which had put me to losses. It may be proper to give their account here.

When I restarted export business in 1973, I had appointed an agent in London. He was an ex-foreign officer incharge of the EEPC London. A very smart and efficient man, he had helped us to secure good business to enable us to make a restart in a big way. Unfortunately for him he committed an unethical act as an agent and I had to cancel his agency agreement in 1975. The man was highly qualified Indian from Andhra Pradesh. The money for which he committed a wrong deed was a few thousand pounds only but I lost faith in him.

Sometime during the year 1975, I was introduced to an Indian family settled in London. The couple came to see me in the hotel I was staying and forcibly carried me to their home. There they treated me like a VIP and during my first stay of few days with them, convinced me that I may continue staying with them whenever I visited London in future. A robust friendship was developed with them mainly by the genial nature of the lady and I continued staying with them during my visits to London for the next two years. In course of my visit in 1977, when we sat for a friendly chat after dinner, the lady asked me about the payment of commission of our London business. When I told her that she could not do any work as an agent, both the lady and her husband became rude.

The background was that in one of my visits, the lady told me that since I had terminated my agency with my first agent, I may appoint them agents and she promised to take out time from the service she was doing and visit our customers regularly. I was obliged to agree. But since the lady could not do anything, I considered it may be just her wishful idea which she was unable to put into practice. But as a result of their rude behaviour in demanding commission, I felt that they were clearly demanding money as their right for accommodating me in their house and looking after me. Therefore, I paid them the commission as the lady wanted and never looked at them after that.

An eyes doctor working in Amritsar Hospital, had come in contact with my brother Raj Paul during his first visit to Amritsar for Gulshan's (his wife) treatment. He came to see Raj Paul once and was introduced to me. That doctor was then settled in London. He invited me to stay with him during my next London visit. He said that he had bought a big house in a London suburb with many rooms. Next time when I went to London I stayed in a hotel, and one of those days I phoned him and told him that I was staying in such and such hotel. The same evening he came to my hotel, had drinks with me and stayed for dinner in my room till late that evening. Early next morning he was again in my hotel, had breakfast with me and offered to drive me to my first appointment in his car. In the afternoon he left me and was present in my hotel again in the evening to have his drink and dinner with me. He made it a routine to be with me as long as I stayed in London and during those days he could convince me to start a company in London which would import our product and deliver ready stock to our customers at better prices. He offered the warehousing of our goods in his large house and took the responsibility to make the deliveries to the customers from there. He took me to the registrar of companies office in London, bought a name of a company for the constitution of which he made me take him as a director. I might have done a few transactions through him but soon disengaged myself from him. But the period I remained under his influence, had costed me a few thousand pounds. I had then known him as a big cheat, very unclean person both in his habits, dealings and living. Only once he took me to his 'big' house. It was an old crumbling building in which he lived with his wife and daughters like dirty uncivilized persons. I felt like breathing a fresh air the moment I came out of his house.

These three betrayals in London were all by Indians and were suffered by Paul Engineers. Those did not hurt much as we came out of their association in a short time. The fourth experience I had was again with an Indian in London whom I appointed as my agent for Garden Tools after my separation from Paul Engineers.

That man took nine years to build up his confidence and wait for the right opportunity to strike and rob us of a fortune. The last episode culminated in 1999. In between I suffered two such instances in Delhi. One by a very friendly high rank government officer with whom I had developed brotherly relations. He retired in 1982, came to my office and told me that he wanted to do some business and had decided to do it under my guidance. He was the most intelligent of the government officers I had dealt with during my tenure with Paul Engineers. I helped him to have a name of his firm, booked orders from abroad in that firm's name and also installed a full-fledged factory for him. In his business he forced me to be a partner and then made me invest liberally in it. I made a big mistake in telling him to bring his young son in that business and that boy proved to be such an evil spirit that he not only defrauded me by a large amount but was also instrumental in making his good father corrupt. I finally parted with them in 1995 after a very stressful time in dealing with the estranged duo. Simultaneously I had been taken for a ride by a son of a very close relative who made me a director in his loss making company. I invested in that company as much as it required and when the company started making good profits after recovering all losses, that young lad pushed me out of that company most unceremoniously. These two episodes combined to hit me so hard that I had to be admitted in Escorts Heart Hospital with a minor attack in September 1995, and had thus become a heart patient for the rest of my life.

In mid 1997, I was admitted in Ganga Ram Hospital to take a 7-day course of injections to clear my badly congested chest, through the outflow of urine. The injections course was completed without any intermediate urine tests. Something had gone wrong and for 2/3 days Santosh, my wife who had been attending on me day and night, complained to the doctor that I had been talking the whole night in sleep and what I talked was totally irrelevant. During daytime, I felt very uncomfortable with no appetite. That doctor did not pay any attention to my wife's complaint. In that bad condition and lack of care, I got into my head the feeling that I had come to a wrong hospital and started insisting that I may be removed to the Escorts Hospital. The Escorts was for heart patients and there my problem worsened and my condition deteriorated to the extent that I regressed into a semi-conscious state.

Santosh was very much alarmed and she spoke to my sons, Pradeep and Sudhir about my condition. After being in Escorts for 4 days, a medical van, with two doctors from the Apollo Hospital, arrived to shift me to their hospital. Pradeep came to me and whispered in my ears that I was being shifted to the Apollo Hospital. I replied in a feeble voice not to disturb me any more. I said that I was very peaceful and wanted to pass away in that state as I was free from all my responsibilities. But Pradeep insisted that they all needed me. Thus ignoring my request, I was carried to the emergency of Apollo hospital. Immediately 4/5 doctors surrounded my bed. I was almost unconscious. After a thorough check-up, they started my treatment. For 10 days I did not know where I was. In those days I had actually reached my end before taking a turn. And I did experience that perfect peace at the border. When I regained a little consciousness I found myself still in the emergency ward. I had a hazy impression that some one important had been visiting me and special care was being taken in my case. After a few more days in the emergency ward, as my condition was brought under control, I was removed to a room and it was then that I was told that

Dr. Reddy, the Chairman of Apollo Hospitals came to see me two or three times. For another 10–12 days, I continued to be in that hospital under very strict supervision. Finally, when I was released I had lost 16 kg weight and was unable to turn sides on my own in my bed. I was reduced to a skeleton. A professional nurse was engaged to take care of me at my residence. She remained with me for 45 days.

During my long hospitalisation in Apollo, Pradeep had been visiting me almost daily. One morning I realised that for three days I had not seen Pradeep. I talked to my wife who told me that he had been busy with some foreign visitors at his factory. On that very day, Pradeep came to my room and sat in a chair near my bed. I saw that his face was pale and he looked much weaker. Santosh told me that the reason for this was that he had been worrying too much about me.

After I came home from the hospital and had gained some strength, only then I was told why Pradeep had not been coming to see me for several days in the hospital. The poor boy was himself admitted in that hospital in a serious condition due to the bursting of his ulcer in his stomach. When he was out of danger, he was removed from the emergency to a room only three rooms next to my own room. Pradeep had developed an ulcer in his stomach during the time he was in USA for his MBA studies. I could not provide him with sufficient funds and he had to complete his studies by working and earning for his fees and other expenses. My serious illness and long hospitalisation had made him work day and night in my service. He had to do lot of running about without caring for his health and diet. That resulted in activating his ulcer and ultimately to its bursting. He had to spend seven days in the hospital. I felt very sorry to hear that my child had to suffer so much because of me.

I was also told the story of my removal to the Apollo Hospital. Sudhir phoned Jagdish, his friend in Madras about my serious illness. Jagdish was one of the Directors of Apollo Hospitals. Dr. Reddy, the chairman of Apollo Hospital happened to be in Delhi those days. Jagdish phoned him to tell that, I, his uncle, was in a serious condition in Escorts and that he may be taken care of. It was Dr Reddy who had specially arranged for my shifting to Apollo and giving me special attention in his hospital.

After convalescing at home for 4–5 months, I started accompanying Pradeep to office. From the car I was carried to the lift in a wheeled chair. The lift took me to the first floor where again the wheeled chair served me to drop me in my office chair. I spent an hour or two in office for a month or so. After that I started walking and attending office for a few hours daily.

But it seemed that all was not well with my mind and body. Every two-three months, I was down with some serious problem and when it could not be controlled at home, I had to be removed either to Apollo or some other heart nursing home near our residence. This went on for the next two years and during this period I had an additional experience of falling sick in London and then getting admitted in two different hospitals of that city too.

Although I was moving on but mine was not a normal life. The fear of falling sick lingered in my mind all the time. That uncertainly made me question the Omniscient God why had he brought me back from the brink of death? Only to eat drink and sleep and thus pass my days? Then one day an unknown doctor was sent to examine me at my home by my youngest brother. The doctor was accompanied by his wife who helped him. He spent a lot of time in examining my pulse, my blood pressure in my positions of sitting, standing and lying down. He asked me whether any of my ancestors suffered from heart problem? In his various queries he came to know that I had been from Sialkot. Hearing this the doctor followed by his wife bowed down and touched my feet telling me that he also belonged to a small village near Sialkot. He finally prescribed for me an Ayurvedic heart tonic named "Arjunarishth". He also told me to continue with my allopathic medicines. His treatment stopped my frequent hospitalisations.

A new life seemed to have begun for me. I stopped thinking like before and questioning God about the purpose of my life. I started reading and writing regularly for few hours a day. My thought channels were diverted towards my social obligations other than those of my family. I started considering compassionately about the poor and suffering of our country and through my sons started discharging those responsibilities in the best way we could. In my mind helping the poor children for their proper sustenance and education assumed the prime place followed by other social causes like helping poor widows, marrying their daughters, donations to various social, spiritual and public health institutions.

In January 2003, my sons had celebrated our fiftieth marriage anniversary by arranging a function which could be called neither ostentatious nor simple. Arranged in Maurya Shereton Hotel, it was a highly enjoyable and very dignified affair. All my family members, my two daughters with their families from USA and all my relatives and friends joined.

Both my sons gave speeches expressing their indebtedness to their parents who they said had made them what they were. Then I was allowed to say only one line in which I could say that I was overwhelmed and enlightened by what my sons had said about us but we had only one regret in our lives. It was that we could not give that attention and love to our children as my sons were giving to their children.

The same year I alongwith my wife and younger son visited Badrinath Temple in the month of May. It was a pilgrimage both enjoyable and elevating. Those two good events were over shadowed by two tragedies, in that year. My younger brother, Satya Paul who suffered for two years after having been caught in the clutches of the cruelest cancer, breathed his last in October of that year. Six months earlier my cousin Balkrishan Puri died with a sudden heart attack at the place where he had served for many years and had that day, delivered a lecture there which was much applauded. He collapsed immediately after finishing his lecture and siting on a chair. Two years back my cousin Madan Lal Sekhri passed away after long illness. Satya Paul and Balkrishan were younger to me by 13 years and Madan Lal by two years. And they were not the only ones who had left from the families of my close relations and of my generation. My youngest sister Daman's husband, Prem Prakash died suddenly of heart attack while he was on an official tour to Chandigarh. It was too tragic for me. The husband of my elder sister Shakuntala died too. He was a saintly person. He was followed by my sister. They were both elder to me. Soon after the death of my sister, her youngest son Sham, died. My sister had lost one son in 1949, suffering from throat cancer. The one after the other my most affectionate cousins much younger to me had died. First to go was Pushpa *bhabhi,* wife of my cousin brother Keval Krishna Chopra, then Pushpa Mago, Krishna Chopra, Sushma Chandhok and Sneh Handa. All these were daughters of my Shanti *bhuaji* with whose family I had the best of my time for several years from 1950 onwards. These deaths were untimely with histories of tragic events in the lives of the deceased. My younger sister Sita's eldest son Vimal died suddenly of an unknown problem while he was alone at some resort. My third sister Prakash lost her 8 years old grandson in few hours and in stunningly sudden manner. That child was special in many ways and was very precocious and lovely. These tragedies of the close kins made a great difference to my life.

Besides the above, there had been many of my close friends who had died during the past years. All those had generously helped me in evolving of my life.

First to go was Brahm Dev Behl, the friend who changed my life. In his later life, he had to go through very bad days. He was found dead in the dry toilet of his small residential quarters in Delhi. Then Charanjit Sachdeva who was working in the International Labour Organisation and was transferred to their Geneva (Switzerland) office. He was alone in his flat where he died in his sleep. His dead body was discovered after two days by some of his office associates who had to break into his house. Raj Kumar Punga who came closer to me in Bombay was a very affectionate friend. He died very young in his house in Ludhiana. Both my school friends Onkar Pandit and Sukh Dev Behl had died one after the other. Onkar Pandit was my first friend made in school and was one of the very close comrades. He died after a prolonged illness. Jagdish Kalra and then Kapur Chand Jain died suddenly of heart failure. Jagdish Sarin died a few years back after suffering long from cancer. Jagdish Abrol and Satish Abrol, both lion hearted companions, had also left. Three close friends I could make after partition in the course of my new business venture in the name of Dipak Agencies (P) Ltd., have all gone. One who was the first to leave was P.S. Kant who resided with his family at Indore. He died there while he was only 51 years. Then died P.N. Behal and last to go was K.K. Chhibber. Kant was from Sialkot, Behal from Gujranwala and Chhibber from Peshawar. Two of my close friends from Sialkot who had settled in Kanpur had both died. First to go was Kuldip Bakshi and the second was Lakshmi Chand Khanna who had died after a long illness in the beginning of 2005. And the other two who had contributed greatly to enliven my life had to go through very painful time. Both died of cancer after suffering from it for years. The one to suffer first was Jagdish Mitra. He was my classmate from Sialkot and was with me in Bombay in 1948, where we lived and worked at the same places. Coming back to Delhi, he became my chum, meeting me almost daily even while he suffered from cancer. He passed away after suffering for the last 15 years of his life. The other to suffer was Sansar Vadehra who lived in Jalandhar where I met him first time after partition in 1976. He was my class fellow in college but when I met him after 30 years he was a totally changed person. He laughed himself heartily and made others laugh with him. He continued with that quality till the time he was not able to speak.

With all those near and dear ones leaving one after the other, life is not as it used to be. I sometimes feel their absence very much and it hurts. I had the best of time with most of my Sialkot friends, and with those who came closer to me in Delhi.

Reverting back to the good old days in my family, I carried a special attachment with my brothers, since the time of their births. They too loved me. Satya Paul, the one younger to me by 13 years, and who died after fighting cancer bravely for two years, was a silent and sober child. But the one next, Raj Paul was a big problem for the family due to his unpredictable pranks. He was a virtual terror for the *mohalla* vendors and for our family barber, Panni, who visited our house once a fortnight to give haircut to all male members. When it was the turn of Raj Paul, Panni always called some one from the family to stand guard there to control Raj. One day I happened to stand there. I knew Raj Paul respected me and he knew that he had to behave properly. I stood there for sometime and saw that there was no problem. He only picked up a comb or scissors lying before him and when I told him to sit quiet without meddling with any of the barber's equipment, he quickly obliged. Thinking that my one time instruction to him would last for the remaining time of his haircut, I went away to attend some work. The haircut completed, Panni lifted the cloth holding the cut hair and went to our front balcony to discard those hair in one corner there. Raj stood up from his seat and vanished. When Panni came back, he found that his haircutting machine had also disappeared with Raj Paul. He gave a loud cry complaining that Raj had gone away with his costly machine. I immediately went to his rescue and assured him that I would get it back. I started to look for Raj Paul in every room of our house but he was not found. I looked on the top terrace of our house, but in vain. Then I went downstairs to look around on the road or in Ram Talai. But before I crossed our large entrance lounge, which was used for keeping our domestic cows and buffalos, I got a glimpse of someone crouching among the animals. I stopped to see and found it was Raj sitting by the side of a buffalo calf and using Panni's machine to shear its hair. When he saw me, he quietly stood up and handed over the machine to me. I went upstairs to pass the same to the worried Panni.

Another time I heard a loud cry from the road with the name of Raj. I rushed down and saw scattered on the road the contents of the entire basket of a poor vendor. He was sitting on the road looking at the eatables of his basket, lying in dust and was cursing his fate. When he saw me, he told me weepingly that he had been very careful and watchful always when he passed under our house for fear of Raj playing mischief with him. That day he could not detect him, hiding somewhere and knew only when he jumped from behind like a prowling big cat and pulled down his basket off his head. He had lost that day's earnings to feed his family. I consoled him and gave him more money than I considered was the worth of all his loss. He stopped crying and started collecting from the road whatever he thought he could salvage. On that day I made Raj sit with me and explained to him the fate of the poor vendor and that while he acted in future, he must remember never to hurt a poor helpless person.

The youngest, Govinder never did any such things like Raj. One day he was looking on the road by leaning over a three foot high railing at our first floor front balcony. Suddenly I heard a loud voice saying that Govinder had fallen from the balcony onto the road. I rushed down and reaching the place of his fall, picked up his inert body. I found no blood on his body nor anywhere on the road where he had fallen. What I found was that the lady luck had favoured us that day and made Govinder fall on the padded front part of a cart lying on the road. I heaved a sigh of relief and with the help of a little first aid, could bring Govinder on his feet.

He had a good sense of timing and the manner in which he used it to his benefit was also a source of enjoyment for me and my friends. Whenever he found me sitting among my friends in my office, he used to come there and addressed me, "*Bhaiji*, can you spare two paisa for me". My friends used to laugh heartily at the kid's sense of timing.

Remembering the episodes of Raj Paul and Govinder Paul's childhood in our old age do provide us with very soothing touch to the much grieved mind and weakened body.

The God Almighty had put in the human body a mind which travelled in a second the distance of time, one had taken 80 years to cover. And again no more time is taken to come to the present reality. That reality in my life may be appreciated better if I write a page or two about my wife and children.

I agreed to the suggestion of my father to get married only when I found myself in a wilderness. Outwardly I looked fine but inside I was just a mass of wreckage. I had failed in my resolve to marry my three marriageable sisters before going for my own. I was also badly frustrated when my intense and sincerest hard work in the joint family business of my father, was ignored.

But I was lucky to get a wife who had no demands and who had merged herself totally into our family from the day she stepped into our house. She too was a God's gift to me in those difficult days. When our first baby was in its early stage of formation in my wife's womb, I got a chance to start my separate business. As my first son was born, that business had also assumed its infant shape, and both started growing side-by-side. In the next two years, two of my sisters were married. A few months after the birth of my first daughter, my third sister was also married. My second son was born in 1957 and the second daughter in 1959. In the beginning of 1959, I managed to send my first son to Nanital for his education.

The house where we lived was too crowded. Twelve humans in three small rooms without the facility of electricity, municipal water tap and flush toilet. The environment there was not healthy and with three growing boys almost crazy. As my sisters left after marriage, my children arrived to fill the gap. The growth of my business and its earning were all spent in the marriages plus in making our living little less harsh by spending on electric facility, municipal water tap and brick-lying on the two open kachacha compounds.

The financial pressure and tumultuous family atmosphere continued to dampen my spirits. I could not give proper attention to my children in a family where my young growing brothers had their first claim on it. It was a situation of my own making and no one other than me can be blamed.

My whole life was spent under one type of pressure or the other, I had developed a sort of immunity to all those adverse developments and allowed the life to take its own course as per my destiny. My children grew up with their own *sanchit karma*. Both my sons had qualified as engineers and then were successful in their business. I could not do anything special for any of my children. My elder daughter after doing her matriculation from Scindhia Girls School, Gwalior, had done her graduation from Dault Ram college, Delhi. The younger one had done her matriculation from Bal Bharati School and her diploma in designing from a Delhi institute. Both are living their own lives in USA. But one thing was very clear. The main responsibility for the upkeep of the children was borne solely by my wife. Not only did she do that but she also gave me full support in all my efforts and stood by me like a rock in my struggling days after marriage. She is the real maker of my family bearing all the extreme odds without even complaining about anything.

All my brothers have grown taller than me and the families of all the four of us are living in separate houses built on the same large piece of land. Every family had to go through good and bad times. The entire older generation, coming from my great grandfather, Jeevan Mal's progeny, are no more. In his lineage I am the oldest male alive. Many of those younger to me have died. Most of my closest friends have also left. I do recognize their part in the drama of my life which I have been able to record as best as I could.

I feel like ending my personal story here. I had started writing about my life from the time of my grandfather and am ending it when I myself am a grandfather. But I feel that I am a grandfather with a difference. I have four affectionate grandsons from my two daughters-in-law. When we are together my grandsons get transformed into our grandfathers; they start kissing our faces from one end to the other. Our two elder grandsons specially act like that. Sometimes in our bedroom, they throw us on our bed and hug and kiss with full affection. Both of us are overwhelmed by their love and sometimes feel perplexed. We had never been kissed by our parents or grandparents. These boys, not only express their unusual love by bringing it out and hugging but they also take a lot of care of us, for our convenience and about our diet. This Beneficence of the Almighty towards us has surpassed every other type. The two elder ones, twins, started treating us that way while they were very young. Perhaps it is God's additional Blessings on us to compensate our loss of such affection from our elders. We bow our heads for all His care for us.

PART - IV

— 19 —

1984 – THE TRAGIC STORY OF MY PUNJAB – THE PERENIALLY SUFFERING STATE

Punjab, the land of my birth is specially gifted by God. At the dawn of history, it was the most favourite abode of many *vedic rishis*. It was a vast fertile area located on the foothills of lush Himalayan mountains of North West, rich with great rivers and healthy robust men and women. But it appeared that this land was also destined to undergo regular sufferings of one kind or the other from time immemorial.

The Punjab of my conception was the one which I saw for the first time on a map in my school and it remained to be so even after it was broken by creation of Pakistan. The Punjab of the British India included the present Pakistan Punjab, the Indian states of east Punjab, Himachal Pradesh and Haryana.

More than five thousand years back on this land the great Mahabharata War was fought at Kurukshetra. It was a struggle between two groups of cousins of one renowned royal family, which resulted in a big war in which almost all the other royal families of India took part. Millions perished in that war and in the end only five Pandav brothers and one Kaurav survived. The entire country especially the Punjab had suffered such a heavy damage that it has taken almost two milleniums to come out of it.

When the country was able to regain some of her past glory, her fauna and flora had also been revived alongwith her general public. Her fame as a very prosperous and spiritual land had again spread all over the world with the result that she attracted some ambitious warriors and rulers. Alexander, a Greek prince, was the first to reach India conquering all the countries on his way. He fought fierce battles in the Punjab before he could reach the river Beas. Having been badly mauled he chose to return from there. He died on the way leaving many of his men in India or on its outskirts. Out of those who were left behind and some other tribes of Central Asia again started invading India. The Greeks, Kushans, Sakas and Huns, invaded through the same north west route and Punjab had to bear the *brunt* of giving their armies stiff resistance and herself suffering a lot. India of those days may not be physically the match for those hungry invaders but it was spiritually strong enough to absorb all those into her social fraternity.

Then on, the whole country experienced an era of development and non-interference from outside for almost a millenium. During those peaceful times in our country, new religions of Christianity and Islam took birth in the neighbouring Western Asia which created a revolutionary effect on its own people as well as on the rest of the world. Christianity chose to spread towards the west after making some mark in the land of its birth. Mohammed the prophet of Islam, preached his religion in Arabia, the country of his birth and saw its rapid spread in his life. He himself had to fight for the spread of his beliefs in the country of his birth. But after his death, Islam spread like a wild jungle fire all around West Asia, North Africa and Europe. The world experienced for the first time the preaching of a religion by sword.

Islamic invaders started invading India in the seventh century but they succeded in establishing their rule here from the twelfth century onwards. After having succeeded in occupying Afghanistan and converting its people who were all Hindus and Buddhists, it started its barbarous invasions on India, killing people, demolishing temples and looting wealth. Punjab was always in the foreground to bear the full brunt of all those rampaging armies. India which had never experienced, such barbarity shown towards its shrines, men and women, was unnerved and she, for the first time, failed in its strength to assimilate these Islamic fanatics. Islam succeeded in converting a small part of its people although it could rule the whole country for almost seven centuries. Finally the Punjab was liberated from the clutches of Muslim rulers by *Maharaja* Ranjit Singh in the beginning of the nineteenth century. At that time the rest of India had been snatched away from the Muslim rulers by the British who came to India by sea and started a trading company in Surat in the seventeenth century. From a trading company they became the conquering company and by AD 1757 they occupied the whole of the country except the Punjab and the North-west areas.

Punjab from the Satluj river upto the Sindh river was in the possession of *Maharaja* Ranjit Singh. As long as *Maharaja* Ranjit Singh lived, he controlled all those areas but ten years after his death, Punjab came under the British occupation. Punjab again suffered devastation in the three fiercely fought battles between the Sikh armies and those of the British. When finally the empire created by *Maharaja* Ranjit Singh came under the British control in the year 1849, the British started consolidating their rule in the country.

In the three Sikh battles, their experience showed the British that the Sikhs and the Dogras were very brave fighters. They managed the Dogras by putting them under the control of *Raja* Gulab Singh, one of the great Dogra generals of *Maharaja* Ranjit Singh, who bought the Himalayan territory of Jammu and Kashmir by paying Rs 70 lacs to the British as Sikh war reparations. The whole of the Punjab including the territory which is now called Himachal Pradesh and Haryana in India and West Punjab in Pakistan rested under the British control.

Hardly eight years had passed since the British had a total control of the Indian territory, when in 1857, Indian soldiers of of the British forces revolted. It spread to many regiments in the Central and Northern India but Punjab which had recently experienced its crushing defeats had remained almost aloof from the revolt which was ultimately crushed by the superior British controlling power.

After the revolt the British rulers decided to enforce, on priority, their policy of divide and rule. They started from the Punjab where they tried to separate Sikhs from the Hindu fold. They invited historians from other countries to write Sikh histories to prove that the Sikh religion was separate from the Hindu religion. They declared Sikhs as a martial community and gave preference to Keshdhari Sikhs in their recruitment in the military services and in allotment of *jagirs* to them in the newly developed areas where canal waters created new fertile lands. They encouraged Sikhs to take control of Gurdwaras and common shrines of Sikhs and Hindus like Hari Mandir of Amritsar, Gurudwara Nankana Sahib, Guru Ka Bagh and others. They encouraged formation of Singh Sabhas and Khalsa Dewans. They carried on those activities for more than 50 years. Simultaneously they had started encouraging Muslims also to form their own separate societies to look after the interest of their religion and warned them that if they remained indifferent to development of their society, they were sure to be gobbled by the majority Hindu community. In due course of time they found that the Muslims were much easier to instigate against Hindus and so for the success of their policy of divide and rule gave prime attention to them. Muslim education was encouraged, plum positions in the British administrative services were thrown their way and by the end of 1920's they created many Muslim leaders to play dominant role in the British administration. Men like Rehmat Ali, Sir Mohamed Iqbal, Sir Mohamed Shaffi and finally Mohammed

Ali Jinnah were won over and were prompted to claim separate homeland by dividing India.

After the end of the Second World War, the British had decided to leave India. They left in August 1947, after dividing the country in two parts. The Muslim majority area were separated from the country to form a new Muslim country, named Pakistan. In the process of division and separation two million people were mercilessly butchered. India was left as a permanently harassed land by the creation of Pakistan. Punjab, the favourite land of the gods was divided into two parts and was made to suffer so much as she had never experienced in her life after existence.

Punjab that remained with India was then called East Punjab. Its size increased with the amalgamation of the many princely states situated within that area. Under the pressure of the Akali Dal, this enlarged East Punjab was again divided into three States viz., Punjab, Himachal Pradesh and Haryana in the year 1967. This much-divided piece of land started boiling in the 37th year of its first bisection. In the year 1984, when the Akali Dal was captured by extremist Sikhs, they started agitation for the creation of Khalistan, an independent Sikh state. It was a very dangerous movement for our country and for those of our people who lived in that area.

Sant Bhindrawale appeared from nowhere in the ranks of the fanatic Sikhs. He was spewing forth fire in his speeches inside and outside the Gurdwaras against the Hindus and the Indian government. He had gathered around him many followers including many disgruntled elements from the retired Sikh military officers. Pakistan was using that unrest to its best advantage in order to take revenge on India for her help to the people of the East Béngal to separate from Pakistan.

Pakistan had created a sort of rapport with Bhindrawale who started enrolling many of the innocent young Sikh boys who were pushed to Pakistan through the long international porous border. They were trained to become militants and were sent back to join the agitating Akalis in India. Those boys were used for looting and murders under the direction of the Sant. A stage reached when law and order in that part of India was completely shattered.

When the state government realized that it was incapable to control the disturbances, it asked the central government for help. The Government of India considered the situation and in response to the request of the state government, sent its armed forces under the command of a Lieutenant General to control the militancy. Bhindrawale and his followers, in order to avoid an open confrontation with the armed forces, took shelter in the Golden Temple, Amritsar. Inside the large precincts of the temple, they had prepared for a sort of armed rebellion. A retired Major General of the Indian Army, who had become a follower of Bhindrawale, had been training the Sikh youths collected inside the temple in the use of various weapons. He had created several pickets in the premises of the temple and on the building of the *Akal Takhat*.

Different types of modern armaments got smuggled from Pakistan into Amritsar, had been sent into the Golden Temple in trucks, hidden under the sacks of the rations going into the temple for daily *langar*. The Golden Temple and the *Akal Takhat* had been converted into a military fortress. The armed forces of the government had to surround the temple but they could not enter it. They found themselves greatly handicapped in the face of a well fortified temple and trained armed men inside it.

When the situation in the Golden Temple worsened, the Indian government headed by Mrs Indira Gandhi ordered the army to clear all the anti-national and anti-religious elements from the Golden Temple. The armed forces announced on loud speakers that all the armed men collected inside the temple should come out and surrender themselves with arms to the army. These announcements were replied with gunshots from inside the temple and from the armed pickets established high up in the *Akal Takhat* building. When the situation further deteriorated and turned into a warfare, the Indian government felt that since the sanctity of the religious place had been defiled by those who had taken control of the temple and who were indulging in the gravest irreligious activities, they should be treated in a befitting manner. The armed forces were ordered to enter the temple. They had to storm into the temple in June 1984. But it was not an usual army operation. They had to confront a well-equipped militarily strong force which had taken shelter in the most respected religious place. Ultimately, the army could flush out the militants from the temple. It was found that bunkers had been created in the man-holes of the temple ground and full military pickets had been organized on all the different storeys of the *Akal Takhat*. In that operation, the army lost many of its officers and men. Bhindrawale and the retired Major General in-charge of the operation inside were killed along with many others. The temple and the *Akal Takhat* were damaged. When it was freed from the militants, it was handed over to the genuine Sikh saints.

But the army's entry into the Golden Temple created deep anger and resentment among majority of the Sikh community all over the world. Pakistan remained active all that time in giving all possible help and provocation to the misguided Sikh youths, and after the raid on the temple, it extended its activities all over the world encouraging NRI Sikhs to be rebellious against their own motherland. Branches of the Khalistan movement were spread all over the world specially in UK, USA and Canada, where most of the NRI Sikhs had been settled and were very well-to-do.

I had personally experienced the effect of that propaganda during my tours in UK. On one occasion I had chanced to visit a Sikh family in London for dinner. My friend Balwant Singh who was invited, took me along. Only three persons from outside and the host were in the party. Beside me and my friend there was one Englishman on the small dining table. As the host served drinks to all and had his first peg, he started talking against the Indian government for their "anti-sikh policies". I was bewildered to hear an Indian speaking against the government of his own motherland in a foreign country, and that too in the presence of a foreigner in his language. I soon recovered from my first shock and spoke in the Punjabi language addressing the host that it was very un-Indian to speak like that before a foreigner. If he must express his grouse he could speak in Punjabi. The hostess, coming near our table supported me and told her husband to stop his irrelevant talk. But the host with the whisky pegs inside him was in a relentless mood. He started talking more vigorously, making me very uncomfortable to sit there. I got up from my seat, told my friend in Punjabi that I was sorry I had come to a wrong place. I left the table and stepped towards the way out, when the hostess rushed towards me apologizing for the absurd behaviour of her husband and requesting me to return to the dinning table. The host regained his senses at my action and promised that he would talk no more. That incident happened sometime before the 'Operation Blue Star' of 1984.

In India, the anger and resentment of the Sikhs penetrated into the army. In some cases, they rebelled and even murdered their commandant Brigadiers and their families. It was a very grave situation which the Government of India had to face. A very important community of India felt badly hurt due to the entry of army men inside the Golden Temple, totally ignoring the aspect of its defilement by militant Sikhs. That resentment culminated into the assassination of the Prime

Minister, Indira Gandhi by two of her own Sikh bodyguards on the morning of 31st October, 1984.

It was an act of a double national tragedy. When the news of the assassination of the Prime Minister by her own Sikh bodyguards, was transmitted to the nation, the people all over the country were extremely shocked and upset. The hot-blooded, especially among the congressmen, turned berserk. In sheer madness, first in Delhi and then all over India, every Sikh found on the road was killed mercilessly. Mobs of frenzied men started attacking the houses where Sikhs were known to be living. Many of those houses were put on fire and the residents inside irrespective of men, women or children, were forced to perish inside. It was the cruelest mayhem, the worst repetition of what had happened at the time of the partition of the country. That time it was the massacre of both the Hindus and the Muslims. This time the only victims were Sikhs, their houses, and their institutions. The police, especially in Delhi, had abandoned their duties and in some cases had encouraged the mad mobs to kill the Sikhs.

It was an unprecedented national calamity. Indira Gandhi's only living son, Rajiv Gandhi, was anointed as the next Prime Minister on the first November when he landed in Delhi from abroad, by the President of India, Giani Zail Singh.

Many Sikh families from all over the country who could survive the mayhem had started migrating to Punjab. The chain reaction of the tragedies continued unobstructed. We lost one of our Sikh workers, Jaswant Singh. My younger brother, Raj Paul, could save the lives of some Sikh families by bringing them to his house in his car, hiding the men-folk locked in his car booth. The Sikh militancy in Punjab was converted into terrorism with open and liberal help from Pakistan and our land of the ten Gurus continued to burn.

Rajiv Gandhi tried to soften the Sikh community's hurt. The Golden Temple and the Akal Takhat, which were damaged in the 'Operation Blue Star', were arranged to be repaired at the central government expense under the supervision of a liberal Sikh saint. An agreement was signed by Rajiv Gandhi with Sant Longowal in which many genuine demands of the Sikhs were accepted. When the Golden Temple was handed over to the reconstituted Sikh Gurudwara Prabandhak Committee, Amritsar, they decided to undo all the repairs done by the Central Government and redid those with their own *kar sevaks*. The Sikh community in general appeared to be pacified. Some diehards among them continued their anti-national activities. The militancy which remained subdued for some time after the tragic events, raised its head again in a worst form of terrorism. There were again murders and looting in the state. Innocent Hindus and some of the Sikhs who appeared to be in favour of peace, were massacred along with their families. Once again Punjab fell into the throes of worst type of unrest which could not be controlled by the state police.

In the next general election, which the Akali Dal had boycotted, a Congress government was formed in the Punjab under Chief Minister Beant Singh. Surindra Nath Malhotra an outstanding IPS officer, was appointed as governor of the state. An unknown DIG of police K.P.S Gill, had been entrusted with full powers, to control terrorism. That police officer proved himself as a brilliant strategist. It took him less than a year to wipe out all terrorism from the state. Time being the best healer, the hurt feelings of the Sikh community have vanished substantially in the course of time. The community has slowly regained its position of pride in the country.

— 20 —

MY ANGUISH

I have ended my book with a general note of a resettled life at the place where we chose to live after being driven out from our ancestral home for the past several centuries. But in my heart I continue to carry an intense love for our lost home. And what I feel today is not my loss alone. It's for the society, the culture which had been thrown out of its homeland. That land where some of the Vedic *Rishies* lived and gave us the Vedic way of life, the land whose social culture and the society withstood centuries of onslaught and atrocities but continued its existence there. Today it had been totally wiped out of their land. What is the value of the grand array of Greats of the nineteenth and the twentieth centuries, that the society gave birth to? All the ministrations of the reformers, the patriotic poets, the novelists, the scholars, the scientists, the Saints, the flag bearers from Raja Ram Mohan Roy to Mohan Das Karam Chand Gandhi had proved ineffective. All the exhortations of Swami Vivekananda, like the one, "She is awakening, this Motherland of ours, from her deep long sleep. No one can resist her anymore, never is she going to sleep any more, no outward power can hold her anymore" (Lectures from Colombo to Almora" from Complete Works of Swami Vivekananda Book 3) did not come true. Similarly, the assertion of Mahatma Gandhi that "Hinduism is a relentless pursuit after truth and if today it had become moribund, inactive, irresponsive to growth, it is because we are fatigued and as soon as the fatigue is over, Hinduism will burst forth upon the world with a brilliance perhaps unknown before" (The young

India from an article by Mahatma Gandhi in that magazine) proved otherwise in his very life. According to these theorized beliefs of those great men the total rout of Hinduism from the area stretching from Peshawar to Lahore could not have been made possible. Swami Vivekananda died in 1902 but Mahatma Gandhi was very much alive to witness the entire cleaning process. Why could that world renowned Hindu with great spiritual power not put a stop to that rooting out of the Hindu. He and hundreds and thousands of the Hindus fought the British to make them leave India. No one at that time could see what way the British had planned to quit. They had left after executing their plan to inflict the greatest harm to the Hindus. In defence of the personage of the Mahatma, I may say that his prime time had passed. He was no more the towering figure that he used to be during freedom struggle of the twenty's and thirty's. He was only a shadow of his reputation at the time of making decision by the Congress Party in favour of allowing creation of Pakistan, he was forced to follow his lieutenants.

The fact is that the English were a very disciplined and organized society. They were ruling the maximum number of the poor and under-developed countries of the world and were too devious for our topmost leaders to understand their subtle moves. They had analyzed thoroughly the situation of our country, its diversity in terms of the people living here, their cultural differences, their regional loyalties and religious beliefs, especially after their experience of the 1857 revolt. And since then, they had planned how they had to deal with our people. Some of our wisest countrymen could only understand that their rulers had a plan for the next 100 years but they could not assess how they had planned to cripple them before leaving within 100 years of the revolt.

After the Revolt of 1857, our rulers were no more the East India Company. We came directly under the Queen of England. The administration, after that change, had started the developments in the country in a big way. The railways, post offices, hospitals, schools, colleges, repairs of roads and construction of canals had all been started with great speed. So much so that even the Indian National Congress was visualized by one of the viceroys of the country. He used the active services of one of his most efficient administrative officers to start the organization in 1885. All those institutions were established and the acts done in such as manner as might win over the general public. They had watched with their astute minds, the regeneration which was taking place in the majority community.

It were the Hindus who turned their education scheme upside down. The government had expected that the English education system would create disenchantment among the Hindus about their ancient scriptures, culture and history. But that education worked to create a renaissance in the majority community and produced a galaxy of enlightened Hindus in all fields to defeat their design. Again, it were the Hindus who were mainly responsible to thwart their scheme of the division of Bengal in the time of Lord Curzon. Finally, it was the majority community again which was the cause of the failure of their objective of starting the Indian National Congress. Because of all this, the Britishers had made up their mind to take revenge on them at any cost.

Simultaneously and silently they were advancing to achieve their purpose. The country was allowed to suffer from famines and diseases as a result of which the people from the vast areas of the country were victimized to the maximum. Famished people were then recruited for the projects started in the country as well as the indentured labourers who were sent out of the country to far off lands to work in the fields under their ruthless English landlords. As those poor people had been dispatched from the country with one way ship journey, they had to helplessly withstand all the atrocities like slaves. When some youths in the country revolted against them, hundreds of those young boys were either hanged or shot dead without any record or semblance of trial. Even then when they could not crush the spirit of the people, they tried to divide them by creating separate areas for Hindus and Muslims in the resurgent Bengal in the beginning of the twentieth century, Somehow they could not put into practice that first experiment.

The developments in the country had served their purpose to strengthen their control on the nerve centres of the economy of the country such as agriculture, industrial production, transport, communication and defence. Once that was established, they felt the need of the controlling hands for which they increased the number of English men for administration and for law and order. I.C.S officers specially trained in England were employed for administration as per the regional requirements of the land. Those officers were as effective in the desert areas as in the plains and in the hilly areas. Then number of English soldiers was increased as also the number of their generals and police commissioners. That much and more on the side of controls.

They had marked long time back, the section of people whom they had to target for punishment and those whom they had to promote to be used for their ultimate purpose.

They executed their plan from A to Z before they left. The demand of a Muslim separate state was the idea which they conceived and put into the heads of those Muslims whom they specially educated and then guided from England. In the managing of the division, it was their plan to see that no Hindu might live in the areas that were called Pakistan. They had assessed the capacities of both Hindus and Muslims and knew that they would successfully manipulate the Muslims to give a practical shape to their wicked scheme.

Muslims were socially much better bound together. Hindus with all their individual merits were a disunited society.

Moreover, the Muslims can be provoked to indulge in the massacres of innocent people without the least compunction. And they used them quite successfully to carry out their plans in toto. In his book "From Curzon to Nehru" Durga Das, the editor of Hindustan Times, had clearly mentioned how an English I.C.S officer opting to stay in Pakistan wrote a letter to Jinnah suggesting that Pakistan's security be ensured by not permitting any Hindu or Sikh to live west of Lyallpur in the Punjab. The suggestion was implemented fully but it stopped at Lahore upto which Pakistan was given the territory. The scheme, to clear all Hindus and Sikhs from the areas upto the Yamuna river could not be implemented. That secret plan was leaked out before it could be acted on. The plan for the East Punjab was to be executed through East Punjab Police. At the time of administrative change over, the police force in every district of East Punjab had Muslim predominance. The Muslim League had conspired that the Muslim constabulary would capture the police armouries between 12th to 14th August, kill the Hindu and Sikh officers and declare that area independent of India. The Hindu officers, having come to know of that conspiracy, immediately held a meeting in which they decided to put more Hindu and Sikh officers at all the places where there were English and Muslim Officers. They took that step in the beginning of August and wherever the Muslim constables had taken possession of rifles, they were apprehended and disarmed. That step worked to demoralize the East Punjab Muslim policemen. Their plan for first offensive having been defeated, they were put on the defensive and thus the East Punjab plan of the Muslim League was aborted. (This episode has also been taken from the above noted book "From Curzon to Nehru".)

In that book another telling instance has been mentioned. Jawaharlal Nehru, accompanied by some Indian officials and journalists, flew to Jhang and Chiniot in West Pakistan, where half a million Hindus and Sikhs had gathered and were waiting for a safe passage to India. They were returning after assuring help to the refugees, and had to stop at the Lahore airport. The Punjab Governor, Sir Francis Muddie met them there. Some journalists asked the Governor why he was not taking steps to protect the Hindus and Sikhs and assure their safe passage to India. His reply was sarcastically curt. He said "You wanted independence. Now have it".

Many English officers and both the Governors of Punjab and N.W.F.P. were blatantly and openly directing the Muslim Leaguers to inflict maximum damage to the Hindus and Sikhs. Such was the extent of the cruel vengeance with which the English were acting against Hindus.

As a reaction to the West Punjab cruelties, the Sikhs and Hindus too paid back in the same coin in the East Punjab. There were massacres of Muslims there also when the refugees from Pakistan reached India and told their tragic tales to their brethren. There were the train loads of Muslims from the Punjab of east of the Ravi river. The total of the exodus of both the Hindus and the Muslims was the largest migration in the history of mankind. There was, however, one difference between the migration of the Hindus and that of the Muslims. The Hindu leaders and the Englishmen in India were protecting the Muslims. And that was the difference.

All said and done, the net result was that all the Hindus and Sikhs were driven out from the West Punjab and N.W.F.P. In Sindh and East Bengal, the Muslim plans worked at a lower scale to begin with but the clearing process is continuing upto this day. The number of Hindus in those areas is now very small. The Hindus there are in such a small minority that they cannot even raise their voice. In contrast, the policies of our leaders in India have not only greatly increased the population of Muslims in India but they have become very vocal and aggressive at various places in U.P., Madhya Pradesh, Bihar,

Maharashtra, Gujarat and in all the Southern states. These are verifiable facts.

No notice was taken of the forced exodous of Hindus and Sikhs from the West Pakistan by the Congress which was the major party being supported by big majority of Hindus. And that party cared more for those for whom Jinnah and his Muslim League had been fighting to secure a homeland. The topmost leaders of the Congress Party had been mesmerized not to see beyond the independence. They had even sacrificed their own most sincere comrades, Khan Abdul Gaffar Khan, Dr. Khan Sahib and all their sincerest followers called the Red Shirts. They were thrown to the Muslim League wolves in Pakistan and were left to suffer for the rest of their lives in sheer helplessness and desperation. Our misfortune was that the large majority of Hindus had placed themselves in the hands of the Mahatma and all his brilliant lieutenants who were thoroughly cheated by Mohamed Ali Jinnah by his false slogans and deceitful rhetoric that the Muslims of the country could not live with the Hindus and wanted their own land. What had happened is that the Muslims of the united India got their own land from which they had killed or driven out all Hindus, Sikhs, Jains and also continue to live in the areas they wanted to separate from. The Hindus of India became the worst sufferers, being under continued menace from both outside and inside, as is very much evident today.

What I see around today is more demeaning. No one in the entire country had ever talked about the tragic "Sweeping out". After Independence, the entire administrative machinery has been thoroughly been corrupted from top to bottom. Selfishness has entered into the lives of the majority of people in the country. Regionalism, factionalism and casteism have spread in all directions. Kashmir continues as the top most unresolved problem from where all Pandits have been thrown out before the eyes of the Congressmen who were masters of the country.

Nobody in the country talks about the Hindus who had been thrown out of the West Punjab at the time of Independence and are still being squeezed out from Bangladesh. But the government and most of the people are europhic about the progress the country has made in several secular fields.

The banishment of all Hindus and Sikhs from their homelands west of Lahore continues to trouble me and I do not understand why me only, a small and an unknown man? I can only hope that this little book may attract the attention of some IGNITED minds and pray that the spirit of ancient Bharat may follow the course as divined by the sage poet Rabindranath Tagore. In his address at ' Shantineketan' on the occasion of the Bengali new year, Vaisakh 1309 (April 1903) he asserted.... "It is Bharatvarsh that will finally triumph, there is not a shadow of doubt in it. The Bharat that is ancient, that which is veiled, that which is vast, that which is magnanimous, that which is silent, that is what will triumph....".

GLOSSARY

A

Abdul Rehman Street : A Bombay wholesale market for stationery items.

Acharya Kriplani : One of the top congress leaders.

Achhut Kanya : A movie produced in 1934 by Bombay Talkies with the main cast of Devika Rani and Ashok Kumar.

Adhikaries : Officers of the volunteers of the RSS.

Agni Hotra : Vedic Havan for purification of environment.

Agra : A city famous for the Taj Mahal.

Aik Nala : A water stream flowing through Sialkot city.

Ajmeri gate : A big crossing in old Delhi near New Delhi railway station.

Allah-Hu Akbar : Muslim religious slogan meaning "God is Greatest".

Alu Bhaji : Potato Curry.

Ambala : A city of pre-independence Punjab now in Haryana State.

Amit	:	Son of my younger brother Govinder Paul.
Amrit Manthan	:	A Hindu mythology picturised by New Theaters of Calcutta.
Amritsar	:	A border city in India near Lahore (Pakistan).
Andheri	:	A suburb of Bombay.
Asha Rani	:	Wife of my brother Govinder Paul
Assam	:	Province of British India also of India after independence.
Avdi	:	Cantonment of Madras.

B

Babe-Di-Ber	:	A famous Sikh temple in Sialkot on the spot where Guru Nanak had stayed under berry trees.
Babu Nathu Mal	:	My great grandfather's cousin brother and a philanthropist of Sialkot.
Badrinath	:	A Hindu pilgrimage in Northern Himalayas on the bank of the river Alaknanda, a tributary of the Ganga. It's a temple of Lord Vishnu, one of the Trilogy of the Hindu philosophy which symbolizes God, the sustainer of Humanity. The other two of the Triology are Brahma, the Creator and Mahesh, the Destroyer.

Bahadurgarh	:	A city near Delhi but in Haryana State.
Baisakhi Mela	:	Festival of the Punjab held on 13th April (1st of the month of Vaisakh) after harvest of wheat crop.
Balaji	:	A famous Hindu pilgrimage temple of South India.
Baldev Raj Sekhri	:	Elder son of Brinda Ban Sekhri. My fathers cousin brother.
Balwant Singh	:	A Sialkot friend. He served in the Second World War in Indian army and had married an Italian wife while he was posted in Italy.
Bangalore	:	A famous city in South India (Karnataka)
Bara Moola	:	A city in J & K state situated near Srinagar. Now part of India.
Basakhi fair	:	A fair held on the first of the Vikram Samwat month of Vaisakh to celebrate the completion of harvest. It falls of 13th April.
Batala	:	A city on Pakistan border near Amritsar.
Begedevadi	:	A satellite town of Poona for residences of military servants.

Bengal : Pre- Independence province of India in the East.

Bhagat Singh : Young Indian Nationalist hanged by the British in 1931.

Bhagwad Geeta : Famous sermon delivered by Lord Krishna to Arjun at the beginning of Mahabharata war.

Bhajan : Spiritual Song.

Bhangi colony : A colony for sweepers in New Delhi.

Bhawani Devi : A Hindu goddess.

Bhopal : Capital city of the princely state of the same name.

Bhuaji : My father's sister.

Birla House : A big Bungalow of Birlas, the top-most businessmen of the time.

Bombay : The largest city and sea port on the west coast of India.

Bombay Talkies : A film company of Bombay.

Brij Lal : My father's third and youngest brother.

Brinda Ban Sekhri : Younger brother of my grandfather.

C

Calcutta : Capital of Bengal Province.

Connaught place : The topmost shopping centre created by the British when they built New Delhi.

Chandni Chawk : A Mughal period shopping centre in old Delhi.

Charsadha : A city in the N.W.F.P. known for being the birth place of Khan Brothers – in Pakistan.

Chenab : One of the five Punjab rivers having source in Himalayas on Indian side and mainly flowing into Pakistan.

Chinniot : A city deep in the West Punjab in Pakistan.

Chnni Lal : My mother's cousin brother.

Chooridar Pajama : An Indian trouser worn by a prince or men of the higher gentry of North India.

Chuni Pehlwan Da Akhara: A wrestling ground bearing name of the master wrestler, in Sialkot.

Colombo : Capital of Ceylon (Sri Lanka).

Conley Park : A well known playing ground in Sialkot. Here Dussehra festival of the Hindus was also celebrated.

D

Daman : My youngest sister

Daska : A Tehsil in Sialkot district.

Dayawanti : My mother.

Dera Baba Nanak : A border town in East Punjab India.

Delhi : Capital of India before and after independence.

Devdas : A movie based on the famous novel by Sarat Chandra Chatterji, produced by New Theaters Calcutta.

Devika Rani : A famous actress of 1930's

Dewan Banwarilal : Husband of the sister of my friend Shiv Kumar.

Dhariwal : A small town in Pathankot district known for a large woollen mill.

Dharowal : A Colony of Hindus in Sialkot.

Dhobi Talao : A large square in Bombay where many famous streets start.

Diya : A small earthen oil lamp still used in rural India.

Don Wilson : My son-in-law, husband of my daughter Rashmi.

Durga Das Sekhri : My father.

Dwarka Das : My father's younger brother.

E

East Bengal : The part of Bengal which formed a state of Pakistan after division.

F

Faiz Road : A road in Karol Bagh locality.

G

G B Road	:	An area mainly occupied by prostitutes & dancing girls in Delhi.
Ganga	:	A great river of India considered sacred for its nectar like water.
Ganga Jal	:	Water from the Ganga considered holy by Hindus.
Gangotri	:	The source of the Ganga in Northern Himalayas – A Hindu pilgrimage.
Gayatri Mantra	:	An important mantra of the Vedas, praying to God for grant of right intellect.
Geeta	:	My elder daughter.
Godpur	:	A small village near Sialkot city.
Gokal Chand Sekhri	:	My grandfather.
Gol Dak Khana	:	A post office in round shape near Gol Market, New Delhi.
Gol Market	:	A well known market of New Delhi built in round shape.
Govinder Paul	:	My youngest brother.
Greenwood Street	:	A mixed colony of Hindu majority in Sialkot.
Gujarat	:	A district town of the Punjab now in Pakistan.
Gulshan Rani	:	Wife of Raj Paul.
Gurdaspur	:	A district city on the border of India near Amritsar.

Guru Gorakh Nath	:	A famous saint of the Nath order of the yogis, known for his promulgation of yogic creations.
Gurudwara	:	A Sikh Temple.
Gwalior	:	Capital city of the princely state of the same name.

H

Hakim	:	A Judge
Hanuman	:	Prince of a South Indian Tribal clan. He became the staunch follower of Lord Ram.
Har Har Mahadev	:	A Hindu religious slogan in praise of Lord Shiva.
Har Ki Pauri	:	The most famous place on the bank of the Ganga at Haridwar. A pilgrimage city in the Himalayas. It is a city included in the newly formed state of "Uttaranchal".
Haridwar	:	A famous pilgrimage for Hindus on the bank of the Ganga when it flows down to planes from the Himalayas.
Hari Sigh Nalwa	:	A famous general in the army of Maharaja Ranjit Singh who conquered Kabul for the Maharaja.
Haripur Hazaara	:	A city of Pakistan in the north of the Punjab.

Harish Chandra : A legendary Hindu king known for his truthfulness and generosity. He gave up all his kingdom, his wife his only son as also himself to a Brahmin who wanted to test his generosity.

Has Kay Liya Hai Pakistan Lar Kay lain gay Hindustan : A new Pakistani Slogan meaning "Pakistan had been secured cheerfully, but shall get India by winning in war".

Hasnabdal : A city towards the northern border of pre-independence province of Punjab.

Haveli : Old large mansion in which several families lived.

Himanshu Roy : Husband of Devika Rani and owner of Bombay Talkies.

Hooka : A north India tobacco smoking gadget.

I

Inder Mohan Chopra : Husband of my sister Prakash.

J

J & K State : Jammu & Kashmir princely state.

Jagdish Abrol : An R.S.S. member of Sialkot who dedicated his life to Sangh work and was

		made incharge of Jammu part of J & K state after he passed his intermediate examination in Sialkot.
Jagannathpuri	:	A famous Hindu temple city in Orissa state.
Jain Mohalla	:	Colony of Jains in Sialkot.
Jalianwala Bagh	:	An open space inside the interior of Amritsar city made famous by the notorious massacre of Hindus and Sikhs on the Baisakhi festival by General Dwyer in 1919.
Jammu	:	Winter capital of Jammu & Kashmir state – about 19 miles from Sialkot.
Jhansi	:	A city of central India.
Jogeshwari	:	A suburb of Bombay.
Juhu	:	A suburb of Bombay.

K

Kalbadevi	:	A busy shopping cum housing street in Bombay.
Kalka	:	A small town and railway station en-route to Shimla.
Kamla	:	My younger sister
Kanyakumari	:	A famous temple town in Southernmost tip of India where three waters mingle– Bay of Bengal, Arabian sea and Indian Ocean, Now famous for Rock Memorial temple of Swami Vivekananda.

Kapur Chand Jain : An important member of R.S.S. and my life long friend.

Karachi : An important sea port and the first capital of Pakistan.

Karnal : A district town in Haryana, India.

Karol Bagh : A famous locality in North West of Delhi.

Kashmiri Basket : A basket with a handle specially made in Kashmir.

Kathua : A second small town on the road leading to Pathankot from Jammu.

Kazi : A Muslim adjudicator of lowest rank.

Kedarnath Sekhri : Youngest son of Tara Chand Sekhri and partner of my uncle Brij Lal in Madan Trunk House, Jammu.

Keshav Duggal : My college and R.S.S. friend.

Khaadi : Cotton cloth made by handloom.

Khan Abdul Ghaffar Khan: The famous Pathan Leader of a Socio-political party of N.W.F.P. called Khudai Khidmatgars. (Servants of God). He became follower of Mahatma Gandhi and established a national government in alliance with Congress in his state in the last election of undivided

India with his brother Dr. Khan Sahib as chief minister.

Khyber Pass : The most popular of the only two passages through the great Himalayas, which connect the Indian sub-continent with Eurasia by land route.

King Porus : The ruler of northern part of the Punjab who gave a stiff fight to Alexander the great around 300 B.C.

Kotli Loharan : A small village near Sialkot city.

Krishan : Hero of the Mahabharata who was said to be a complete human being nearest to God.

Kul Bhushan : 2nd Son of Pandit Sudarshan.

L

Labhu Ram Sekhri : The third and youngest brother of my grandfather.

Laddoos : A most common Indian sweet.

Lahore : Capital of pre-independence Punjab, now in Pakistan.

Laila Majnu : A love story famous in Arabian countries.

Lakhanwal : A third small town on the road leading to Pathankot from Jammu. Situated on the bank of the river Raavi.

Lakshman : Younger brother of Lord Ram.
Lakshmi Chand Khanna : R.S.S. member and my life long friend and relative.
Landi Kotal : A city at the end of Khyber Pass towards Afghanistan.
Langer : A free community mess run in Sikh temples.
Lathies : Long bamboo sticks.
Leela Devi : My father's third sister.
Ludhiana : An industrial town in East Punjab famous for Hosiery goods. Now it has earned more fame as a city of cycle manufacture and other engineering goods.

M

Madan Lal : The only son of uncle Brij Lal
Madras : The largest city and a sea port in South India.
Madrassa : Muslim style school run in a Mosque.
Mahabharat : An epic of Hindus famous for a great war between cousin princes.
Maharaja Hari Sigh : The last prince ruler of J & K state.
Maharaja : Prince of an Indian state.
Mahim : A locality of Bombay.
Malan Devi : My grandmother.
Manali & Manikaran : The popular hill stations and also Hindu sacred places in Himachal Pradesh state of India near Punjab.

Manendra : Another Greek Invader of India in 1st or 2nd century B.C.

Masjid : Muslim Mosque.

Masterji : Teacher in school.

Mathura Brindaban : Twin cities famous as the places where Lord Krishna was born and brought up.

Maulana Azad : One of the top Congress leaders and education minister of the first Govt of free India.

Maulvi : Muslim priest of a mosque.

Minerva Talkies : A film production co. run by Sohrab Mody.

Mohalla : Colony.

Montgomery : A city of Pakistan.

Mulla : Muslim teacher in a Mosque.

Murree : Hill station in Pakistan.

N

Narowal : A tehsil town, in district Sialkot from where my maternal parents village was four miles.

Nawa Shehar : A city of N.W.F.P. on the Northern side of the Attuck bridge on the Sindh river.

Nizamabad : A small town near Wazirabad now in Pakistan.

Noakhali : A city of Bengal Province now in Bangladesh.

O

O.T.C : Officers Training Camp organised by R.S.S.

P

Pagri : Turban

Pakistan Zindabad : Long live Pakistan – a Pakistan slogan.

Pandas : Record keepers at all famous Hindu pilgrimages.

Pandit Sudarshan : A well known story writer in Hindi in the middle of 20th Century.

Panditji : Used here for Pandit Jawaharlal Nehru.

Pandu : Father of five princes named Youdhister, Bhim, Arjun, Nakul and Sehdev of Mahabharata.

Panipat : A district town in Haryana, India.

Pathankot : A city in India on the border of Pakistan and Jammu state.

Pathans : A Muslim clan who resides in N.W.F.P.

Patilas : Cooking vessels.

Paush : The name of a month of Vikram Samwat. It starts from 15 December and ends on 13 January .

Pamento Mrs. : A Goan Christian lady who kept paying guests in her house, in Parel, Bombay.

Peshawar	:	Capital city of the pre-independence province called North Western Frontier Province.
Phoolanwanti	:	Wife of my father's youngest brother Brij Lal
Pinki	:	My eldest daughter in-law, Sudhir's wife.
Poori	:	An Indian Fried Bread.
Pradeep	:	My younger son
Prakash	:	My younger sister
Prem Prakash	:	Husband of my sister Daman.
Punjab	:	Pre Independence province.
Purohit	:	A priest.

Q

Quid-e-Azam Zindabad	:	Pakistans called Mohammed Ali Jinnah as Quid-e-Azam

R

R.S.S	:	A Social organization of Hindus called Rashtriya Swayam Sevak Sangh.
Raj Ghat	:	A place on the bank of Yamuna river where Gandhiji's body was cremated.
Raj Guru	:	Young Indian Nationalist hanged by the British in 1931.
Raj Paul	:	My younger brother.
Raja	:	Ruler.

Ram : Hero of Ramayana and a noble king.

Ram Dhun : Bhajan with repetition of Ram.

Ram Lal Marwah : My eldest brother-in-law. Husband of my sister Shakuntla Devi.

Raman Ashram : A place sanctified by the great 20th Century Saint Raman Maharshi. It is in Tiruvanmalai, a well known temple city in Tamil Nadu, state of South India.

Ramayan : An epic of Hindus narrating life of Lord Ram.

Rameshwaram : A famous temple city on the sea near Sri Lanka.

Rangoon : Capital of Burma (Mynamar) eastern neighbouring country of India.

Rani : Queen.

Rashmi : My younger daughter.

Ravan : King of Lanka (Sri Lanka) in Ramayan time.

Ravi : One of the five famous rivers of the pre-independence Punjab. It has its source in Himalayas on Indian side but flows mainly into Pakistan.

Ravi Varma : My son in-law, husband of my daughter Geeta

Rawalpindi	:	A prominent city in Pakistan near which Islamabad, the new Pakistan capital has been built.
Red shirts	:	The followers of the political party of Khan Abdul Ghaffar Khan of N.W.F.P.
Renu	:	My younger daughter in-law, Pradeep's wife.
Rishi Kesh	:	A famous pilgrimage, 20 km to the north of Haridwar on the Ganga bank.
Rohtak	:	A city of pre-independence Punjab now in Haryana State.
Roop Kaur	:	Wife of Brinda Ban Sekhri

S

Saint Xaviour's college	:	Famous higher education technology college in Bombay.
Samba	:	A small town on the road leading to Pathankot from Jammu.
Sant Fateh Singh	:	An Akali Sikh Leader.
Sarais	:	Community resting places in India where travellers stay usually without payment.
Sardar Patel	:	One of the top Congress leaders and minister for home affairs and states in the first government of free India.

Sardarji	:	A word of respect used for Sikhs.
Sare Jahan Se Achcha Hindustan Hamara	:	Our India is supreme in the entire world.
Satya Paul	:	My younger brother.
Shaikhupura	:	A city on the border of Pakistan near Lahore.
Shakha	:	R.S.S. assembly held daily at a place.
Shakuntla Devi	:	My eldest sister.
Shanti Bhuaji	:	My father's second sister.
Shanti Dev Katyal	:	Husband of my sister Sita Devi.
Shashi Bhushan	:	Youngest son of Pandit Sudarshan.
Shishu Mandir	:	Primary School.
Shiv Kumar Sharma	:	An R.S.S. member and a life long friend.
Shivratri Mela	:	A Hindu Festival for the worship of Lord Shiva.
Shreefpura	:	A Muslim colony in Amritsar deserted by Muslim to go to Pakistan.
Sialkot	:	A city of pre-independence Punjab now in Pakistan.
Simla	:	The summer capital of pre-independence Govternment of India now the capital city of Himachal Pradesh, an Indian state.
Sindh	:	A province of Pakistan.
Sita	:	Wife of Lord Ram.

Sita Devi	:	My younger sister
Samadhi	:	A burial place where saintly persons or their ashes are buried.
Som Nath Khanna	:	Husband of my sister Kamla
Sonipat	:	A district town in Haryana, India.
Srinagar	:	Summer capital of J & K state, renowned for its beauty as a Hill station.
Subedar	:	The administrator of a province in Muslim rule.
Sudhir	:	My eldest son
Sukdev	:	Young Indian Nationalist hanged by the British in 1931.
Sumitra Devi	:	My father's fourth sister.
Surinder	:	My cousin brother and son of my Shanti Bhuaji.
Swayam Sevaks	:	Volunteers (members of R.S.S.).

T

Tarachand Sekhri	:	My grandfather's uncle, his father's cousin.
Tata Memorial Hospital	:	Famous Cancer Hospital of Bombay.
Tibia college	:	A college teaching Unani Medicine – vacated for the use as a government servants colony.
Tonga	:	One horse carriage in India.
Trunkawala	:	The one who deals in steel trunks,

U

Unionist	:	The Punjab government before partition.
Usha Rani	:	Wife of Satya Paul.
Uttar Kashi	:	A city on the river Bhagirathi, name of the Ganga before the river Alaknanda meets it.

V

V.T. Station	:	Victoria Terminus, a great terminal railway station of Bombay.
Vaishno Devi	:	A famous Hindu pilgrimage. A sacred cave deep on top of Himalayan mountain in Jammu part of J & K state.
Vas Dev Sekhri	:	My father's cousin brother and younger son of Brinda Ban Sekhri.
Ved Kaur	:	Wife of Labhu Ram Sekhri.
Vidya Bhushan	:	Eldest son of Pandit Sudarshan.
Vidya Devi	:	My father's eldest sister.
Vijay Dashmi	:	Dussehra festival of Hindus celebrated 20 days before Diwali almost all over India.
Vikram	:	Son of Satya Paul.
Vikram Samwat	:	The era beginning from the reign of King Vikramaditya of the Hindu period of the Indian history.

W

Wah : An estate in the North of pre-independence Punjab owned by Khizer Hayat Khan, the chief minister of the province before partition.

Wazirabad : A city in the Punjab and a large railway junction in the centre of Lahore and Rawalpindi.

West Punjab : The Divided Punjab other part in Pakistan.